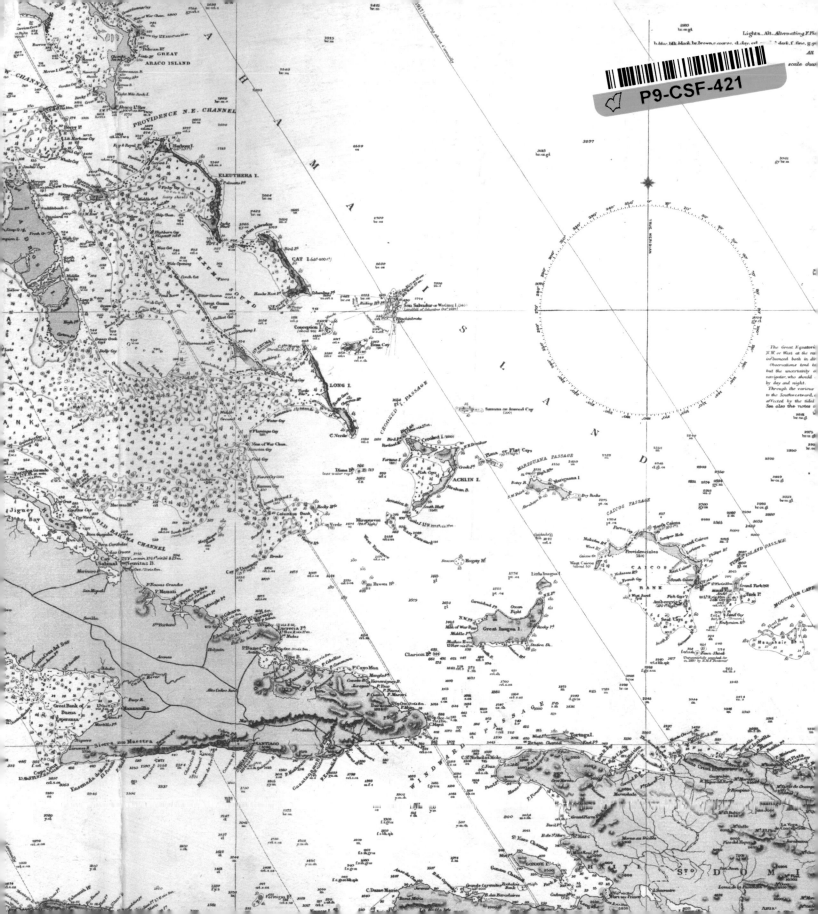

Cuba, America and the Sea

The American Maritime Library: Volume XVI

Cuba, America and the Sea

The Story of the Immigrant Boat *Analuisa*
and 500 Years of History Between Cuba and America

Dr. Eric Paul Roorda

MYSTIC SEAPORT · THE MUSEUM OF AMERICA AND THE SEA

Mystic Seaport
75 Greenmanville Ave., P.O. Box 6000
Mystic, CT 06355-0990

www.mysticseaport.org

Designed by Darcy Magratten
Printed by Thomson-Shore, Inc.

ISBN (cloth): 0-939510-98-7

Roorda, Eric Paul.
    Cuba, America and the sea : the story of the immigrant boat Analuisa and 500
years of history between Cuba and America / Eric Paul Roorda.—1st ed.—Mystic,
CT : Mystic Seaport, c2005.
        p. : ill. ; cm.—(American Maritime Library ; v. 16)
        Includes bibliographical references and index.

    1. Cuba — History. 2. Cuba — History, Naval. 3. Cuba — Emigration and im-
migration. 4. United States — Emigration and immigration. I. Title.

 F1776.R6 2005

Endpapers: *West India Islands and Caribbean Sea*, Royal Hydrographic Office, 1876,
1914. (G.W. Blunt White Library, Mystic Seaport)

Dedication

To *Analuisa* Fernandez Cuadras, who was a fountain of love for her family and their neighborhood of Mariel, Cuba, a seaside community of hard-working people.

And to Nuestra Señora de la Caridad del Cobre, "Our Lady of Charity of Cobre" (pronounced CO-breh), the patron saint of Cuba. In 1620, three shipwrecked men in an open boat prayed for deliverance from a storm, and survived. Afterward, they found a statue of the Virgin Mary floating on a plank in Nipa Bay, on the northeast coast of the island, near the town of Cobre. The sacred statue of Caridad del Cobre now resides in the cathedral in Cobre, and is a familiar and beloved image in Cuba, worn on medallions and displayed in homes. Pope John Paul II traveled to Cobre to pay homage to Caridad during his 1998 visit to Cuba, an event that drew hundreds of thousands of pilgrims from all over the island. Caridad del Cobre represents both the Madonna of Catholicism and Ochum, one of the "seven African powers" of the religion of Santería. Ochum (or Oshun) is the river goddess of the Yoruba people of West Africa, many of whom were swept up in the transatlantic slave trade, survived its horrors, and were deposited in Cuba. There they lost their freedom, but not their religious traditions, combining African beliefs with the Catholicism of their masters to create a new religion, Santería. Both Oshum and Caridad del Cobre are associated with water. Caridad del Cobre is always shown coming to the aid of three men in an open boat in heavy weather. The scene evokes the experience of two groups for whom Caridad del Cobre holds special significanace: fishermen and the hundreds of thousands of Cuban immigrants who have made passages to the United States in small boats in recent years. Miralys Milian Gonzalez, one of those who came to the United States in a small boat named *Analuisa*, said, "We call [Caridad] the lady that's going to save all the Cubans that come in boats." The image of Caridad del Cobre rescuing the three frightened mariners reminds us of the perils faced by millions of people who crossed the ocean in the past to come to America.

Finally, this book is dedicated to another inspirational woman, Pearl Elaine Roorda, 1929-2005.

Contents

Preface

This is a book about a boat. A small, graceful, wooden boat, which arrived at Mystic Seaport in 1994 from a Coast Guard impoundment yard in south Florida, with some scraps of clothing and a sack of blackened oranges still sitting in the bilge. *Analuisa*, from the port of Mariel, Cuba, was a mystery, abandoned after having brought someone, somehow, from there to here. Once the boat and its contents were duly catalogued and added to the Museum's collection, and the new immigrants were located and their families back home interviewed, it was not the end of the story. The questions remained. What did *Analuisa* represent? Could this boat's story help to explain the motivations for immigration on the high seas, in waves over decades? Could it tell us why the centuries of close ties between Cuba and America ended in such acrimony, like a romance gone sour? The answers caused ripples, which expanded into more questions, until the boat herself was practically lost in the broader context, like a speck in the Straits of Florida, floating away from the shadow of a towering cruise liner.

Cuba and America have influenced each other for almost five hundred years. Separated only by the Straits of Florida, the histories of these two nations are intertwined through geographic proximity, active commerce, and massive immigration. Maritime connections between the largest of the Caribbean islands and the mainland of North America originated with the earliest European colonization. Trade and travel between Cuba and America contributed to heavy ship traffic in the Gulf of Mexico and along the East Coast, closely linking the cities of New Orleans, Havana, New York, and Boston. The development of Florida had a strong Cuban flavor, as well, especially in Key West, Tampa, and later Miami, all accessible to Havana by ferryboat. The countries' shared interests on the seas remained strong until the early 1960s, when the Cold War interfered. The United States broke off relations with the government of Fidel Castro in 1962, imposing a trade embargo that severed almost all maritime ties with Cuba. Since then, movement on the high seas between the estranged neighbors has been confined mostly to sporadic Cuban immigration.

In August 1994, a wave of maritime immigrants to America embarked from Cuba in fishing boats and improvised rafts. Crossing the Straits of Florida and the turbulent Gulf Stream is always risky, but to attempt the passage in over-crowded small craft, as they did, is particularly perilous. Only ninety miles separate Cuba from Key West, but that is "plenty of water," as Ernest Hemingway said, and it does not stand still, but flows parallel to the land at a rate of two to five knots per hour. Many who set out to cross the Straits of Florida in small craft have drowned, died of thirst, burned to death from gasoline explosions at sea, or been run down by passing ships. By braving these risks, Cuban immigrants who come by sea follow in a long tradition of maritime immigrants to America, who often came under desperate circumstances, but did not allow the dangers of the voyage to stop them.

Acknowledgements

AE Doyle and Alida Anna Roorda played the key roles in the research leading to this book, especially during a long and challenging trip to Cuba. AE Doyle also contributed her photography skills in Havana and Mariel, her technical knowledge in recording interviews and unearthing data, and her editing abilities during the long process of investigating and composing this book. Frances Elizabeth Roorda has contributed more recently.

Our friends in Cuba helped us in many ways. We thank them all fondly. Angel Luís, Teresita, and Jorge housed us, fed us, and encouraged us during the weeks we spent in their home. Norge led us around Havana and translated for us. Guido drove us where we wanted to go in his 1959 Ford Zephyr, and managed to get enough gasoline to travel down the coast to Mariel.

In Mariel, we found the man who built *Analuisa*, Luciano Cuadras Fernández, who told us the story of his boat. He passed away in July 2004, but has our admiration for building a handsome and durable craft. Since that trip to Mariel, many members of the Cuadras and Alfaro families have assisted me in assembling the story of *Analuisa*. They have all been friendly and welcoming, and more than that, they have been inspirational. My deep thanks to these sweet people, who represent the very best of the long tradition of American immigration, in the order in which I met them: Luciano Cuadras Fernández, Caridad Alvarez Sánchez, Luís Cuadras Fernández, Maribel Hernández Montenegro, Yadira Cuadras Hernández, Luís Cuadras Hernández, José Antonio Cuadras Fernández, Amarilys Pita Cuadras, Leonardo "Victor" Milian, Miralys Milian, Julio González, Julito González, Leonardo Milian hijo, and Juan José Alfaro.

The Johns Hopkins University Cuba Exchange Program made my research in Havana and Mariel possible, and Wayne Smith and Franklin W. Knight both provided guidance and served as role models. Lauren H. Derby offered invaluable advice prior to our departure for Cuba, and through introductions shared with us her lovely friends: Angel Luís, Teresita, Jorge, and Norge.

Special credit goes to Marifrances Trivelli, director of the Los Angeles Maritime Museum, who was instrumental in bringing the *Analuisa* story to light when she worked at Mystic Seaport. Many other people on the museum staff worked to bring the boat to Mystic Seaport and to tell her tale to the public, especially Dana Hewson, Revell Carr, Andrew German, Bill Peterson, Jane

Keener, Peter Glankoff, Chris Cox, and Quentin Snediker. Peggy Tate-Smith worked diligently to obtain photographs for the book.

Thanks to Gail Swanson of Key West for sending me her rich collection of press clippings and photographs on the subject of Cuban rafters, and to Joe Wojtas of the *New London Day* and Al Lara of the *Hartford Courant* for sharing information with me. Thanks also to the U.S. Coast Guard for their cooperation in preserving *Analuisa* in 1994, and to the U.S. Treasury Department for their policy of permitting research trips to Cuba in 1995.

The Munson Institute of American Maritime Studies at Mystic Seaport, a program for graduate university students, provides me with a maritime base of scholarly operations. The Williams College-Mystic Seaport Maritime Studies Program for undergraduate students supported me during the initial stages of this research, with particular nourishment coming from Jim Carlton and Katrina Bercaw. Thanks to Glenn S. Gordinier of both the Munson Institute and the Williams-Mystic Program for many years of generosity with his knowledge of the sea.

Bellarmine University in Louisville, Kentucky, is my academic home, granting me a sabbatical leave to complete this manuscript. Fond thanks to my colleagues Margaret Mahoney, John Oppelt, Timothy Welliver, Michael Krukones, and Robert Pfaadt.

Pearl Elaine Roorda and William Simon Roorda hosted me during my research in Florida, and clipped numerous newspaper articles on Cuban-American relations for me. They are also my parents, so I thank them for much more than that! For example, I thank them for taking me to Mystic Seaport, letting me roam the shores of the Great Lakes, providing me with the entire Hornblower series by C.S. Forester to read and re-read, and visiting coastal fortifications all over eastern North America at my behest, such as Forts Mackinac and Michilimackinac, Fort Henry, Fort McHenry, Fort Sumter, and Fort Wagner. Those experiences were the sources for my fascination with the water and maritime history, which has led to this book and much more in my life.

Prologue

The "feet wet/feet dry" policy governing United States policy toward Cuban immigrants since 1995 leads to scenes like the one being acted out live on cable TV as I write this. Off the coast of Rodríguez Key near Key Largo, Florida, the United States Coast Guard is apprehending a group of six Cubans who have arrived in a small fishing boat. One of the television anchors covering the "news flash" remarks that the boat "looks like a day-sailer you'd use to putter about on a lagoon." But he does not know what he is looking at, because the vessel is a handsome little craft of the Mariel type, like *Analuisa*. The clean, curved lines of the boat are obscured a bit aft, in the back part of the vessel, where a box-like cuddy has been rigged to project over the transom, probably to store food and water for half a dozen adults. But this is no raft cobbled together out of empty oil drums and plywood, like so many others that have attempted the Florida Straits crossing in the past, about which the TV reporter says, "rickety is a nice word." Rather, this boat was made to fish all day, every day, and when the fishing was good, to haul a heavy catch. It rides high now, dancing on the sunny surface of the ocean, because the passengers are gone.

The refuge-seekers nearly made it to land before sunrise, getting so close that they tried to swim for the beach when the Coast Guard showed up. Now a Coast Guard launch is about to "round them up," as a TV reporter on the scene describes what is taking place on the live satellite feed. Two swimmers are already on deck, while two more tread the dazzling blue water and elude the lines thrown at them by the Coast Guard, knowing that if they can swim a mile and touch the sand of the United States, they will get to stay. But if they are captured now, the Coast Guard will return them to Cuba, and their desperate bid to cross the Straits of Florida in a little skiff will have been for nothing. There are four Coast Guard vessels on the scene now, three of them busily "triangulating" around one of the two remaining swimmers, who looks young and athletic, probably able to swim the mile to the beach if unimpeded. The other looks portly and middle-aged, and he is visibly tiring. Neither of "these guys," as the reporter on the scene invariably calls them, has a life preserver, or a chance, really.

José Basulto, president of Hermanos al Rescate, is interviewed on the telephone. Brothers to the Rescue is an organization that used to fly small aircraft over the Straits of Florida, looking for Cuban emigrants in distress, dropping supplies, and contacting assistance for them if they ask for it. Basulto, a veteran of the Bay of Pigs invasion of 1961, says that the Brothers to the Rescue suspended their flights because of the policy of returning would-be immigrants to Cuba, saying that the "United States Coast Guard is doing the work of

Castro's Frontier Guard!" He takes indignant exception to the word "migrant" used by the reporters to describe the men in the water, insisting that they are "refugees." Congressional Representative Lincoln Díaz Ballart of Florida is then telephoned for his comments. He hopes the men in the water do not drown (they have been dodging the rubber-gloved hands of Coast Guardsmen for an hour now), and he hopes the "totalitarian nightmare that Cuba has been living for forty-four years will end," and the flow of "rafters" from Cuba will stop.

The tide has turned, and the Cubans are being drawn farther away from the land, as the power launches circle around, kicking up turbulent wakes that exhaust the swimmers, a technique refined by the Coast Guard to tire out and detain Cubans under the "feet wet" provision of the Cuban Adjustment Act. Three other Cubans trying to swim to shore from a small boat were taken into Coast Guard custody in exactly the same kind of "op" last week, a TV news caption informs the viewers. After an hour and a half of treading water, the last of the swimmers is fatigued. He had been diving like a dolphin to get away from the swooping Coast Guard launches, but now he allows himself to be plucked from the lucid waters and handcuffed.

He and the others now begin the trip to Krome Detention Center in Miami, like so many Cuban refugees before them, where they will await a hearing before an immigration judge. The magistrate will likely determine that they are economic refugees, not political refugees, and will order their deportation to Cuba. In the meantime, the little fishing boat that carried them from Cuba will be towed to the Coast Guard Impoundment Yard in Key West and burned. Perhaps it was named for someone's mother!

Louisville, Kentucky
May 15, 2003

As displayed at Mystic Seaport, *Analuisa* is shown with members of the Cuadras family on board and the cruise ship *Ecstasy* on the horizon.
(Judy Beisler photo; Mystic Seaport 1994.130)

Chapter 1: **The Crossing**

When the sun rose over *Analuisa* on the unbroken surface of the ocean, with no land in sight, they began to get worried.[1] After a frantic departure in the middle of the night, the companions had buoyed each other's spirits by cracking jokes and bantering back and forth, but now a mood of quiet anxiety prevailed among these friends and close family members. Nineteen of them and a pet dog were crowded into a wooden boat just twenty feet long, and though the sea was relatively calm by the standards of the volatile Straits of Florida, the motion of the vessel plowing through the low swells and the insistent Gulf Stream made several of the passengers on board seasick. The two youngest children, just five and nine years old, were sound asleep, tucked under the small deck at the stem of the fishing boat.

Analuisa was the creation of Luciano Cuadras Fernández, who named his new boat after his mother on the day he launched it some thirty-five years before. But Luciano was not aboard *Analuisa* for this, her longest voyage ever; he was still back in Mariel, Cuba, while his crowded *lancha*, still sturdy, chugged farther away. His niece and nephew, Luís and Amarilys, together with their spouses, Maribel and Victor, had loaded *Analuisa* with their four children, a son-in-law, and ten others from town, along with a few hastily assembled provisions, then launched the skiff toward Key West in the dead of night. Luís and Maribel gave their daughter and son, Yádira and Luís Jr., some sedatives to calm their nausea and fear. Amarilys's husband Victor Milián, a veteran fisherman, steered the boat. Their teenage son Leonardo sat quietly along the gunwale, and their daughter Miralys held her puppy Sisi. Miralys's husband Julio González took his place on the hot wooden engine box, stooping down to bail out the seawater that seeped through the seams. As a former national champion canoeist, he had ample strength and endurance for the seemingly unending task. Because *Analuisa* had been out of the water for ten sunny days prior to departure, she was not as watertight as usual, the planks having shrunk, opening the seams. Also, the little launch was dangerously overcrowded, there was little drinking water on board, and some problems with her 1956 Briggs and Stratton engine had given her passengers a fright soon after departure.

Luís Cuadras and his brother-in-law Victor navigated with Victor's compass, judging the angle of their course against the Gulf Stream to make headway to the north. Not wanting to risk turning off the motor, they had been refueling while it continued to run, despite the fact that a small spill of gasoline hitting the spark plugs could ignite and explode, killing everyone. In fact, they would find out later that exactly such an explosion destroyed a boat much like theirs, which had set out with a group from their hometown just hours before they did. The blast left only one infant survivor. Remarkably, that baby lived to be plucked from the charred wreckage by passengers in another skiff. *Analuisa* did not go up in flames, but there were other causes for worry.

The Gulf Stream begins as the Florida Current, which flushes out of the Gulf of Mexico between Cuba and Florida, moving thirty million cubic meters of water per second at five miles per hour.

Ships began to appear as the sun continued climbing in the sky, but the ships ignored or did not see *Analuisa* and her people waving colorful clothing to attract attention. Noon came and went. Twelve hours had passed since they had left Mariel Bay, and still there was no sign of help. *Analuisa* puttered along far from Florida, and some of the people aboard argued over what to do next. Some also prayed, asking Nuestra Señora de la Caridad del Cobre, Cuba's own Lady of Charity, to intercede for them, to deliver them from the dangers of being in a very small boat on a very large ocean.

The Gulf Stream flows through the Straits of Florida with the volume of one thousand Mississippi Rivers.[2] It is a half-mile-deep stream of water fifty miles wide, moving at the pace of a slow jog, a leisurely paddle, or a lazy sail under lights winds—three to five miles per hour. The water surges by at the rate of thirty million cubic meters of water per second, but its course is parallel to land, making it difficult for boats with little or no propulsion to break free of its relentless grasp on anything that floats. People caught up in the northerly current watch the lights of Florida's neon coastline slide by, out of reach. The Gulf Stream's dynamic motion also creates miniature gyres, which are really giant eddies, within its midst. These swirling spots can be particularly dangerous for small craft to encounter. During the summer, the prevailing winds blow from the south, which helps rafters and encourages them to try their luck at that time of year. But if summer breezes turn stormy, they often back into the southeast

The 855-foot cruise ship Carnival *Ecstasy* was launched at Helsinki, Finland, in 1991 and registered in Liberia. With capacity of more than 2,000 passengers, and a crew of more than 900, the *Ecstasy* was making her routine passage between Miami and Cozumel, Mexico, when she sighted the *Analuisa*. (Courtesy Carnival Cruise Lines)

and blow in gusts, building up choppy seas and pushing boaters into the Gulf of Mexico and into oblivion.

Small boats and rafts are extremely difficult to see from other boats and from the air. Anyone who has tried to keep their eyes trained on a dinghy or lifeboat from the deck of a larger vessel knows how quickly a twenty-foot boat, even a bright orange one containing many people wearing yellow foul weather gear, will disappear to the naked eye. Within minutes, as the distance between the two vessels increases, the small craft becomes intermittently lost behind waves and swells, then begins to look like a wave itself, and soon thereafter is lost from view entirely. Even with calm conditions, it is not easy to keep one's eye on an object the size of a typical Cuban small craft as it gets farther away. In the choppy conditions characteristic of the Straits of Florida, only a few hundred feet of distance is required to render such a thing virtually invisible to someone on another boat. Spotters in airplanes also have trouble seeing small boats. An airplane searching for rafters can fly no closer than five hundred feet above the water, or the humidity prevents the engine from running smoothly. Yet the airplane can cruise no higher than a thousand feet above the surface of the ocean if a spotter is to have any hope at all of detecting a small craft or inflatable object on the surface. Even if a trained person is scrutinizing the water diligently on a sunny day, and the people drifting below are waving their arms and their brightest clothing, for the one to discern the others is still a matter of finding a floating needle in a giant haystack of salt water.

Now here was *Analuisa*, all twenty feet of her, slowly motoring into the heart of the Gulf Stream. She was packed stem to stern with anxious people, but only a small amount of gasoline remained for the old engine, and an even smaller supply of fresh water remained for the nineteen passengers, whose own store of hope was rapidly depleting. They had already rationed the precious liquid only to the children, and the adults were feeling parched. With fifteen hours behind them and nothing but salt water in front of them, the odds of their survival seemed to be diminishing faster than their fuel, their drinking water, and their once-abundant optimism. *Analuisa* had reached a point on the mighty, moving waters from which few floating objects of her diminutive size and lack of power ever emerge with anyone living on board. As the saying goes and statistics predict, only something like a miracle could save the people of the *Analuisa* in their desperate circumstances.

The miracle, in this case, came in the form of an enormous blue-and-white cruise ship rising from the limitless seas. The agonies of death by thirst or exposure had scarcely begun for the helpless group of Cubans when they saw the *Ecstasy*. The Carnival Cruise liner approached over the horizon to the northeast, navigating a westerly course toward them. Once again, as before, every person on the comparatively tiny *Analuisa* waved their clothing, especially the orange garments some had chosen to wear, because they had heard orange was the best color for the purpose of attracting attention at sea. They had very few other personal possessions with them, having no room to spare, but Amarilys had a mirror in her small bag. Now her brother Luís used the mirror to reflect sunlight, trying to signal the quickly moving cruise ship for help. But for all their waving and reflecting, it seemed as if the dream-like ship would pass by without seeing *Analuisa*, still a faraway speck on the gathering waves, when an attentive lookout on the bridge of the *Ecstasy* spotted the flickering mirror in the distance. Hearing the report, the captain ordered the giant ship, towering nine decks above the surface of the water, to change course, and in the ancient tradition of mariners helping anyone lost at sea, he went to aid the *Analuisa*.

After fifteen anxious hours at sea in that small launch, the Cuadras family and their companions clambered out of Luciano's little fishing boat and away from the hellish potential of untold hours adrift in her, with nothing to drink, eat, or pour into the empty engine. But before their salvation from near disaster was assured, everyone in the group had to climb a steep, swaying, ladder-like set of stairs up the side of the towering ship, a prospect that terrified several of them. But summoning the courage to step from the rocking skiff to begin the climb, all of the late-embarking passengers made their way to the safety and comfort of the luxurious floating city. The incredible abruptness and scale of the transition became evident immediately upon their having set foot—or paw—on deck. At first, it looked as if Sisi the dog would have to be left behind on *Analuisa*, but the cruise ship captain gave instructions to bring the puppy on board, so Julio made the ascent with his wife's pet under his arm. Once she was on board, a member of the crew presented the hungry animal with a plate of roast chicken, a rare treat for humans in Cuba, to say nothing of dogs, during the long years of hardship and shortages on the island. Then the exhausted travelers were shown to cabins where they would stay for the duration of the cruise to Mexico and on to Florida. They exulted in the hot showers and the rich abundance of food and beverages readily available aboard the ship, things so rare in Mariel. Meanwhile, the Carnival Cruise Line *Ecstasy* continued on her majestic way to Cozumel, leaving the abandoned *Analuisa* bobbing in the Gulf Stream in her wake.

Like the sailors being saved by Caridad del Cobre in statues and images of the patron saint, four terrified men felt themselves pushed and pulled by the restless seas of the Straits of Florida. The engine had died in their small fishing skiff named *Carmencita*, and now they despaired, believing they were doomed to the same agonizing fate of thirst or drowning that had claimed so many others from Mariel, their home. Grimacing from pains in his chest, the boat's owner, Juan José Alfaro, feared a heart attack would strike him before he could reach land. His cardiac problems had caused him to leave his wife and young son back in Cuba to seek medical care in Florida, where his brothers and sister lived, but he never counted on his motor failing the way it had. He and his three friends left from the little dock on Mariel Bay behind the house where his mother Caridad lived. She saw him off, the seventh of her eight children to embark on a voyage to the United States.

Carmencita's engine trouble had started when Juan and his friends were only about fifteen or twenty miles into the voyage. They limped along for a while, but the motor finally sputtered out, and all efforts to revive it had failed. The men began to cry from rising frustration, fear, and regret. Juan Alfaro thought of his mother Caridad, and of her namesake, Caridad del Cobre, the charitable lady of the immense waters of the world, as the tears came.

That's when he saw *Analuisa*. A few hours earlier, nineteen of his neighbors from Mariel had deserted the sturdy boat to climb the *Ecstacy*'s ladder, leaving *Analuisa* behind. Her white hull and orange trim showed her to be one of the Cuadras family boats, immediately recognized by Juan Alfaro, who grew up in the close-knit neighborhood of La Puntilla with the other fishing families. *Analuisa*'s old engine was still warm, and after some urging it fired up again. There was some gasoline left on board, and even a little bit of water. Juan and his three companions left *Carmencita* in their wake as *Analuisa* chugged off with them into the darkening seas. Juan lay down to relieve the stabbing pains in his chest as night fell, but in a few hours one of his friends awakened him excitedly to show him the glow of lights just over the horizon, the lights of a city. It was Key West. They had made it, thanks to *Analuisa*!

As symbolized in this 1580 wood engraving by Theodore de Bry, Christopher Columbus arrived with his three ships in the New World, which he believed was Asia, expecting to spread Christianity among the natives and to receive the gold and jewels of the region in return. (Courtesy Library of Congress)

Chapter 2:   **Fourteen Colonies:**
Cuba and British North America

The native people of Cuba were accustomed to amazing sights. Huge storms they called *hurracán* (hurricanes) uprooted entire forests and caused the sea to rise and rush onto the land. Fish and whales sending plumes of spray into the air regularly passed by their shores. Clouds of seabirds dense enough to obscure the sun congregated at rookeries along more than two thousand miles of seacoast. But the people in Cuba who witnessed the approach of three caravels from Spain during the autumn of 1492 were unprepared for the spectacle. They had seen dugout canoes fashioned from a single tree before, but the *Niña*, *Pinta*, and *Santa María* were an unexpected phenomenon, with steep hulls up to ninety feet long, tall masts and stout yards like trees themselves, and spreading expanses of sail reflecting the light.

Christopher Columbus landed on the island of Cuba for the first time on October 28, 1492. He and his little flotilla sailed along much of the north coast of the island during that first voyage of exploration. They spent six weeks feeling their way first to the west, then back to the east, interacting with the native people along the way. This island could be Cipango, Columbus hoped, a large outlying island of Asia reported by Marco Polo and in other travelers' accounts, perhaps what we know as Japan. Columbus dispatched two of his mariners as envoys to the interior, where he imagined the king of the island would be found in his capital, but they returned with reports only of more villages of thatched houses like those they had come across during their coastal exploration. As the three vessels passed by the beautiful beaches and inviting harbors of Cuba's north coast, the possibility that this was a peninsula of the Asian landmass occurred to Columbus. The Italian navigator, who called himself "Colón" in the Spanish of his adopted nation-state, later claimed to his patrons King Fernando II and Queen Isabela that he had indeed reached Asia. Actually, he had encountered an island about 730 miles long, only 160 miles wide at is broadest, but much narrower in most places, averaging about 50 miles across. Cuba is the largest island in the Caribbean, and in fact it is not a single island, but an archipelago of more than sixteen hundred islands. Even so, Columbus had in mind much more significant landmasses than Cuba.

Columbus returned to the Caribbean the following year, this time with seventeen ships and about fifteen hundred men. Again sailing in his favorite ship, the *Niña*, Columbus explored the south coast of the island, continuing to hope it was the fringe of Asia. The shallow and labyrinthine waters around the islands and inlets of southern Cuba frustrated him after many weeks of looking for a passage or strait to the riches of "the Indies." But before returning to Spain again, Columbus forced his crew to swear an oath that Cuba was not an island, but an appendage of the mainland of Asia. He threatened to slice their tongues if they said differently, but no kind of threat, no matter how dire, could make his cherished dream of oriental wealth come true in the islands of the Caribbean.

Columbus continued to nourish the notion that Cuba was part of Asia throughout his third voyage of exploration, which took him along the coast of South America, and his fourth voyage beginning in 1502, which brought him near Cuba one final time. On that last long and beleaguered expedition, Columbus was shipwrecked on the island of Jamaica, eighty-five miles to the south of Cuba. He and the survivors were rescued only because Diego Méndez and some other members of the crew paddled off in a dugout canoe to find help. They made the hazardous 400-mile crossing to the Tiburón Peninsula in present-day Haiti, and from there they trekked overland to Santo Domingo in the present-day Dominican Republic, to summon assistance.[1] The Admiral of the Ocean Sea returned to Spain for good in 1504, just as it was becoming evident to the legions of navigators who sailed in his wake that Cuba was not part of Asia at all. Instead, the rough outline of two continents previously unknown in Europe was slowly revealed to these men, who swelled the wave of exploration and conquest set in motion by Columbus.

One of these conquerors was Diego Velázquez de Cuéllar, a wealthy adventurer who sailed with Columbus on his second voyage. He led the Spanish invasion of the island of Cuba from 1511 to its completion in 1514. Velázquez and his comrades-in-arms encountered a large population of people on the island. The native people were descendants of ancient mariners who ventured onto the ocean from the coast of what is now Venezuela, paddling dugout canoes made from tree trunks. They reached the Caribbean islands and settled there, from Trinidad to the farthest Bahamas, to the western tip of Cuba. Fifteen hundred years later, when the Spanish arrived, millions of native people inhabited the Antilles.[2]

Three groups of people lived among the islands of the Caribbean when the Spanish arrived: the Ciboney, Taino Arawak, and Carib. Only the Ciboney and Taino Arawak lived on Cuba, far from the warlike Carib inhabiting the eastern part of the Caribbean archipelago. The Ciboney were a Neolithic culture, cave-dwelling hunters and gatherers who used stone tools. The more numerous Taino Arawaks, on the other hand, lived in large towns that included permanent houses and large sports fields. They practiced versatile ceramic skills, fished with hooks, spears, and impoundment nets, and raised crops of beans, corn, squash, and cassava. The Spanish under Velázquez went about seizing control of this population and their homes. They met fierce resistance, led by Hatuey in the mountainous eastern region of Cuba. Hatuey was a *cacique*, a chief of the local Taino Arawak, whose armed opposition to the Spanish ended when Velázquez pursued, captured, and executed him in 1514. Hatuey is still remembered in the name and logo of the leading beer brewed in Cuba.

Diego Velázquez divided the native people of the whole island among his followers as workers for gold mines and sugar plantations. Becoming the first colonial governor of Cuba, he ruled until 1521, then returned to office in 1523 for the last year of his life. He is best known for dispatching Hernán Cortés to Mexico in 1519, then changing his mind and ordering him to return to Cuba. Cortés refused to obey the governor because he and his small army had already reached the capital of the Aztec empire and were not about to stop. Velázquez sent his most experienced general, Panfilo Narvaez, who had led the campaign against Hatuey during the conquest of Cuba, to apprehend Cortés. Cortés attacked Narvaez upon his arrival and defeated him, then went on to overthrow Moctezuma and conquer Mexico. The incredible wealth of the mainland societies shifted the focus of the Spanish empire away from the relatively poor native people of the Caribbean and toward the Aztecs of Mexico and the Incas of Peru, conquered in the 1530s, with their mountains of gold and silver.[3]

Within fifty years of the Spanish invasion of Cuba, the Ciboney and the Taino Arawak both were virtually extinct, victims of diseases brought from the "Old World," against which their bodies had absolutely no immune defenses. Smallpox, influenza, and ninety other maladies arrived with the Europeans and the animals that came along with them. Harsh treatment of the native population by the conquerors, who slaughtered many at the outset and divided up the survivors as slaves, also contributed to the demise of the native people.[4]

African workers brought unwillingly from West Africa replaced the dwindling numbers of Taino Arawak in the fields and mines of Cuba, beginning in 1523, when the King of Spain ordered three hundred slaves sent to the colony. Seven hundred more followed in 1528, at the request of the colonists. The flow of captive immigrants from Africa to Cuba continued for the next three hundred and fifty years, making the island the largest slave society in all of Spanish America. At its height in the 1830s, the Cuban slave trade would take fourteen thousand unfortunate people away from their homes in Africa every year.[5]

The principal vehicle for moving people, goods, and treasure around the Spanish empire was the galleon, a large three-masted vessel with high forecastle and sterncastle. For protection, these lumbering vessels gathered at Havana to make up the annual *flotas* (convoys) that carried the treasures of the Americas back to Spain. Detail from John Ogilby, *America* (1671). (G.W. Blunt White Library, Mystic Seaport)

La Habana, or Havana, was one of the first cities the Spanish conquerors built in what was being called the "New World." Diego Velázquez first founded a settlement called San Cristóbal de la Habana in 1514 on the south coast of Cuba, but the original location was swampy and unhealthy, so the city was relocated to La Chorrera on the north coast. That site had the disadvantage of being vulnerable to attack, which prompted a final move down the coast in 1519, when the city known as La Habana found a permanent home on the edge of a deep harbor, a mile wide and two miles long. The Spanish colonizers situated what became their capital on a peninsula there, between the harbor and the sea. Havana would benefit from the harbor's spacious anchorage and its convenient proximity to the Gulf Stream, which flows like a conveyor belt of warm water east and north to Europe. The port city grew rapidly, ranking third in Caribbean trade behind Santo Domingo and San Juan, Puerto Rico, by mid-century, when a total of seventeen vessels reached Spain from Havana over a span of seven years. Permitted from the outset to build boats for trade with other Spanish settlements—unlike others that had to rely on Spanish-built vessels—the city became the center of shipbuilding in the region. Havana was the most important port in the Caribbean area by 1600 and had earned the designation "Key to the New World and Bulwark of the West Indies" by royal decree a century after being founded. "Ships of no matter what size are practically moored to the houses of the city," marveled a traveler to Havana in the mid-1600s.[6]

Havana became the home port of the *flota*, or fleet system, in which galleons brought goods from Spain to the colonies and carried the exports of the Spanish-American empire back to Spain. These "great unruly" treasure ships, loaded with silver, gold, and valuable tropical commodities, convened in Havana harbor to form convoys before attempting their return voyage across the Atlantic. Staying together for protection, the annual flotas left Havana, which was guarded after

1538 by the fortress called the *Castillo de La Fuerza Real* (Castle of the Royal Arms), and rode the Gulf Stream north. Once past the point later occupied by St. Augustine, Florida, which was guarded after 1565 by the *Castillo San Marco* fortress, they shaped an easterly course to Cádiz, Spain.[7] A squadron of fighting ships called the *Armada de la Carrera de Indias* protected the convoys on their dangerous transatlantic passages.

A former commander of the treasure fleets, Pedro Menéndez de Áviles, founded St. Augustine in 1565 to guard the route of the Spanish galleons from English, French, and Dutch sea raiders, then went on to become governor of Cuba. The first permanent European settlement in what would become the United States, Spain's Florida outpost at St. Augustine stemmed from the same root as Havana, Cuba. It predated England's Virginia colony by nearly a half century, but beginning with the first three ships to arrive at the site christened Jamestown, Virginia, in 1607, an increasing number of British colonies sprang up on the mainland coast to the north, along with settlements planted by the Dutch and French.

The northern European competitors of Spain—England, France, and the Netherlands—also preyed on the biannual Spanish fleets emanating from Cuba. Naval forces of these imperial rivals, considered pirates by the Spanish, laid in wait in the Florida Keys and the islands of the Bahamas for the passing flotas, and sometimes attacked Havana itself. French raiders held the city for ransom in 1555, despite the "Twelve Apostles" battery of cannons at the newly constructed Cabaña Fortress guarding the entrance to the harbor. Another form of piracy was slave smuggling to the domains ruled by Spain, an activity pioneered by John Hawkins (or Hawkyns) and Francis Drake. These two became the most renowned of the English "sea dogs," figures despised by the Spanish but idolized

As one of the first Spanish cities in the New World, La Habana was established alongside a good harbor on the north coast of Cuba in 1519. Well fortified to defend against sea raiders, Havana repulsed an English expedition in 1655, not long before this fanciful image of the port was published. (Detail from John Ogilby, *America* (1671); G.W. Blunt White Library, Mystic Seaport)

in England. Drake attempted to sack Havana in 1585, but was repulsed. The formidable and famous fortifications guarding the entrance to the harbor, *El Morro* to the east and *La Punta* to the west, were constructed soon after, to guard against future incursions. During the undeclared war between Spain and England that began in 1570, and particularly after the outbreak of formal hostilities in 1585, Spanish vessels had to waste long periods of time in Havana harbor waiting for the coast to clear before crossing the Atlantic to Spain.

The Dutch became the main threat to Cuba in the early 1600s. Admiral Piet Heyn of the Dutch West Indies Company, founded in 1621, forced the entire Spanish treasure fleet into the Bay of Matanzas, soon after it left Havana in 1628, and captured every ship. The cargo included indigo, tobacco, dyewood, and so much silver that it required several days to count it all. The capture of the "silver fleet" inspired Dutch nationalist pride during the Eighty Years War (1568-1648), when the seven northern provinces of the Netherlands fought for independence from Spain. Sometimes the treasure seized in raids on the Spanish was a surprise, as it was when a Dutch vessel chased down a sloop bound from Yucatán to Havana with a load of cacao in 1627. Not knowing that the pods were the raw material for chocolate, the corsairs thought they were sheep manure and threw them into the sea. Within a few years, however, the secret of chocolate had been discovered in other raids on Spanish Caribbean ports, and cocoa became a popular beverage in the Netherlands. Dutch *zee-rovers* harassed Spanish shipping and port cities in the Caribbean so tenaciously that the fortifications in Havana and Santiago de Cuba (the second-largest city in Cuba, on the southeastern coast of the island) were expanded twice, 1602-06 and 1640-43.[8]

The defenses of Havana and Santiago prevented English forces sent by Oliver Cromwell from seizing Cuba in 1655. The English invasion force, commanded by the Puritan governor of Massachusetts Bay Colony, retreated from Havana to take weakly defended Jamaica from the Spanish instead. Kingston and Port Royal, Jamaica, became bases for raiding the Caribbean commerce of other nations, especially Spain. One of the most famous Jamaican pirates, Henry Morgan, became royal governor of the colony, revealing the high level of official support enjoyed by the marauders. Woodes Rodgers also made the transition from "pirate" to royal governor in the Bahamas islands, which like Jamaica were seized from Spain as the imperial rivalry with Great Britain heated up in the late 1600s. Nassau on New Providence Island, the heart of the Bahamas colony, offered convenient access to Spanish shipping lanes from Cuba. Major Smith, governor of New Providence, continued to dream of seizing Cuba for Great Britain after visiting the island as a captive in 1665. "This great Island is easier to be conquer'd, and would make the best Plantation, beside the prejudice it would be to the *Spaniards*, and the great advantage to our Nation," he wrote.[9]

While raiding was one way to tap the wealth of the Spanish empire, commerce was another. Spanish colonial policy on the subject was inconsistent, sometimes cracking down on illicit trade, sometimes permitting the colonists of the different New World empires to supply each other's needs. Bureaucrats across the empire colluded with the movement of contraband. Spanish officials in the Canary Islands allowed ships from Amsterdam to sail to Havana, and some of them even traveled to the Netherlands with false ship registers to sell. Cuban officials accepted bribes from foreign traders to market goods in the colony or to sail on to another colony with their written permission, among many other forms of corruption. By the early 1700s, "hardly a single official did not implicate himself" in the rampant smuggling in Cuba, although most of it flowed through the southern parts of the island, not Havana. Then as now, Cuban tobacco was one of the most heavily traded commodities in the black market. Almost two-thirds of the annual crop of ten million pounds "surfaced illegally" in England and the Netherlands, with barely a third finding its way through the cumbersome official system to Spain.[10]

While the Caribbean islands, including Cuba, did not fulfill Columbus's dreams of an endless source of gold and jewelry, they became fertile grounds for the development of a colonial agricultural system nearly as significant as the gold and silver mines of the mainland Spanish colonies. Sugar came to the Caribbean from the Canary Islands, transported by Columbus on his second voyage in 1493. Colonial North American trade with the Caribbean followed the movement of the "sugar frontier" from the smaller to the larger of the Antilles between the 1600s and the 1800s. Sugar dominated Caribbean agriculture, and its expanding cultivation created steady demand for land and slaves. Slave labor was integral to the plantation economies of the Caribbean. Slaves performed all the grueling tasks of sugar production, many of which were very dangerous, exposing the workers daily to the risk of severed limbs, broken bones, cuts, burns, infection, and disease. The slaves dug holes to sow the sugar crop and used sharp machetes to harvest the fields, which were dense with razor-like foliage ten feet high. They crushed the cane in large, exposed rollers, and boiled the juice in four infernal stages, which required ladling the molten, bubbling liquid (at temperatures around 300 degrees Fahrenheit) from one gigantic open kettle to the next. The process yielded raw sugar, which British colonial North Americans traded for and took home to refine into white "loaf" sugar, as well as molasses, which they distilled into rum.

West Indian sugar and molasses powered the vibrant colonial North American maritime economy for two centuries, while the thirteen colonies on the mainland served as a warehouse supplying the Caribbean plantation system. Although it was nearly 1800 before sugar became a major export from

Columbus introduced sugar into the Caribbean in 1493, but its cultivation did not become significant in Cuba until the 1700s—100 years after the sugar economy was established in British islands. This illustration by Theodor de Bry shows the labor-intensive process of sugar production, with field hands to plant, tend, and cut the cane, others to strip and grind the canes in the mill, and still others to boil the juice, separate the molasses, and crystallize the sugar. A dangerous industrialized process, sugar production began to rely on slave labor in the 1500s and was the principal reason for the persistence of slavery in Cuba until 1886. (Courtesy Library of Congress)

Cuba, other tropical exports, such as coffee and tobacco, competed for the attention of plantation owners in Cuba as they pushed back the fringes of the natural environment to cultivate cash crops. The residents of Havana and other Cuban coastal cities, where goods were continually scarce because of the mercantile policies of Madrid, were willing to conspire with American smugglers, who brought everything from fish to furniture to their shores, looking for local tobacco, sugar, and coffee.

The trend of the 1700s, during which the Bourbon dynasty came to power in Spain, favored the gradual opening of ports in the Americas, but under close official scrutiny. The Spanish crown encouraged legal trade from Cuba, the "Pearl of the Antilles," by forming the *Real Compañía de la Habana* (Royal Havana Company) in 1740, a move that tried to divert commerce away from the illicit channels through which it habitually ran. More stringent enforcement of the trade restrictions within the empire led to conflict. At the time the Royal Havana Company was formed, Spain was at war with England over the issue of smuggling in the Caribbean region. "The War of Jenkins' Ear" began in 1739, when the Spanish coast guard apprehended an English trader named Robert Jenkins operating on the coast of the "Spanish Main," off Venezuela. Accusing Jenkins of violating the trade laws of the Spanish empire, the Spanish captain lopped off his ear as a warning, telling him to send it to Parliament. Jenkins did just that, precipitating the war with the very strange name. Residents of the North American colonies blamed the War of Jenkins' Ear on King George II of England, calling it "King George's War." Many colonists were swept up in its bloodshed, including George Washington's brother Lawrence, who took part in Admiral Edward Vernon's 1741 expedition against the walled city of Cartagena on the Spanish Main, in present-day Colombia. Lawrence named his Virginia estate after his former commander, but the fever he contracted while serving with the

British forces in the Caribbean during the war deteriorated his health long after his return from the unsuccessful campaign. He returned to the Caribbean, this time to Barbados, in hopes of recovering from tuberculosis, but died there in 1751, leaving Mount Vernon to his younger half-brother George, who had accompanied him on the trip.

A group of free Cuban soldiers of mixed African and European descent was captured by the British during the War of Jenkins' Ear and sent as slaves to New York, where they participated in an uprising known as the Conspiracy of 1741.[11] Teaming with other enslaved people of color and "black Irish" co-conspirators, the Cubans burned the governor's mansion and other buildings around the city before being put down and publicly executed. The New

In 1749, 14-year-old Brook Watson (future lord mayor of London) was a sailor aboard a Boston vessel when he lost his leg to a shark in Havana Harbor. In his 1778 painting, artist John Singleton Copley exaggerated the grandeur of Havana, but he accurately depicted the mix of seafarers engaged in colonial trade to Cuba when it was permitted. (Photograph © 2005 Museum of Fine Arts, Boston)

York Conspiracy of 1741 highlighted the different perspectives on race that would distinguish Cuba from the neighboring colonies to the north. The Cuban soldiers who had been captured during the War of Jenkins' Ear were free men of color, a common status for individuals of mixed race in Spanish America. But there were few non-White people in the British American colonies who were free, because of laws called "black codes," dating from the 1680s, which identified dark skin color with slave status in society.

Ties between the North American mainland and Cuba increased greatly after 1762, when the British captured Havana during the Seven Years War, a global conflict with a North American theater of action known as the "French and Indian War." British statesman William Pitt the elder told his countrymen that, with possession of the great port city, "all the riches and treasure of the Indies lay at our feet."[12] Great Britain restored Cuba to Spain at the close of the war in 1763, in exchange for the colony of Florida, which at that time comprised the fortress city of Saint Augustine, the entire peninsula, the Florida Keys, and the Gulf of Mexico coast all the way to Louisiana.

Although the British occupation of Havana lasted only ten months, it changed the way Cuba did business. The occupiers' declaration of free trade brought an unprecedented flow of goods to the previously sheltered colony, resulting in greater prosperity and heavier ship traffic than ever before. The presence of thousands of North American soldiers among the invaders strengthened personal contacts that facilitated future commerce with the island. The King of Spain declared his own version of *comercio libre*, or free trade, shortly after the British departure from Havana, opening Cuba and a few other Caribbean colonies to trade from nine Spanish cities, and ending the monopoly held by the port of Cádiz since the time of Columbus.

The reign of the most reform-minded Bourbon, King Charles III, began in 1759 and lasted nearly thirty years. At the end of that time, forty thousand people lived in Havana, making it the third largest city in the Americas. Under Bourbon rule, the city ceased to be a *gran aldea*, or big village, as attested by the University of Havana (founded 1728) and the imposing new city hall (completed 1792), among other urban embellishments.[13] Development fanned out to the west from Parque Colón, a plaza located where legend said Columbus had first come ashore in 1492. Havana's growth was geographically limited to the north by the wave-wetted coastline, and to the east and southeast by the curving margin of the harbor, where the infrastructure of shipping—wharves, warehouses, and workshops—occupied more and more city space as the Cuban economy expanded with each passing decade. The town of Regla came into existence across the harbor to the east. After Cuba was opened to the international slave trade in 1789, it would become the center for the Cuban slave trade, with *barracones*, or slave pens, and auction houses concentrated near the waterfront. A royal decree permitted Havana to expand its shipbuilding industry around the same time.

Cuba prospered during the last years of the 1700s, as the Bourbon monarchy of Spain continued to carry out colonial economic reforms that increased the island's maritime links with the world. After years of deterioration, the flota system ended once and for all in 1778, and most of Spanish America gained the same level of "free trade" enjoyed by Cuba since 1765.

During the same period of Spanish "Bourbon reforms" in the colony of Cuba, the thirteen colonies of North America went through a more violent series of transitions in their relationship with "mother country" England. While the Bourbon monarchs loosened their grip on colonial trade practices, the British government clamped down on the widespread smuggling of the American colonists. The trouble began with what the colonists called the French and Indian War, which they interpreted very differently from the legislators in London. The British won the war in 1763, taking Canada from the French and Florida from the Spanish in the peace settlement. The acquisition of these territories removed the threat of raids from the French and Spanish along the seacoasts and frontier borders of the thirteen colonies. But the war had been very expensive, driving the British treasury into debt; in response, Parliament went about trying to increase government revenue. Reasoning that the North American colonists in particular had benefited from the war because the danger of attack from hostile French and Spanish neighbors had been removed, the lawmakers passed a series of acts to enforce the taxes already on the books. They included tariffs on foreign sugar and molasses that Yankee traders habitually evaded. In fact, the Sugar Act of 1764 that so outraged so many colonists in North America actually reduced the rate of taxation on sugar imports, but provided for strict adherence to the new, lower duty.

From the point of view of many colonists, they had already paid their dues during the recent war. Not only had they faced off against the French and Indians at home, they had launched ambitious and successful naval expeditions to seize the stronghold at Louisbourg in Nova Scotia and the Caribbean island of Martinique, and they had contributed to the attack on Havana and its subsequent occupation. Far from feeling indebted to the metropolitan government, many colonists thought they should be rewarded with the right to settle on the lands recently wrested from France and Spain, especially the rich region west of the Appalachian Mountains. Instead, King George III proclaimed that land to be under the stewardship of the Indians who lived there, prohibited the colonists from crossing the mountains to claim it, and commanded frontiersmen like Daniel Boone, who had already forged ahead in pursuit of furs, to return to the eastern side of the peaks. When the majority of colonial traders continued to ignore the customs collectors, tension mounted in the seacoast cities of the colonies, which were the destinations for smuggled cargoes from Cuba and other Caribbean markets. Common "Jack Tar" sailors from the waterfront escalated the violence of the confrontation between the imperial forces and the willful colonists in the streets of America's ports. Clashes between salty colonial mobs and the "lobsterback" soldiers of the empire, such as the "Boston Massacre" of 1770, presaged the warfare of the American Revolution.[14]

Trade between Cuban and North American merchants boomed during the American Revolution, when Spain sided with the United States and threw its colonial ports open to the new nation. Maritime traffic from the thirteen newly independent states to Havana surged from four vessels in 1776 to 368 in 1782. But Spain reasserted its imperial restrictions against foreign commerce when the war ended, expelling American agents and barring U.S. ships for a decade.[15]

Also at the close of the American Revolution, Spanish King Charles III pressed King George III of Great Britain to return to him the fortress of Gibraltar, gateway and strategic key to the Mediterranean. A British fleet had seized "The Rock" back in 1704, and its garrison had since defended it successfully during three sieges by the Spanish. The most recent siege, lasting three years and seven months, began in July 1779, part of the hostilities triggered by the war for United States independence, and did not end until several months after the Siege of Yorktown, Virginia, which culminated in the surrender of the British army in October 1781 and concluded with ratification of the Treaty of Paris in 1783. But when King George III asked for one of "the limbs of Spain," Puerto Rico and Cuba, in exchange for Gibraltar, King Charles III refused to make the trade.

In its demand for slave labor, Cuba jumped into prominence in the last quarter of the eighteenth century. The cultivation of sugar, which occupied just three thousand acres in 1762, had expanded to cover half a million acres in 1792. Coffee was becoming an important Cuban product as well, particularly with the resettlement of French coffee planters from Saint-Domingue after the slave revolt led by Toussant L'Overture that resulted in the new nation of Haiti. The number of slaves in Cuba rose from around forty-four thousand in the 1770s to eighty thousand in 1792, three years after foreign-flag slave ships were first permitted to land in Cuba. American slavers were partly responsible. Although U.S. law prohibited American captains from carrying slaves to other nations after 1794, American captains such as James De Wolf of Bristol, Rhode Island, became substantial suppliers of African slaves in Cuba. The De Wolf family alone made 84 slaving voyages between 1784 and the end of legal slaving by Americans in 1807, and James De Wolf became one of the first Americans to establish a sugar plantation on the island of Cuba. His plantation, Mount Hope near Matanzas, commemorated his home in Bristol.[16]

"Neutral trade" between Cuba and the United States was again permitted during the portion of the Napoleonic Wars when Spain was at war with France. The number of American ships calling at the island increased from 150 in 1796 to more than 600 in 1800. The intimacy of the commercial connection with Cuba had a cultural influence on the early American Republic as well, seen in events such as one held in Salem, Massachusetts, in 1801, when the local Marine Society held a well attended fund-raising turtle dinner. The guest of honor that night—the turtle!—had been a gift from a "gentleman in Cuba."[17]

The rise in U.S. trade with Cuba came about in part because of the simultaneous slave revolt in the French colony of Saint-Domingue, soon to be renamed Haiti, which had been the principal source of tropical produce for the United States. Thereafter, Cuba would be the leading destination for American ships in the Caribbean. Spain would open the colony to world trade in 1818, then formalize the commercial relationship with the United States with a treaty the following year. Partly as a result of this easing of imperial restrictions, Cuba did not take part in the revolutions that swept the rest of the Spanish empire between 1810 and 1825, remaining a colony until the War of 1898.[18]

By the time the colony of Cuba threw open its ports to the trading ships of the world, a diverse and numerous people called the island home, with more coming every year. Two out of every five of the 700,000 individuals in Cuba in 1820 had been born in Africa and brought unwillingly across the Atlantic, stripped of their possessions and their liberty, but not of their memories and intellects. New arrivals from Africa continued being dragged to Cuba until 1860, when the nefarious slave trade was finally suppressed, but the practice of slavery itself was not phased out until the 1870s. Through the experience of 600,000 Middle Passage survivors, Afro-Cuban culture maintained the rhythms and religious beliefs of those regions of Africa where the original unwilling immigrants had been born and raised. Salsa and rumba music have helped to perpetuate African influences in Cuban culture to the present day, and the practice of *Santería* keeps the deities of West African people alive in the New World. These examples of musical and religious vestiges of African culture in

La Caridad del Cobre, the patron saint of Cuba and those in peril on the sea. This statue was donated to Mystic Seaport by *Analuisa* passengers Miralys Gonzalez and Luciano Cuadras. (Mystic Seaport 2000.151, Dennis A. Murphy photo)

Cuban society also demonstrate the blending that takes place with elements of the dominant Spanish culture. Salsa and *rhumbas* have the same syncopation as the rhythms of West Africa, but now the lyrics set to them are sung in the Spanish language. The gods and goddesses of Santería endured the suppression of African religious practices by the Spanish with their identities intact, but had to acquire Catholic disguises, such as the river goddess Oshun masked as Our Lady of Caridad del Cobre. Such blending of African and European traits also characterized the Cuban people, as a collective Cuban identity took shape among them over the years, despite wide disparities in the distribution of wealth and freedom from the top of the social pyramid to the bottom.

Perched at the apex of Cuban colonial society, a small set of self-consciously non-Cuban officials, sent from Spain, governed the island's affairs. These military men and career bureaucrats came and went without putting down roots in Cuba. But the top segment of local society, the wealthy planter class, put down roots quite literally, by managing the cultivation of coffee, tobacco, and especially sugar. These elite landowners traced their lineages to Spanish nobility, with twenty-nine families claiming titles as of 1810, including thirteen at the level of marquis and sixteen headed by counts. Plantation families pushed the sugar fields across much of the island, using forced labor to produce almost a third of the world's supply by 1860. This clannish, light-skinned group guarded their social status at the top by arranging marriages within their number.

At the base of the social triangle were the slaves, who represented a quarter of the Cuban population in the 1770s, but whose numbers grew to more than half of all Cubans by the middle of the 1800s. In the middle strata of Cuban society, between the few upper-crust families and the numerous slaves, could be found white artisans, farmers, and merchants. The Cuban population boomed in the late eighteenth century, as new immigrants from Spain, many from the regions of Andalusia, Galicia, and Asturias, helped to turn new settlements into thriving towns and cities, or turned small plots to the meticulous cultivation of tobacco. Free people of color, many of them freed sons and daughters of slaveholders and their slaves, also occupied a middle layer of Cuban society. Often openly recognized, educated and provided for by their fathers, this class of Cubans occasionally owned slaves of their own. Other slaves purchased their own freedom, a right called "co-articulation," which was encoded in a Spanish law that derived from a Roman slavery practice. Still other people of color earned their freedom through military service. While a person with one black parent and one white parent was called "mulatto," that common term was just one of many designations for different proportions of European and African blood, which suggests how rigidly conscious Cubans were of the status conferred by comparatively light skin. The large number of black and mixed-race people among the free population of Cuba, about fifteen percent, differed from the society of the Southern United States, where dark skin color of any shade almost always conferred slave status on a person.[19]

The distinction between black and white skin colors, like the contrast between dark tobacco and light sugar, imposed a deep cultural divide in Cuba long after the abolition of slavery in the 1870s. The famous Cuban writer Fernando Ortiz, known as the "Third Discoverer" of Cuba (along with Columbus and the liberator José Martí), noted this black/white, tobacco/sugar dichotomy in his best-known book, *Cuban Counterpoint: Sugar and Tobacco*. Ortiz identified many differences between the principal agricultural crops of the island and between the two main races of people living there. "Tobacco is dark, ranging from black to mulatto; sugar is light, ranging from mulatto to white. Tobacco does not change its color; it is born dark and dies the color of its race. Sugar changes its coloring; it is born brown and whitens itself, at first it is a syrupy mulatto and in this state pleases the common taste; then it is bleached and refined until it can pass for white, travel all over the world, reach all mouths, and bring a better price, climbing to the top of the social ladder."[20] Tobacco and sugar both shaped and mirrored the pattern of life for Cubans in all social classes in the countryside, while trade in those two commodities energized the cities.

Commerce in smokes and sweetness also brought cosmopolitan influences into the lives of Cuban city-dwellers, especially those in the many ports that sprang up wherever there were decent harbors during the late 1700s, and grew with the surge in agriculture that took place in the early 1800s. People and goods from around the world came ashore at these burgeoning entrepôts, with their rich hinterlands covered in sugarcane and tobacco leaves. Heightened race and class consciousness came along with the greater human diversity of the urban population, which comprised people of every shade of complexion and every economic state. The richest Cuban families shifted their residence with the seasons from their plantation mansions to stately homes in the city, where they gathered at exclusive clubs. But other clubs at lower levels of the social ladder also maintained their own kind of exclusivity, such as the practice of welcoming free mulattos but excluding any slave or person with a very dark complexion. The complexities and inequities of Cuban society provided the subject matter for the most famous novel in Cuba, *Cecilia Valdés* by Cirilo Villaverde, which took the author four decades to complete. The first part of the book was published in 1839, making it perhaps the earliest anti-slavery novel, and it was later translated into English as *The Quadroon*, meaning a person of one-quarter African ancestry, three-quarters European, in this case the heroine Cecilia. The culture of free, mixed-race people in Cuban cities comes through vividly in such scenes from the book as a "Fashionable Dance for the colored people." The lovely protagonist, daughter of a Spanish slave trader and a mulatto woman, is the center of attention at the crowded party, where "from early in the evening, the floor was crowded with people of all colors, sexes and conditions, that jammed both windows of the porch and made a lively picture." Some of those who admire Cecilia's beauty do so with "expressions of pity because, taking her for a white girl, it was natural that people would be surprised to see her there and would suspect of low taste anyone who mingled so intimately with colored people."

Everyone at the dance, of whatever hue, follows a strict dress code demand-ing white satin dresses with blue sashes and feathers in the hair of the women, black frock coats, white silk ties, and shoes with silver buckles for the men. When a less-nattily attired fellow with particularly dark skin intrudes, managing to enter after the ticket-takers desert their post at the door, his appearance makes him "the target of all eyes from the moment he entered the ballroom," and when he dares to ask the elegant Cecilia for a dance, an altercation ensues. Señorita Valdés has such bias that "even a casual observer could notice that there was a difference in her treatment of Negroes and mestizos [people of mixed race]. The latter often led her in a contradance. With the blacks, however, she danced only minuets." When fair Cecilia snubs the ill-clad interloper entirely, he gets angry, yelling that "she scorns me because she thinks that on account of her white skin, she is white. But she's not. Maybe the Young Lady can fool others, but not me!" Her boyfriend intervenes and kicks out the presumptuous stranger, cursing him as he goes: "You dog. You must be a slave! Get out!" The hostilities and jealousies deeply ingrained in Cuban society emerged so clearly in Villaverde's narrative of Cecilia Valdés, that it continues to resonate with readers today.[21] Although a supposedly color-blind revolutionary government has broken up the wealthy landowning class in Cuba, it cannot erase racial prejudice from a population so deeply impacted in the past by slavery and discrimination.

From very disparate human sources—native American, European, African, and even Asian—emerged a hybrid population unique to Cuba, immersed in a culture equally diverse in its origins. The Spanish word for such a blending—of people, language, food, religion, or music—is *criollo*, or creole, which basically means "homegrown." Through the ups and downs of a difficult history, the Cuban people remained buoyant in spirit, and continued to increase in their numbers, until today there are more than one hundred million homegrown souls on the island. Despite the richness of their culture and the beauties of their homeland, many of these people have made bold attempts over the years to leave Cuba and cross by boat to the United States. The attraction of the neighboring country to the north is based on the long relationship between the United States and the Cuban people, a relationship that grew stronger during the tumultuous years of the nineteenth century.

Chapter 3: "Take Her, Uncle Sam!": Cuba and the United States

Cuba boomed in the first quarter of the nineteenth century. When Spain lost most of its American empire, it tightened its control over its two remaining colonies, Cuba and Puerto Rico. By 1827, Spain was shipping as much merchandise to those two islands as it had to its entire hemispheric empire before the Latin American independence movement disrupted the relationship. The colony became the principal market for the flour of Bilbao and Santander, the textiles of Barcelona, and the wine and olive oil of Málaga, Seville, and Cádiz. Havana was among the five largest cities in the Western Hemisphere at that point, along with New York, Boston, Mexico City, and Lima, Peru. The first railroad in the Spanish-speaking world began operating in Cuba in 1830, only five years after the world's first functional steam railroad in England and a mere three years behind the first United States line. By the mid-1800s, Cuba alone provided a quarter of Spain's revenues, generated by trade with the increasingly sugarcoated colony. Cuban prosperity was linked to the exploding sugar industry, which produced enough sugar to satisfy the entire world market by itself.[1]

Cuba experienced a large military build-up and increased Spanish naval presence in its coastal waters, partly in response to a wave of invasion attempts from the United States in the 1840s and 1850s. Newspapers such as the *Louisville Daily Courier*, expressing the sentiments of the expansionist Young America wing of the Democratic Party, urged the seizure of Cuba from Spain. "She [Cuba] admires Uncle Sam, and he loves her. Who can deny the banns? There she sits on her throne of Cleopatra, pouting her rosy, sugared lips. She is of age. Take her, Uncle Sam!"[2]

The Spanish colonial authorities imposed strict censorship on the domestic press and tried to prevent provocative foreign publications like the *Louisville Daily Courier* from entering Cuba. Americans and other visitors coming to Cuba were warned not to carry sensitive publications with them into the colony, at the risk of fines and imprisonment. The captain of the U.S. steamer *Crescent City* lost

Along the Havana waterfront, vessels moored with bows to the quay in European fashion, making cargo-handling a problematic process. (*Gleason's Pictorial*, December 17, 1853; G.W. Blunt White Library, Mystic Seaport)

his permission to land in Havana because he published in New York what the authorities said were "gross lies" about Spanish rule in Cuba.[3]

Despite the tense political atmosphere, American ship owners and captains found a variety of ways to make money trading with Cuba. For instance, George Washington Lee of Norwich, Connecticut, employed his brig *Jerome* in an active trade between Havana and Marseilles, France, in 1824. The vessel carried Cuban sugar, coffee, and cocoa to the Mediterranean, returning with garlic, hats, and wine for the burgeoning Havana market. Silas Beebe of Groton, Connecticut, commanded the schooner *LaGrange* in a network of trade linking the ports of New York, Havana, New Orleans, and Veracruz, Mexico. In December 1826, he cleared New York with a cargo of flour, apples, cider, beef, pork, and cod, which he exchanged in Havana for 400 boxes of raisins that he took to New Orleans, along with a multinational group of passengers: four of them French, two "Creole" Cubans (including "Yago, Color Boy"), one "Connecticut mariner," and an Irishman. After a side trip to Veracruz with candles and more passengers, Beebe took on cotton in New Orleans and returned to New York. Soon he was outbound again, this time with barrel staves, candles, soap, and four barrels of tripe for Cuban gourmets. Loading with the island's delicious coffee, citrus, pineapples, and bananas, he again made the New Orleans-Veracruz round-trip circuit before clearing once more for New York with Louisiana cotton on board.[4]

Fishing smacks from New London County, Connecticut, also made the trip to Cuba. These sloop- or schooner-rigged vessels had a "wet well" in the hold—a watertight compartment with holes allowing the flow of seawater through it—where fishermen stowed live fish to keep them fresh until they reached market. Artist Winslow Homer documented a later generation of these smacks in a series of watercolors, picturing them at their work on the dangerous waters of the Straits of Florida. At least nine smacks sailed south from Long Island Sound in November 1824 to spend the winter in the Florida Keys, delivering their catch to the fresh fish market in Havana. The Connecticut smacks made weekly runs from Key West to the Cuban capital, often in groups of three or more vessels, each smack bearing a stalwart-sounding name such as *Alert, Energy, Eagle,* and *Perseverance.* They unloaded hundreds of live fish at a time and sold them for high prices, then returned to the Keys to catch more.

The log of the Stonington fishing smack *Gallant* chronicles many such visits to Havana, including Christmas Day 1824, spent there in the company of several other smacks. Most of the trips were only overnight stays, but in March 1825 the *Gallant* remained in Havana Harbor for nearly a week to be "careened." The crew unloaded the ballast and guided the boat in to the beach, then tipped it to clean and paint one side of the bottom, tipped it again to paint the other side, re-launched and reloaded the boat, and finished by painting the deck. Captain Hiram Clift of the *Gallant* took the opportunity to purchase a new supply of lines and hooks in the city, and even "went up to Castle Blanco" one squally afternoon, a rare bit of sightseeing for a busy fisherman. Stormy weather necessitated other maintenance; one gale left the *Gallant* with a "sprung" mainmast, and another sent the topmast crashing down

New England fishermen spending the winter in the Florida Keys to serve the Havana market were among the first to see the profitability of salvaging the merchant vessels snared by the reefs. With increasing trade to the Gulf of Mexico, "wrecking" became a principal occupation for the new settlement of Key West, which retained strong ties to Cuba, just 90 miles south. (*Harper's New Monthly Magazine,* April 1859; G.W. Blunt White Library, Mystic Seaport)

on deck. But bad weather could mean windfall profits, too. Captain Clift's journal describes how smacks supplemented their lucrative fishing enterprise by "wrecking," or salvaging vessels that stranded on the treacherous reefs along the Florida Keys. The *Gallant* spotted the schooner *Ceres* of Norfolk, Virginia, which had run aground during a northeast gale while bound from New Orleans to Havana in November 1824, and went to its rescue. Captain Clift and his crew tried to haul the *Ceres* free by "Kedging"—carrying anchors offshore and winching the schooner to them—but when that failed they concentrated on removing the cargo of flour and hams before everything was "bilged," or spoiled by salt water. Clift received half the value of the cargo he and his men saved. The *Ceres* was the first of three vessels the *Gallant's* crew helped to salvage before heading back to Connecticut in May. One of them, the Boston brig *Creole,* was en route from New Orleans with a cargo of cotton. The *Gallant* and a number of other smacks unloaded cotton bales from the stranded *Creole* until they were able to float her over the reef to deeper water, becoming the owners of the discharged cargo as they did so. Their share of the salvaged cotton paid Clift and his men more than two thousand dollars, a fortune at the time.[5]

Around the time vessels like *Jerome*, *LaGrange*, and *Gallant* sailed their routes to Cuba, piracy revived in the Caribbean. Pirates preyed on shipping in the waters around Cuba in the 1600s, but were suppressed by an international effort for a century preceding the Latin American wars for independence in the 1820s. But then the two sides taking part in those wars—the rebellious republics fighting Spain and the royalists defending her—both sanctioned privateers to attack each other's commerce. The privateers fighting on both sides attacked whatever vessels they encountered near Cuba and Puerto Rico, the remaining bastions of Spanish control. When their prey began to include American vessels, the U.S. Navy responded with the formation of the West India Squadron in 1822, the first of its many squadrons around the world. Commodore James Biddle was the first commander of the squadron, based in Key West, but he resigned after finding out that big frigates, which needed deep water to operate, were ill suited to operations close to the Cuban coast. The next commander was Commodore David Porter, a bold officer who had taken the U.S. frigate *Essex* into the Pacific Ocean to attack British whaleships during the War of 1812. He penetrated the inlets of the Cuban coast in a "mosquito fleet" of shallow-draft sloops, schooners, and barges to pursue and destroy pirate vessels close to their lairs in Cuba and Puerto Rico. Porter also employed the first steam-powered vessel ever used in naval action, a small, four-year-old steamboat built at Hartford, Connecticut, and named *Sea Gull*. Porter's violation of Spanish sovereignty in Puerto Rico led to his court-martial, but his tactics curtailed piracy, allowing the further proliferation of merchant vessels voyaging to Cuba, like the busy *Jerome*, *LaGrange*, and *Gallant*. When Commodore Porter sailed into Key West aboard the sloop of war *John Adams* in December 1824, the crews of the *Gallant* and the other fishing smacks gave him three cheers! Sailors from Porter's patrol boats, such as the schooner *Terrier*, boarded these same fishing smacks to be sure they were not disguised pirates, too.[6]

During these years, Cuba came increasingly under United States influence through maritime means. The voyage to Havana from New Orleans took two or three days, and that from New York four to six, whereas the transatlantic trip from Spain required two or three weeks. This geographic advantage over the distant "mother country" gave the United States a dominant role in Cuban trade, with food, wood, and manufactured goods flowing south, and sugar, tobacco, and coffee flowing north. Mississippi and Ohio River port cities also took an active part in the relationship, especially in supplying flour. For three decades before the Civil War, Cuba ranked third in imports and fourth in exports among American trading partners, and the United States ranked first among Cuba's. [7]

High tariffs and shipping fees cut into this growing trade, especially after the outbreak of a trade war between the United States and Spain in the 1830s. Exorbitant duties on flour pushed the price of bread beyond the means of most Cubans, reduced the trade of the Mississippi and Ohio River valleys, and fuelled the movement in the United States calling to annex the island. Spain also tried to exclude American rice from Cuba, reducing its connection with the Southern states, though nearly three-quarters of the Cuban rice market was still supplied by the United States. Washington retaliated by raising duties on Cuban coffee and restricting trade in Spanish—mainly Cuban—vessels to U.S. ports. This navigation act, passed in 1834, weakened the maritime links between Cuba and Southern ports of America, destroying the nascent Cuban merchant marine and impeding the Cuban shipbuilding industry, which relied on the carrying trade to its northern neighbor. Even so, more than two hundred ships sailed between Cuba and New York in 1835. [8]

One of the most audacious maritime entrepreneurs was Frederic Tudor of Massachusetts, who pioneered the global ice trade. This business involved harvesting ice on New England ponds during the long, cold winters, storing it in insulated icehouses, and sending it by ship to the tropical regions of the world. Tudor eventually earned the nickname "the Ice King" for his success in spreading the pleasures of ice cream and chilled drinks to the torrid zones, but it took a long time to sell his unlikely scheme to the Caribbean and beyond. In 1807, the second year of his efforts, Tudor had some initial success with ice at Havana, but the 1808 Embargo delayed the business until 1810. Helped by a monopoly on ice sales in Cuba, Tudor persevered, though storm, yellow fever, and unreliable business associates kept his "shipping speculation" a tenuous one for years. Until his business spread to Charleston, to New Orleans, and ultimately to Calcutta, Havana taverns and hotels were the principal customers for American ice, some of which went to keep fish from the Straits of Florida fresh for consumption by an international clientele. [9]

Sugar was of the greatest importance in the trade linking the mainland with Cuba, especially after the "sensational" increase in Cuba sugar production in the 1770s. The pace of sugar cultivation intensified after the hurricanes called St. Francis of Assisi and St. Francis of Borja, named for the October days of the Catholic calendar when they hit, destroyed most of the mature coffee trees on the island in 1844 and 1846. Rather than replanting with coffee, which took at least three and as many as seven years to yield a harvest, landowners put in sugarcane, which matured in as little as a year. By the 1860s, sugar accounted for more than eighty percent of Cuban exports, with each harvest producing

A modern Cuban sugar plantation of the 1850s, powered by steam and served by hundreds of slaves. (*Harper's New Monthly Magazine*, 1865; G.W. Blunt White Library, Mystic Seaport)

a half million tons. Fast-growing sugarcane found a ready market in the United States, where it became a prominent part of the national diet. Sugar consumption soared before the Civil War, reaching the level of nearly thirty pounds per person annually. Most of this came from the proliferating plantations of Cuba. In contrast, the average Spanish citizen ate less than two pounds of sugar each year. When new U.S. tariff rates discriminated against refined white sugar in favor of unrefined brown sugar, the American refining industry flourished as a result. There were only four domestic sugar refineries in 1848, but by 1856 there were twenty-seven, most of them in the Northeast. The tremendous expansion in Cuban sugar production created other maritime connections to the United States. The grinding machinery and steam plants required by the factory system of the sugar industry came on ships from the North, as did everything required for the railroad construction that supported the spread of sugarcane cultivation: iron rails, ties, cars, and locomotives. Still, even sugar was subject to the vagaries of the weather, as Captain William Walker of the brig *New Era* found in Cuba in 1857: "Nothing doing here in Freights, and nothing to ship, there is no Sugar in the place for they have had so much Rain that the Cane will not yield." Insurance rates for ships bound to Cuba climbed during the hurricane season of late summer and autumn, and passages punctuated by "gale after gale," as the *New Era* encountered, were common. [10]

The sugar boom also fueled a voracious market in slaves. By international agreement leveraged by Great Britain, the legal transatlantic trade in slaves ended between 1817 and 1820. More than a hundred thousand African slaves were rushed to Cuba in those last three years, including an unusually high percentage of females, imported in the hope of sustaining the slave population. With a thousand sugar plantations by 1830, the largest of which would grow to run on the nearly endless labor of 800 slaves, the Cuban demand for slaves became almost insatiable. "It is the worst sort of slavery I have seen anywhere," wrote the British consul in 1850. Indeed, the annual mortality rate was about ten percent. Though Spain had agreed to cut off the slave trade in 1820, the illicit traffic in African captives continued with the tacit, and well paid, permission of the colonial authorities. [11]

The illegal Cuban slave trade victimized an average of fourteen thousand people a year during the 1830s. Kidnapped and gathered in crude barracoons by slave dealers near Sierra Leone, up the Congo River, and in Angola, the Africans

The Cuban slaver *El Almirante* was in the Bight of Benin on the African coast with 400 captives on board when the ex-slaver, HMS *Black Joke*, attacked and captured her in 1829. (Mystic Seaport 2001.49)

were packed in small, fast vessels flying the Portuguese or Spanish or sometimes American flag for the Middle Passage trip of perhaps two months to Cuba. The bloody traffic defied growing efforts by Great Britain to exterminate the slave trade and continued throughout the 1850s, bringing thirteen thousand Africans to Cuba annually during that last decade of the Middle Passage. Slaves accounted for forty percent of the Cuban population, with more arriving all the time. The slave trade became a salient issue between the United States and Cuba, as many vessels involved in the smuggling were constructed for that purpose in Baltimore, and such prominent firms as G.G. & S. Howland of New York openly cooperated with Cuban slave traders. A high percentage of the crews who manned these disreputable vessels came from the United States, as well.[12]

Free black and mixed-race sailors, on the other hand, faced mounting intimidation from the authorities in Cuba and the cotton ports in the Southern United States. Since the late 1700s, the threat of slave insurrections in the U.S. had heightened the alertness of civic authorities in the Southern states. Alarmed by the success of the revolution in Haiti and worried about the role of free black sailors as bearers of tales of freedom to the closed slave societies, they clamped down. After Denmark Vesey's planned uprising in Charleston, South Carolina, was discovered and the leaders executed in 1822, South Carolina quickly imposed a set of Negro Seamen Acts to discourage sailors as agents of resistance. Intended to eliminate contact between black sailors and slaves, the acts required that ship captains place their black sailors in the local jail, at the expense of the ship, during their stay in port. A Spanish royal order in 1837 imposed similar restrictions in Cuba and Puerto Rico, and Alabama and Louisiana followed suit. In 1846 alone, one hundred free blacks from the Northern United States languished in Cuban jails.[13]

The other issue in Cuba was the *emancipados*: Africans liberated from slave ships. With the Royal Navy cruising on the African coast and in the Caribbean, and the U.S. Navy providing intermittent patrols with its African Squadron, hundreds of Africans were freed before being delivered to a life of slavery. If freed near Africa, Sierra Leone became home to those liberated by the Royal Navy, while those freed by the U.S. Navy were deposited in Liberia. When the Royal Navy caught a slaver off Cuba it delivered the Africans to Cuban authorities, who were expected to place them in the hands of benevolent overseers who would Christianize them and employ them. But those put to work on sugar plantations were barely distinguishable from slaves, and some were actually enslaved when their bogus benefactors gave them the names of dead slaves. [14]

The *Amistad* incident of 1839-41 highlighted the major points of the slave controversy. At Havana, the Cuban-built, Baltimore-style coasting schooner *Amistad* was loaded with fifty-three Africans who had recently survived the Middle Passage aboard the Portuguese slaver *Teçora*. The *Amistad* would deliver them to the plantations of their new owners near Puerto Principe, 300 miles east of Havana. During the passage, Sengbe Pieh, whom the Cubans had renamed Joseph Cinque, unlocked his shackles and led an uprising against the small crew, seizing the schooner. The Africans then tried to make the survivors (two of whom had purchased them) sail them back to Africa, toward the rising sun. Instead they ended up as the "prize" of a U.S. revenue cutter off Montauk, Long Island, New York, and their case entered a labyrinth of U.S. courts of justice. While abolitionists championed their freedom and their owners and the Spanish government sued for their return as property, the legal case turned on their identity as slaves as indicated by their inability to understand Spanish. Though listed as *ladinos*—Spanish-speaking slaves native to Cuba or imported before 1820—it was clear that they were *bozales*—newly arrived, and thus illegal slaves who only spoke the Mende language of Africa. The case gave expression to the diametrically opposed perspectives on Cuba, slavery, and the slave trade held by Americans before the Civil War. Congressional Representative and former President John Quincy Adams, who represented the Africans before the Supreme Court in the last round of the legal contest for their freedom, articulated the abolitionist argument that Cuban collusion in the slave trade was immoral, slavery on sugar plantations was brutal, and the unwilling *Amistad* passengers were victims of kidnapping who should be allowed to return home. The opposing, mainly Southern view, held that the Africans were the legal

This 1839 lithograph by John Childs depicts the principal figures in the *Amistad* case. At center, Singbe Pieh (Joseph Cinque) address his fellow African captives, who wear clothing found on the *Amistad*. Behind Singbe is the *Amistad*'s 16-year-old cabin boy, Antonio, and to his right is Jose Ruiz, who had purchased the males captives in Havana. Ruiz was wounded in the uprising on board the *Amistad*. At far right is Pedro Montes, who had purchased the African children in Havana and who collaborated with Ruiz in the suit to have the Africans returned as their property. The U.S. Navy officer may represent Lieutenant Thomas Gedney, who commanded the brig *Washington* that took the *Amistad* captives into custody, and who sued for salvage of the vessel and cargo. At left are several of the U.S Navy sailors from the *Washington*. (ICHi-22004, courtesy Chicago Historical Society)

property of the planter who bought them, and furthermore, such difficulties as those posed by the *Amistad* case could be avoided by annexing Cuba and reopening the U.S. slave trade, illegal since 1808. The Supreme Court ruled in favor of the Africans, who were eventually returned to Africa by missionaries, but the judgment did not impede slave smuggling to Cuba. In the years of the secession crisis in the United States, 1859-61, the Mixed Commission for the Suppression of the Slave Trade in Havana counted 58,705 kidnapped Africans and ninety-four Middle Passage voyages.[15]

As the international slave trade drew to a close, the demand for labor intensified in the proliferating sugar fields, along the lengthening railroads, and in the mechanized sugar factories of Cuba. One new source of sugar workers was China. More than a hundred thousand Chinese men signed contracts to work in Cuba from 1847 to 1871, many of them recruited and transported by American shipping companies participating in the "coolie trade." The *ku li*, or bitter strength, of these Chinese workers explains their being called "coolies"

After 1850, Asian contract workers, hired for a specified number of years, increasingly helped meet the demand for manual laborers in Cuba. Frederic Remington drew these Chinese "coolies" preparing to load coal on a steamship at *Havana*. (*Harper's Weekly*, November 7, 1891; G.W. Blunt White Library, Mystic Seaport)

in the harsh industries they manned: mining Peruvian guano, building American railroads, and producing Cuban sugar. Mexico sent Mayan and Yaqui Indians taken prisoner in wars in Yucatán and in northern Mexico to be forced laborers on Cuban plantations, as well. The mix of labor is suggested in a list of fifty-six *cimarrones*—fugitive slaves (also, in a linguistic commentary on maritime culture, the word for lazy sailors)—captured at Cardenas in 1857-58. The largest number, thirty-eight, were Asians, while six were Cuban-born *Criollos* and two were apparently Central American Indians. Among the ten Africans, most of whom were too young to have arrived before the end of the legal slave trade, seven were from the Congo region and one was a Mandingo. No matter their race, every one of the *cimarrones* had a Spanish name.[16]

The development of the sugar industry, port facilities, and railroads led to the colony of Cuba being "overrun by Americans," who resided in the cities and on the growing plantations. One of the resident Americans, William King, became vice president of the United States in the Franklin Pierce administration in 1853—he was sworn in at his plantation near the port of Matanzas! Although the U.S. absorbed most Cuban commerce, Spain still controlled its politics, resulting in a kind of "dual colonialism" that kindled conflict between the two nations over the fate of the island. Many Americans advocated annexation of Cuba from Spain, especially those in the South who favored the extension of slavery, and those in New York who emphasized the importance of Cuban trade and investment to the prosperity of that city. Cuban trade was pre-eminent in New York, the most active port in America; 967 vessels arrived there from Cuba in 1857, 400 more than from second-place England. A great number of Cuban slaveholders agreed that annexation would extend the life of slavery, and they conspired to detach the colony from Spain and apply for acceptance into the Union, as slaveholders in Texas had done after their revolt against Mexico in 1836.[17]

As Spain lost its mainland empire in the Americas and became "the sick man of Europe" in the 1820s, it seemed likely that Cuba would slip away, too. When Spain considered turning Cuba over to the United Kingdom in 1823, Secretary of State John Quincy Adams predicted that the island colony would instead become an American possession. Adams, who drafted the famous Monroe Doctrine asserting protection over the Latin American republics, newly independent from Spain, said that as "an apple severed by the tempest from its

The New York & New Orleans Steam Ship Company launched the similar wooden side-wheel steamers *Black Warrior, Cahawba, De Soto*, and *Bienville* in the early 1850s. They normally called at Havana for mail and passengers during the run between New York and New Orleans. When the *Black Warrior* was detained at Havana in 1854 for trade violations, President Franklin Pierce came close to calling for war against Spain in order to seize Cuba. (Mystic Seaport 1997.29)

native tree, cannot choose to fall to the ground, Cuba, forcibly disjointed from its own unnatural connection with Spain, and incapable of self-support, can gravitate only toward the North American Union, which by the same law of nature cannot cast her off from its bosom." Rather than wait for the apple to fall from the withered Spanish tree, some Americans tried to pluck it by force.[18]

The constant threat of invasion from the United States during the 1840s and 1850s kept Cuba and the waters around it in a state of intrigue and tension. On several occasions, private seaborne armies composed mainly of American mercenaries, called "filibusters," descended on the Cuban coast in steamships that came from New Orleans via Key West. The conspiracies led by Narciso López, a Cuban exile, and John Quitman, a Mississippi planter and politician, complicated navigation and diplomacy in the region. In 1854, the Havana port authorities detained the steamer *Black Warrior* of the New York & Atlantic Steamship Company on a technicality, interrupting her regular run between the Gulf port of Mobile, Alabama, and New York, and inciting a fresh war scare.[19]

At the same time, three proslavery diplomats posted in Europe pressured Spain to sell Cuba to the United States outright, implying in their "Ostend Manifesto" that the Americans would simply seize the colony if its mother country refused to name its price. Future president James Buchanan, future Confederate envoy James Mason, and their counterpart Pierre Soulé met in

49

the Belgian port of Oostende (Ostend) to put their thinly veiled threat into words, and though both political parties in the United States disowned their annexationist gambit, President Franklin Pierce asked Congress to appropriate fifty million dollars to offer Spain for Cuba. But Cuba was not for sale, and the Spanish resented the implication that they would voluntarily give it up.[20]

Julia Ward Howe captured the prevailing air of suspicion in her 1860 account of entering the port of Havana on the British mail steamer *Karnak*.

And here is the Morro Castle, which guards the entrance of the harbor—here go the signals, answering our own. Here comes the man with the speaking-trumpet, who, understanding no English, yells to our captain, who understands no Spanish. The following is a free rendering of their conversation:
"*Any Americans on board?*"
"*Yes, thank Heaven, plenty.*"
"*How many are Filibusteros?*"
"*All of them.*"
"*Bad luck to them, then!*"
"*The same to you!*"
"***Caramba***," *says the Spaniard.*
"---- ----," *says the Englishman.*
And so the forms of diplomacy are fulfilled.[21]

Havana was the eighth busiest port in the world in the 1850s, with nearly one thousand U.S. vessels arriving annually. It was the foreign port most frequently visited by U.S. vessels, with an influence such that English novelist Anthony Trollope commented in 1859 that the city would "soon become as much American as New Orleans." [22]

Passengers wanting to travel between the Cuban metropolis and the principal American cities could book passage on the side-wheelers of the New York & Atlantic Steamship Company (New York), the Atlantic Mail Steamship Company (Philadelphia), the Baltimore-Havana Steamship Company, and the French Imperial Mail Steamship Company (New Orleans). On the busy inland riverfront of Louisville, Kentucky, travelers could buy their tickets direct to Havana, boarding a riverboat steamer for the trip down the Ohio and Mississippi Rivers, then changing to a bluewater steamer in New Orleans for the crossing to Cuba. Spain subsidized shipping from its colony in Cuba back to the mother country on the *Compañia Transatlántica Español*, the Spanish Transatlantic Line, or

The Iron Warehouse and industrial waterfront on the east side of Havana Harbor, ca. 1862, show well in this view from the fortified heights near El Morro, *La Fortaleza de San Carlos de la Cabaña.* (Mystic Seaport 1985.3.3)

simply "the Spanish Line," as it was known in Havana. The island's foreign trade was dominated by Spanish merchants who took advantage of the reduced rates on the Spanish Line to import their products from Europe. [23]

Though steamships took the lead in carrying people, bulk cargoes mainly went under sail until late in the century, experiencing the vagaries of weather and the marketplace. One voyage of the brig *New Era* of Providence, Rhode Island, is representative of this business. The trip south in December 1857 was uneventful for Captain William Walker, "the best passage this year," but once in the port of Cienfuegos, he found there was "little sugar on the island" to purchase because of heavy rain during the growing season. On the way back north the brig encountered "gale after gale," and seawater damaged some of the sugar Walker had been able to obtain. American ships and masters also dominated Cuban coastwise shipping; the first U.S. steamship in service outside the country ran between Havana and Matanzas, beginning in 1819. [24]

Sail or steam, ships making the voyage to or from Havana faced a variety of navigational risks. One example of these hazards taking a heavy toll was the wreck of the British steamer *Tweed*, which left Havana for Veracruz and Tampico in February 1847, loaded with a cargo of more than one thousand bottles of mercury (used in mining operations) and a supply of coal to refuel HMS *Hermes*, a Royal Navy steamer stationed in the Gulf of Mexico. A gale closed in not long after the *Tweed* cleared Morro Castle, and the weather was so foul for the next two days that the captain lost track of the ship's position. Early on the third day, the lookout spotted waves breaking on a reef barely awash in the storm and, though he screamed a warning, there was no time left to react. The *Tweed* struck hard and broke in half. The overloaded lifeboats swamped, but some swimmers found calm water inside the reef. A few crew members subsequently patched up the mailboat and sailed it to Campeche for help, leading to the eventual rescue of seventy-nine dehydrated and sunburned people.[25]

A particularly vivid description of travel to Cuba was left by one of the greatest chroniclers of American maritime history, Richard Henry Dana Jr., whose *Two Years Before the Mast* (1840) is a classic account of both the culture of American seamen and the maritime expansionism of the antebellum United States. In *Two Years*, his first book, Dana portrayed California as a region ripe for U.S. influence and acquisition; in *To Cuba and Back: A Vacation Voyage* (1859), Dana portrayed Cuba as a society corrupted by slavery, and he warned against U.S. involvement there. Dana began his narrative with the voyage from New York to Havana aboard the U.S. mail steamer *Cahawba*. The "motley group [of] passengers," included: "shivering Cubans... Yankee shipmasters going out to join their 'cotton wagons' at New Orleans and Mobile; merchants pursuing a commerce that knows no rest and no locality;... invalids wisely enough avoiding our March winds; and here and there a mere vacation-maker, like myself."[44]

Dana found the *Cahawba* to be "an excellent sea boat, and under the best of discipline," on which "the rule of quietness prevails, almost to the point of an English dinner party. No order is given unless it be necessary, and none louder than is necessary for it to be heard." Steaming south "down the outer edge of the Gulf Stream," Dana observed a parade of vessels "as in a dioramic show," including a "heavy cotton droger," a "saucy little Baltimore brig," and a bark under a "pile of white canvas" on the horizon.

Arriving at Havana, with its "houses running down to the coral edge of the ocean," the *Cahawba* passed the Morro Castle at the narrow entrance to the port and came into view of "the spreading harbor and the innumerable masts," which formed a "dense forest along the edge of the city." The scene, wrote Dana, was a "magnificent spectacle," with vessels from Spain, France, Great Britain, the United States, the Netherlands, Portugal, Italy, Brazil, Colombia, and Venezuela. "What a world of shipping!" he exclaimed.

Dana encountered the resident Americans, who were "chiefly engaged in commerce, banking, or trade," but who viewed themselves as "sojourners," not "citizens," in Cuba. This "class of persons," he wrote, impeded the growth of "patriotism and philanthropy" in Cuban society, because they were faithful only to "the strong tap-root of interest." This might be said of the subsequent generations of American shippers, investors, and developers who shaped the history of Cuba for a century after Dana's 1859 visit. After sampling plantation life and witnessing a slave auction, Dana was eager to leave Cuba behind, but not without partaking of the fruits of slave-based agriculture: he took home a barrel of oranges and several boxes of cigars.[26]

The Civil War disrupted the routine of commerce between Cuba and America on the sea, as the Union built up a naval blockade of every port in the Confederacy and gradually captured them all. Up until the war, sixty-two percent of Cuban exports found their market in the United States, which supplied twenty percent of Cuba's imports.[27] But the war disrupted much of that trade, and it nearly disrupted relations with Great Britain, as well, in an issue concerning Cuba. Two Confederate envoys to Great Britain and France slipped out of Charleston, South Carolina, aboard the blockade-runner *Theodora* in October 1861, making it to Havana. From Havana, the two Southern diplomats embarked on the British mail steamship *Trent* for the voyage to England. But the day after leaving Cuba, November 8, the *Trent* was stopped on the high seas at the order of Captain Charles Wilkes of the U.S. Navy sloop-of-war *San Jacinto*. Wilkes was already famous for leading a five-year maritime expedition of scientific and economic exploration in the Pacific, 1838–42, that had resulted in American claims on Samoa and confirmed that Antarctica was a continent, among other things. The Wilkes Expedition also resulted in a court martial for its commander on charges such as burning two native villages in Fiji, but he was acquitted. (Gene Roddenberry based his *Star Trek* series in part on the officially named United States Exploring Expedition, including the starship *Enterprise*, which bore the same name as Wilkes's flagship.) The *Trent* affair ensued when Wilkes arrested the two Confederate agents, James Mason (of Ostend Manifesto fame) and John Slidell, and removed them from the British ship, which was a violation of international admiralty law. Although Wilkes permitted the *Trent* to continue on to England, he took the two Confederate passengers to prison in Boston. Prime Minister Lord Palmerston in London mobilized an army of 8,000 men to send to Canada over the issue, but Abraham Lincoln defused the war scare when he released the prisoners and disowned Wilkes's actions.

As the naval noose around the Confederate States of America slowly tightened between 1861 and early 1865, the business of running the Union blockade generated huge profits for those willing to take the risk. During the first year or two of the war, the blockade was inefficiently enforced because there were not enough ships and too many harbors to guard. The fast steam side-wheelers called blockade-runners left the primary blockade-running ports of Havana, Bermuda, and the Bahamas with a variety of destinations from which to choose, but the list grew shorter as the fortunes of war turned against the South. Both the likelihood of capture and the profits to be made increased as the war went on and fewer port cities remained in the hands of the Confederates. In any port involved with running the blockade, Confederates, Europeans, and unscrupulous Northerners conducted a brisk trade in guns, medicines, cotton, and sugar, which brought fantastically inflated wartime prices in their respective markets. Sugar that sold for three cents a pound in Havana sold for eleven dollars in the Confederate capital of Richmond, Virginia. The U.S. consul in Havana reported that blockade-runners departed the port at an average of one a day during 1863; in the late stages of the conflict, virtually all trade to the South came via Havana. New Orleans initially was the most attractive destination for the Havana blockade-runners, but the city fell to Admiral David G. Farragut's fleet in April 1862. Attention then shifted to Mobile, Alabama, until Farragut's forces captured the bay in July 1864. The final haven for blockade-runners until the end of the war was Galveston, Texas.

The Confederate States Navy responded to the Union blockade by raiding Northern commerce. Confederate commerce raiders captured or destroyed many vessels bound to Northern cities with Cuban sugar, and found shelter and repair facilities in Cuban harbors. The CSS *Florida* visited Cuba twice during her destructive wartime voyages, refitting the first time, and the second time burning the Boston-bound sugar brig *Estelle*, melting her cargo into salty caramel before calling at Havana. Navigation from Havana to Matamoros, Mexico, a neutral port close to the Texas border, also increased during the war. After Appomattox, steamers from Mexico contributed to the stream of Confederate war refugees (planters, politicians, and military officers) to Havana.[28]

Heavy maritime traffic between Cuba and the United States resumed soon after the end of the Civil War. Slavery had been abolished on the mainland as a result of the bloodshed, and during the war Union naval forces worked with the British Royal Navy to finally suppress the slave trade to Cuba, but slavery still survived on the island. Since the Haitian Revolution, 1791-1804, even a rumor of slave insurrection could bring a brutal preemptive assault from slaveholders, such as occurred in the Matanzas and Cárdenas areas in 1834. An abolition movement gained momentum in Spain during the 1860s, however, and the Cuban slaves themselves resisted their harsh treatment in every way they could. Spain passed the Moret Law in 1870, which freed all slaves born after 1868, and all slaves over the age of sixty. But the fact that Cuban plantation owners were deeply in debt to politically powerful Spanish merchants and shippers helps to explain why the Spanish government refused to eliminate slavery in Cuba, even though it was abolished in Puerto Rico in 1873.

Slavery was one of the major issues leading to the outbreak of Cuba's violent Ten Years War, fought between 1868 and 1878. During that long struggle against Spanish colonial rule, rebels (many of them escaped slaves) burned sugar plantations and caused Cuban cane harvests to decline, yet the sea-lanes to the United States remained busy.

With the outbreak of rebellion against Spanish rule in Cuba in 1868, Spanish authorities came to the U.S. to obtain patrol boats to seal the Cuban coast. Built to a design by innovative naval architect John Ericsson, 30 of these gunboats were launched in 1869. Held up during diplomatic negotiations by the Grant administration, the gunboats were finally delivered for use in the guerrilla war that flared for ten years. (*Harper's Weekly*, October 16, 1869; G.W. Blunt White Library, Mystic Seaport)

Americans came down on both sides of the Ten Years War. To help suppress the Cuban rebels, the Spanish government contracted with prominent New York shipbuilder Cornelius H. Delamater to construct thirty gunboats for the Spanish Navy in 1869. At sixty thousand dollars in gold apiece, they were a windfall for a struggling U.S. shipbuilding industry. Delamater had the innovative marine engineer John Ericsson, best known for designing the revolutionary Civil War ironclad *Monitor*, plan these fast, shallow-draft vessels. Delamater engaged Charles Mallory of Mystic, Connecticut, to build fifteen of the hulls at several of the shipyards in Mystic. Before they were completed, the Peruvian government complained that delivering the gunboats would be a violation of U.S. neutrality in the ongoing war between Spain and Peru, as they could be used against Peru, or free Spanish ships for that service. For two months U.S. marshals impounded the vessels until the Grant administration certified its observance of neutrality laws. But, at the same time, sympathy for the Cuban rebels was increasing in the U.S. After the last gunboat headed for Cuba in early 1870, a former U.S. consul wrote to the Mystic, Connecticut,

American Captain Joseph Fry, a Tampa, Florida, native, had graduated from the U.S. Naval Academy and served in the Confederate Navy and aboard blockade-runners. In 1873 he accepted command of the ex-blockade-runner *Virginius*, which was running arms to the Cuban rebels. Captain Fry was among more than 50 crew members of the *Virginius* executed at Santiago de Cuba in November 1873. This incident brought the U.S. and Spain close to war again. (G.W. Blunt White Library, Mystic Seaport)

paper, "thirty gunboats sail from New York harbor to crush the struggling Cubans, causing tyrants to rejoice, liberty to weep and Americans to blush!"[29]

Other Americans found opportunities to profit by supplying the rebels with the arms and ammunition they needed. One of them was Captain Joseph Fry, a native of Tampa who grew up in Key West, whose long career at sea included years in the China Trade and a stint commanding a blockade-runner during the Civil War. Fry accepted command of the *Virginius*, another blockade-runner built in 1864 on Scotland's River Clyde specifically for the Havana-to-Mobile run, which had proven to be unprofitable in the peacetime trade from New Orleans to Cuba because of its coal-hungry engines. Sold to a U.S. company in 1870, the *Virginius* was soon thereafter chartered by the Cuban insurgents in New York, led by General Manuel Quesada, who used the vessel to deliver a load of arms and twenty-one rebel fighters to eastern Cuba in June 1871. Two years later, having earned a reputation with the Spanish authorities as a gun-runner, the *Virginius* was pursued by the Spanish warship *Bazan* to the port of Aspinwall (now Colón) in Panamá and blockaded there. But because the vessel was registered in New York and flew an American flag, the U.S. Navy steamer *Canadaigua* escorted it to safety, permitting a second illegal landing on the south coast of Cuba with weapons and ammunition in July 1873. In October, Captain Fry took command of the *Virginius* in Kingston, Jamaica, and set out for Santiago de Cuba to deliver the largest cargo of arms and men yet attempted, more than a thousand rifles and revolvers and sixty men, in October. After putting into Haiti for repairs, the ship was intercepted upon its departure by the Spanish warship *Tornado*, which gave chase. *Virginius* and *Tornado* were both built to be fast blockade-runners;, in fact, they came from the same shipyard. The *Tornado* caught up with *Virginius*—its bottom fouled with marine growths—and forced its surrender, despite the ham and bacon that the engineer of the *Virginius* threw into the furnace to help make steam. After their capture, more than fifty of the Cubans and Americans aboard were shot by firing squads in Santiago de Cuba, including Captain Fry. The execution of American citizens in Cuba nearly precipitated war between the United States and Spain. The tiny United States Navy mobilized during November and December 1873, but Secretary of State Hamilton Fish negotiated a resolution to the incident. As a result, the weak United States Navy, which had been reduced to a shadow of its Civil War strength, was not required to build any more "floating palaces" of war, at least not for a while. [30]

The upheaval of the Ten Years War sent thousands of Cubans north to more stable circumstances in the U.S. The movement had begun earlier, with the migration of cigar makers to Florida. Cuban immigrants began rolling cigars in Key West in the 1830s. The population of the little island increased from 2,800 to 18,000 in the next few decades, and Tampa expanded from 2,000 to 23,000 inhabitants, largely as a result of the Cuban influx. During the Ten Years War, the wealthiest members of the planter class, who had been in the practice of maintaining second homes in Paris, France, simply relocated to the City of Light when the violence increased in Cuba. Many of them remained in Paris after the Ten Years War as absentee landlords, later supporting independence from afar when the Revolution of 1895 broke out. Educated and professional members of the Cuban middle class tended to prefer the northeastern cities of the United States for their expatriate homes, especially the metropolis of New York, with its steamship connections to Cuba. The Corona, Elmhurst, and Jackson Heights neighborhoods of Queens would attract a dense population of Cuban immigrants. Working-class Cubans made their way to settle in Key West and Tampa, and later in Jacksonville and Ocala, as well, when the cigar industry expanded to the northern part of Florida. Vicente Martínez Ybor, a Spanish immigrant to Cuba, moved his successful tobacco rolling operations from Havana to Key West when the Ten Years War intensified in 1869, and in 1886 he opened another factory in Tampa. A manufacturing community called Ybor City sprang up around the factory, where the cigar workers and their families re-created the same kind of social clubs, restaurants, churches, and other urban amenities that they had known in Cuba. The clubs included the Spanish Club, the Asturias Club (named for the province on the north coast of Spain where many immigrants to Cuba originated), the Cuban Club, and, later, the Patriotic Union of Martí and Maceo, named for the heroes of the Revolution of 1895. [31]

One of the steps that Spain took to extinguish the rebellion of the Ten Years War was to free all the slaves who fought on either side during the war, and to promise an end to slavery for all other slaves when hostilities ceased. When slaves in the east refused to work after the war, the government declared them to be "apprentices" and ordered their masters to pay them for their labor,

With its white limestone façade and location on an ancient plaza, the Cathedral of Havana reminded some of a bit of old Spain set down in the Caribbean. Built by the Jesuits, 1748-1777, this church was consecrated as the Cathedral of Havana in 1789. (© Mystic Seaport, Rosenfeld Collection 1984.187.11808F)

but they still were compelled to remain working wherever they were. Although many "apprentices" negotiated the purchase of their own freedom from small operators, the reluctance of the largest sugar planters to relinquish control of their core workforce delayed full abolition until 1886. These estates had purchased many slaves in the last years of the transatlantic trade, and they wanted a return on their investment. Other sugar planters had already converted to hired labor, such as Chinese immigrants, or had reduced their labor needs by purchasing new sugar technology to replace the inefficient methods of the past. These estates had no attachment to the institution of slavery.[32] In fact, at the time apprenticeship was easing the transition from slavery to free labor, a depression in the world sugar market bankrupted many slaveholders. They were glad to emancipate their slaves and be rid of captive laborers whose upkeep they could no longer afford. The freed slaves filled the ranks of the rebel forces again a decade later, when the Cuban Revolution of 1895 successfully challenged Spanish domination of Cuba.

The U.S. deep-water merchant marine declined after the Civil War, but vessels of many other national flags strengthened the connections between the major American ports and Cuba. Cuba provided twelve percent of all U.S. imports in 1870, mainly sugar, which arrived in nearly 500 U.S. sailing vessels and 101 U.S. steamers. There was little competition from foreign carriers at that point, but twenty years later, when seven percent of U.S. imports originated in Cuba, foreign ships entering U.S. ports from Cuba outnumbered American ships in the categories of both sail and steam. As Spanish control of the colony slipped in the last quarter of the century, the Munson Line and the Ward Steamship Company competed for an increasing share in the traffic between New York and

Cuba. The Ward Line dominated the route to Havana, while the Munson Line served the other coastal cities, such as Santiago. During the sugar depression of the 1880s, U.S. bankers and investors acquired vast tracts of bankrupted Cuban sugar land, holdings that were soon to be threatened by the outbreak of another destructive war, the Cuban Revolution of 1895. [33]

Despite recurring conflict and the uncertainties of the international sugar market, the city of Havana prospered in the late 1800s. English historian James Anthony Froude praised the Cuban capital in exalted language in 1888: "Havana is a city of palaces, a city of streets and plazas, of colonnades and towers, and churches and monasteries.... The Spaniards built as they built in Castile; built with the same material, the white limestone they found in the New World as in the Old. The palaces of the nobles in Havana, the residence of the governor, the convents, the cathedral, are a reproduction of Burgos or Valladolid, as if by some Aladdin's lamp a Castilian city had been taken up and set down again unaltered on the shore of the Caribbean Sea." [34]

Anti-Spanish sentiment ran high in the United States after 1895, as the war for *Cuba Libre*, or "free Cuba," intensified again, fuelled in part by the publicized abuse of American travelers and U.S. citizens living in Cuba by Spanish colonial authorities and military forces. In one sensational case in 1896, a schooner named *Competitor* was seized in Cuban waters while delivering arms and mercenaries to the rebels, with two Americans caught red-handed on board, and two more apprehended on shore a few days later. The four U.S. citizens were prosecuted as pirates under admiralty law, convicted in a Cuban court, and condemned to death. Despite the weight of evidence against them, the U.S. State Department eventually obtained a pardon for the filibusters, but the friction between the United States and Spain continued to heat up nevertheless. By early 1897 there were seventy-three legal cases involving U.S. citizen protection claims, seven cases of American journalists being expelled from Cuba, and ten million dollars of personal and property compensation claims deriving from a total of eighty-three suits.

The growing Cuban communities in Florida and New York supported the nationalist movement in their home country actively. The Cuban Revolution of 1895 was a war for independence led by a trio of national heroes: Martí, Gômez, and Maceo. Intellectual leader José Martí, one of the most important writers and thinkers in all of Latin America in the 1890s, exiled himself from Cuba to raise funds and consciousness among his compatriots in New York and Jacksonville, employing the network of steamship lines to move between the Cuban expatriate enclaves of the United States. With the Revolution of 1895 in full swing, Martí vowed to return to Cuba to join in the fighting, but he died in combat soon after his arrival, making him a martyr for the patriotic cause.

Originally planned as an armored cruiser, the second-class battleship USS *Maine* was launched at New York in 1889. Commissioned as the second U.S. battleship in 1895, the 318-foot *Maine* was sent to Havana in January 1898 to protect American citizens in case of violence. On the evening of February 15 she exploded, killing 260 American sailors and precipitating war. (Mystic Seaport 1997.86.24)

The military chief of the revolution was Máximo Gômez, an immigrant from the Dominican Republic, who went on to lead the resistance to Spain in the wake of Martí's death. The third member of the revolutionary trinity of Cuba was Antonio Maceo, a charismatic and successful Afro-Cuban general, who led an army of angry former slaves. After his tragic death, José Martí became the central figure for Cuban nationalism as it developed over the next century, a George Washington–like figure whose portrait is still on the one peso bill, and whose bust can be found in every school and government office on the island. Martí envisioned a unified Cuban society free of racism and racial discrimination. He also understood the deep interest of the United States in Cuba, and warned that the larger country might replace Spain as an imperial master. He wrote in 1895, the year the revolution began, that "Cuba must be free, from Spain and the United States." [35]

Another cause for war arose over the Spanish tactic of "reconcentration," which was the precursor of the twentieth-century "concentration camp." The Spanish "concentrated" the civilian population of Cuba in cities and in improvised camps, while anyone outside the designated zones of civilian "reconcentration" could then be considered a rebel. Health, sanitation, and food supplies all deteriorated badly under this system, resulting in mass starvation among the civilian population. Captain George A. Converse of the USS *Montgomery* visited the port of Matanzas in early February 1898, reporting that starvation had killed nearly sixty thousand residents in the previous three months, while a hundred thousand more out of a population of two hundred fifty thousand were in imminent danger of perishing from hunger. Even the few Americans living in the city were within two weeks of running out of food.

Captain Converse urged authorities in Washington to help as soon as possible, and he was not to be disappointed.

Rioting broke out in Havana in December 1897, prompting the Navy Department to dispatch the battleship USS *Maine* from the naval base at Norfolk, Virginia, to stand on alert in Key West, Florida. The *Maine* was barely two years old, but because it had taken six years to construct in the outdated New York Navy Yard, the battleship was already obsolete, and had been downgraded to "second-class" status. Still, with its two turrets with two ten-inch guns each, the USS *Maine* was an imposing sight. The warship waited at Key West, ready to steam to the Cuban capital at the request of the U.S. consul general, for the purpose of protecting American lives and property. The consul general was Fitzhugh Lee, a nephew of Robert E. Lee who had served as a cavalry general under his famous uncle during the Civil War and later as governor of Virginia. The North Atlantic Squadron gathered at Fort Jefferson in the nearby Dry Tortugas for winter exercises in the Gulf of Mexico that year, the first war games in the region after a two-year hiatus. President Grover Cleveland had not wanted to appear to threaten the Spanish by dispatching the fleet to the waters near Cuba, but his successor, President William McKinley, went ahead with them. The Navy Department organized the North Atlantic Squadron into fighting groups instead of dispersing the ships for "good will" cruises and port calls, as the likelihood of U.S. intervention in the Cuban revolution increased. When the street riots resumed in January 1898, the *Washington Star*, which had a reporter in Havana, editorialized that the United States should station a ship in the harbor there rather than at Key West in case of trouble, because the "dirty work" of an upheaval in the city would take place in the six hours required for a battleship to steam across the Straits of Florida. U.S. Consul General Lee cautioned against the arrival of the *Maine* because of the political tensions in Havana. He worried that the appearance of the battleship would enflame anti-American sentiment on both sides of the revolution. If the ship had to come, he advised, it should enter the harbor either when another foreign warship was present on a cordial visit, or in the pre-dawn hours when the city was asleep, reducing the emotional impact that the intimidating entrance of a battleship would have on the local population. Instead, when President McKinley dispatched the battleship *Maine* to Havana, Captain Charles D. Sigsbee intentionally stalled in order to arrive there late in the morning of January 25, 1898, when no other nation's warships were in the harbor, creating a very public stir as his menacing vessel shouldered past Morro Castle to its berth.

The U.S. government explained the appearance of the *Maine* as a visit symbolic of friendship with Spain, notwithstanding the fact that the battleship's departure from Key West had been so sudden that Captain Sigsbee had no

yellow fever certification to present to the Spanish port authorities, as required by law.
They allowed the ship to enter anyway, but the Spanish press denounced its presence
as a provocative act that would encourage the Cuban revolutionaries. Several hundred
Cubans visited the *Maine* after its arrival, and while their individual interpretations of
what the mammoth warship was doing there remain unknown, they probably enjoyed the
opportunity to clamber around and admire the view of the city and the harbor from its tall
steel superstructure.

Three weeks later, just after nine o'clock in the evening of February 15, 1898, the
battleship *Maine* exploded at its mooring, killing 266 men. Fire in the ship's coal bunkers
ignited the forward munitions magazine, which was directly beneath the crew's quarters
in the forecastle, so that all of those who lost their lives, except for two officers, were
common seamen. They came from all over the United States, from East Deering, Maine, to
Los Angeles, California, and from West Bay City, Michigan, to New Orleans, Louisiana.
Others among the dead were natives of Denmark, Sweden, Norway, Finland, Russia,
England, Ireland, Canada, Greece, Romania, and Japan, and even included one of the
numerous Hassel family from the tiny island of Saba in the Dutch Antilles in the Caribbean. [36]

News of the catastrophe on board the USS *Maine* reached the United States almost
immediately, when an intelligence agent in Havana telegraphed another agent in Key West,
who then reported personally to Captain Albert Gleaves of the USS *Cushing*. The *Cushing*
was a speedy torpedo boat built by the Herreshoff company in Bristol, Rhode Island,
which was famous for racing yachts and fast steam yachts. The *Cushing* itself might have
been damaged or destroyed by the explosion on the *Maine* but for a twist of fate. Capable of
going at a speed of twenty-three knots, the vessel was supposed to begin service as a kind
of messenger boat for the *Maine* on February 15, going back and forth between Havana and
Key West regularly, but a mistake in telegraphing orders to Captain Gleaves caused him to
take the *Cushing* to Havana four days earlier than intended by his superiors. For that reason,
the little torpedo boat had already begun its duties and was not alongside the *Maine* when
the battleship exploded. Several hours later, Captain Gleaves received a cable from Captain
Sigsbee of the *Maine*, who had survived the blast. [37]

Rescuers transported the wounded survivors aboard two vessels moored nearby, the
Ward Line steamer *City of Washington* and the Spanish warship *Alfonso XII*. Within forty-
eight hours of the disaster, the Navy Department convened a court of inquiry to investigate,
as required by regulations. Presided over by Captain William T. Sampson, the court met
aboard the lighthouse tender USS *Mangrove*, which came to Havana to serve as a kind of
floating courthouse. The court consisted of five naval officers, one of them a judge advocate,
another an ensign in charge of diving operations on the wreck, and three regular members,
none of them a specialist in the fields of munitions or naval architecture. Jurisdiction over
the wreck of the *Maine* led to a dispute with the Spanish authorities, because the wreck
itself was the property of the U.S. Navy, but it lay in Spanish waters. The two countries
conducted their own separate investigations, but cooperated in diving operations and in

Part of the U.S. Navy's "fleet of experiments" off Cuba: (Top) The USS *Vesuvius*, a yacht-like 252-foot vessel, was armed with three "dynamite" guns at the bow for launching highly explosive shells with compressed air. Her silent bombardment of Santiago in June 1898 caused widespread panic, but the ship's short range and limited arsenal made her impractical. (Mystic Seaport 1997.86.11) (Top right) The USS *Gloucester* had served as J.P. Morgan's 240-foot steam yacht *Corsair* for seven years before the U.S. Navy purchased her as a gunboat for the war. The speedy USS *Gloucester* dispatched two Spanish torpedo boats in a 17-knot engagement during the Battle of Santiago. (Mystic Seaport 1958.1172) (Bottom) Built in 1890 as the steamer *El Sol* of the Morgan Line, this 404-foot ship called peacefully at Havana during her years as a freighter on the New York-to-New Orleans run. Purchased by the U.S. Navy, renamed USS *Prairie*, and armed as a commerce raider and blockading ship, she served off Cuba during the war. (Mystic Seaport 1959.1372.23)

policing the wreck site. The murky water and deep mud of Havana harbor hampered the divers as they tried to conduct their investigation on the hulk of the *Maine*, which had sustained massive damage from the explosion. The wreck site resembled an underwater jungle of jagged, twisted metal, which threatened to entangle and cut through the air hoses of the divers as they tried to make sense of the debris. The 400-page report produced by the naval court of inquiry concluded inaccurately that the destruction of the *Maine* was caused by an external explosion, perhaps a mine, which implicated the Spanish in the disaster, because they must have either caused it or failed to prevent it, both explanations being justifications for war. In fact, spontaneous combustion in the poorly maintained coal bunker was most likely to blame, but the damage was done.

While calling for a Spanish armistice in hostilities against the rebels in Cuba and for an end to the concentration camp method of securing the population, the McKinley administration at first denied any intention of invading Cuba. Spain agreed to an armistice in its war against the rebels, but already McKinley had been swayed by public demand for war. The U.S. then demanded independence for Cuba and withdrawal of Spanish forces. Spain broke diplomatic relations on April 21, and the U.S. proclaimed as naval blockade of Cuba the next day. Spain retaliated with a declaration of war, which the U.S. matched on April 25, making it retroactive to April 21. [38]

The naval War of 1898 would be fought by a weak force, according to the standards of the great navies of the time, a club that included neither the United States nor Spain. the state of the United States Navy had improved since the the time of the *Virginius* affair in 1873, but it was far from being a world power on the high seas. There were only four "first-class" battleships (*Indiana, Massachusetts, Iowa, Oregon*), one "second-class" (*Texas*), two armored cruisers (*Brooklyn, New York*), sixteen cruisers lacking armor plating (including *Mongomery*, sent to Matazas when the *Maine* went to Havana) and twenty-eight assrted others: fifteen gunboats, six monitors, five torpedo boats, one ram, and one unique "dynamite cruiser."

These vessels were now mobilized for a war against Spain, and were joined by many other vessels acquired or chartered by the U.S government for the emergency. This assemblage of fighting ships was an odd assortment, a "fleet of experiments," in the words of the British minister to Washington at the time. Lord Julian Pauncefote's characterization can be illustrated by a few examples from the ships that fought the War of 1898. The "dynamite cruiser" USS *Vesuvius* was an experimental fighting ship launched a decade earlier, which used compressed air rather than gunpowder to fire high-explosive shells, so its cannons "coughed" almost noiselessly when they fired. The attack of the *Vesuvius* on Santiago de Cuba on June 13, 1898, had a similar, terrifying effect to the V-2 rockets that struck London during World War II, causing widespread panic when bombs suddenly started blowing up in the city, without the usual warning sound and flash of firing to precede the impact of the shells. Another unusual vessel in the 1898 fleet was the USS *Gloucester*, formerly the luxury yacht of millionaire J.P. Morgan, who had called the sleek, 240-foot steamer the *Corsair*. Sold to the Navy and fitted with rapid-fire guns, the *Gloucester* would chase down the two Spanish torpedo boats at a speed of seventeen knots, sinking the *Pluton* and driving the *Furor* aground during the battle of Santiago. The USS *Prairie* was one of several first-class ocean liners built with government subsidies, which were designed for easy conversion to commerce raiding or other naval missions. Launched at the technologically advanced Cramp shipyard in 1890, the ship served on the New York to New Orleans route for the Morgan Line, owned by the Southern Pacific Railroad, under the name *El Sol* until purchased by the government for wartime use in 1898. With the addition of artillery, the fast steamer took part in the naval war off Cuba. The twenty-one-knot greyhound of the fleet was the 400-foot armored cruiser *Brooklyn*, commissioned just a year and a half before the war. With her high freeboard, extreme tumble home and side-mounted turrets with eight-inch guns, and three stacks that rose a hundred feet above her boilers, the *Brooklyn* was a distinctive ship. Her crew (totaling more than five hundred officers and enlisted men) loved her for her modern electrical conveniences and her spacious living quarters. [39]

The most sensational aspect of the mobilization for war with Spain was the voyage of the USS *Oregon*, one of the U.S. Navy's four "first-class" battleships armed with thirteen-inch guns, and the fastest battleship in the small navy. Setting out from San Francisco, California, on March 12, 1898, under the command of Captain Charles Clark, the *Oregon* sprinted nearly fifteen thousand miles in sixty-six days, despite almost wrecking during a gale in the Strait of Magellan. The newspaper press, especially the Hearst Syndicate publications that were beating the drum for war with Spain, followed the progress of the battleship with breathless

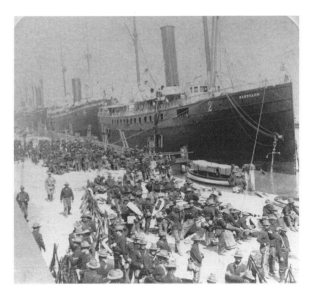

Teddy Roosevelt's "Rough Riders" prepare to board the Mallory Line steamer *Santiago* and other transports for the passage from Tampa, Florida, to Santiago de Cuba in June 1898. The *Santiago* and her sisters were accustomed to calling at Cuba, but under more peaceful circumstances. (Mystic Seaport 2000.50)

coverage throughout the voyage. Off the coast of Brazil, the *Oregon* encountered Captain Joshua Slocum in his little thirty-six-foot yawl *Spray*, homeward bound to New England after sailing alone around the world. Captain Slocum had not heard about the declaration of war, so he was surprised to read the battleship's signal flags asking him, "Are there any men-of-war about?" hoisted together with a bright yellow Spanish flag. Slocum recalled: "When I had read her flags I hoisted the signal 'No,' for I had not seen any Spanish men-of-war; I had not been looking for any. My final signal, 'Let us keep together for mutual protection,' Captain Clark did not seem to regard as necessary. Perhaps my small flags were not made out; anyhow, the *Oregon* steamed on with a rush, looking for Spanish men-of-war, as I learned afterward." [40]

The *Oregon* found the Spanish warships. Averaging close to twelve knots, the 350-foot battleship arrived in Florida on May 24, ready to participate in the war that had been declared a month before. The *Oregon* immediately joined the naval blockade of Havana, then steamed to the south coast of Cuba in time to play an active role in the decisive Battle of Santiago on July 3, 1898.

The War of 1898 was a boon to the New York & Texas Steamship Company, the "Texas Line" of C.H. Mallory & Company, third-largest steamship operation in the United States. Charles Mallory of Mystic, Connecticut, began as a

Launched at San Francisco in 1893, the 350-foot battleship, USS *Oregon*, steamed 14,700 miles around South America to join the U.S. Navy blockade of Cuba. Fast and heavily armed, with four 13-inch guns firing 1,100-pound shells her crew called "railroad trains," she helped destroy two Spanish warships in the Battle of Santiago and drove another ashore. In this view of her stern, she lies in New York Harbor for the grand naval parade celebrating the armistice in August 1898. (J.S. Johnston photo; Mystic Seaport 1958.1175)

sailmaker after the War of 1812, moving into ship management and shipbuilding on the banks of the Mystic River. While he stayed in Mystic, operating whaleships and building clipper ships and wooden steamboats (including some of the 1869 Spanish gunboats), his son Charles Henry broadened into owning and operating steamships, and moved to New York City. The wooden hulls of "Mystic-built" ships were too deep for the shallow approach to Galveston, Texas, the terminus of the line's routes, so in the 1870s the younger Mallory purchased shallow-draft iron ships from the Roach shipyard in Philadelphia, naming them for American cities.

The Mallory Line used Key West as its transit hub and communication center between New York and the ports of New Orleans and Galveston. Mallory was already a familiar name in Key West. Charles Mallory's distant relative, Stephen R. Mallory—late Confederate States secretary of the navy—had settled there in the port's early days to begin a thriving law practice based on salvage claims for ships stranded in the Keys. The open space where the Mallory Line docks and warehouses once stood on the west shore of Key West is still known as Mallory Square, a place where locals and visitors now gather nightly to watch the sunset. After the telegraph cable linked Key West with Havana in 1868, offering up-to-the-moment knowledge of Cuban markets, the freight ships of the Texas Line often called at Havana during their passages to New York. C.H. Mallory & Company survived the late 1800s, an era of brutal competition and sweeping consolidation in the steamship industry, largely from the profit made from shipping war materiel and men from Tampa via Key West to the Cuban theater of the War of 1898. Chartered by the government, eight of the Mallory Line's "city" ships participated full-time in supply or hospital service during the period of hostilities. Overall, the company received twenty percent of the business generated by war mobilization.[41]

The naval phase of the War of 1898 ended with one battle off Santiago de Cuba, where the new generation of U.S. warships destroyed the decrepit Spanish fleet. Two memorable naval officers, William Sampson and Winfield Scott Schley, competed for the initiative in the campaign preceding the battle,

(Top) Commissioned just 17 months before the war began, the 400-foot armored cruiser USS *Brooklyn* combined great speed with a functional grace. Her 100-foot stacks increased the draft in her boilers for efficient steaming, her high freeboard raised her guns and gave her plenty of berthing space, and the extreme tumble home of her sides allowed her side-mounted turrets to fire in a 180-degree arc. The *Brooklyn* and *Oregon* shared the glory in the victory off Santiago on July 3, 1898. (Mystic Seaport 1958.1171)

(Middle) Sailors on the *Oregon* pose atop her 13 inch gun turret during the battle of Santiago. (Mystic Seaport 1997.86.23)

(Bottom) Celebrating victory, U.S. Navy sailors pose by the turret and fallen mast of the Spanish cruiser *Vizcaya*, which was driven ashore by the USS *Oregon* and *Brooklyn*. (Mystic Seaport 1997.86.40)

and for the glory in its victorious wake. Both Sampson and Schley attended the Naval Academy in classes a year apart as the Civil War broke out; then after graduating, they served together on the USS *Potomac*. They did not work together again until almost a half-century later, becoming the two major figures in the Battle of Santiago. In the meantime, Sampson survived the sinking of the USS *Patapsco* after it hit a mine in Charleston Harbor. After the Civil War, as head of the Naval Observatory, he masterminded "Standard Time" in the United States by organizing the fifty-three chronological systems in use around the country into the five time zones still used today. Schley was one of the most popular officers in the Navy, proving his fighting mettle in action under Admiral David Farragut on the Mississippi River against Port Hudson during the Civil War, and as commander of an expedition against Korea in 1871, to avenge the crew of the American schooner *General Sherman*, who had been killed after landing there. Afterward, as head of the Bureau of Equipment and Recruiting, Schley standardized the Navy's familiar "bluejacket" uniform and set up the Navy's first cooking school. He was also among the founders of the National Geographic Society.

Spanish Admiral Pascual Cervera y Topete recognized that his fleet was completely over-matched by American naval forces, but his orders nonetheless were to steam across the Atlantic to take them on, which he did under protest. It was something of an accomplishment merely to coax six of the Spanish vessels all the way to anchorage in Cuba. The Spanish fleet made its Atlantic crossing in May and took shelter in the deep, well-fortified harbor of Santiago de Cuba, on the southeast coast, before Schley's squadron took position to blockade the island's south shore. The American expeditionary force left Tampa on board a convoy of chartered passenger vessels and arrived off Santiago late in June. Army forces, including Teddy Roosevelt's "Rough Riders," fought their way into control of access routes to Santiago and within artillery range of the Spanish ships. Rather than allow the doomed fleet to surrender, the Spanish governor of Cuba ordered Cervera to face the U.S. Navy head-on.

Cervera's flotilla consisted of two small torpedo boats, the speedy *Pluton* and *Furor*, and four armored cruisers: *Vizcaya*, which had been visiting New York a week after the *Maine* disaster, *Infanta María Teresa* and sister ship *Almirante Oquendo*, both of them with defective turrets that refused to rotate, and *Cristóbal Colón*, an Italian-built warship that completely lacked the four guns for its main batteries. Facing them off Santiago was an impressive array of battleships and cruisers that included the *Oregon*, *Texas*, *Iowa*, *Massachusetts*, *New York*, and *Brooklyn*. When Cervera steamed forth on the sunny Sunday morning of July 3, 1898, it required only four hours for the superior might of the U.S. ships to completely destroy the Spanish fleet. The torpedo boats went down almost immediately, while the *Oregon* and *Brooklyn* ran the four larger vessels to ground along the coast west of the city, three of them on fire, all of them total losses. Six hundred Spanish sailors lost their lives, while only a single American died in the battle. The carnage was such that Captain John Philio of the USS *Texas* stopped his men from exulting as they battered the crippled and burning *Vizcaya* on the Cuban shore, saying "Don't cheer, boys! Those poor devils are dying." Only the *Cristóbal Colón* escaped bloody destruction by beaching and surrendering, but the Spanish crew scuttled their ship as the Americans tried to tow her back to sea.[42]

Credit for the lopsided victory was disputed between Sampson, the commanding officer of the fleet—who had been absent during the battle itself for a meeting with his Army counterpart, General William Shafter—and Schley, who had directed the action from the bridge of the *Brooklyn*, but who as junior officer was prevented by Sampson from submitting his own report of what had happened. A subsequent court of inquiry by the Navy did little to enhance the reputation of either man, or to cast a more positive light on a battle fought for a spurious reason, the accidental sinking of the poorly maintained *Maine*, against an unequal and unprepared opponent, Cervera's pitiful flotilla.

Santiago fell two weeks later, and Spain called for U.S. peace terms as hostilities were ended by a protocol signed on August 12. With the signing of the Treaty of Paris in December, Spain freed Cuba while assuming the island's $400 million debt (which was one-twentieth of the price the U.S. paid Spain for the Philippines by terms of the same treaty). Spain ceded Puerto Rico and Guam to the U.S. as indemnity for the war. For health reasons, most U.S. troops had left Cuba in August 1898, but an occupying force remained until 1902, when the Republic of Cuba gained independence.

The United States intervened in the Cuban Revolution in 1898, but as José Martí had feared, American forces did not cooperate with Cuban rebel forces in the war they were calling the "Spanish American War." General William Shafter, commander of the Fifth Army Corps, had met with General Máximo Gómez near Santiago de Cuba to plan the American amphibious landing, but after the city fell relations between Cuban insurgent forces and the invading Americans deteriorated, and joint operations ceased. An American officer denounced the Cuban soldiers as "mango-bellied degenerates," and General Shafter prohibited them from entering Santiago. The American commander declared the city to be "part of the Union," and did not allow any Cubans to participate in municipal government. General Gómez, feeling betrayed, led his army away from the city they had besieged. In glaring contrast, American soldiers could be seen walking arm-in-arm in the streets of Santiago with the Spanish soldiers who had so recently been their enemies, and carousing with them at the Spanish Club. Nor did the American authorities permit any Cuban representation in the peace negotiations with Spain, which led to the Treaty of Paris.[43]

As brief as it was, the War of 1898 had broad implications for the U.S. Navy and its mission to maintain fleets on both the Atlantic and the Pacific. The slow, arduous route taken by the USS *Oregon* and its near disaster in the Strait of Magellan along the way showed that a canal connecting the Pacific and Atlantic Oceans was necessary for rapid movement of naval forces. An isthmian canal ranked high on Admiral Alfred Thayer Mahan's prescriptions for American naval strength, part of his influential Sea Power Thesis, first articulated in 1890. Mahan argued that combined fleet operations were the key to command of the seas, so the United States had to have an interocean waterway to face threats in both hemispheres of the globe. The failed French effort to create a water route across Panama would soon be revived under terms of the Hay-Pauncefote Treaty of 1900, by which Great Britain conceded to the U.S. the sole right to build a canal across the isthmus and maintain its neutrality.

Mahan also called for technologically advanced warships like the *Oregon*, which required large amounts of coal to fire their steam engines. In order to fight sea battles with a large fleet of steam-powered battleships anywhere in the world, it was essential to stockpile fuel at naval bases or "coaling stations" in strategic places. The War of 1898 represented a large step toward fulfilling Mahan's formula for American sea power. Not only did the dramatic and widely publicized voyage of the USS *Oregon* hasten the national momentum toward building the Panama Canal, but the Navy acquired excellent naval bases in Cuba, Puerto Rico, and the Philippines.[44]

General Leonard Wood succumbs to seasickness during an inspection tour of Cuba in 1901. (Mystic Seaport 1993.132.2.19)

Chapter 4: **"See You in C–U–B–A": The Twentieth Century**

Several factors strengthened the "ties of singular intimacy" between the U.S. and Cuba called for by William McKinley in his state of the union message of December 1899. Under the military governorship of General Leonard Wood, U.S. forces occupied Cuba during the creation of an independent Cuban government and a constitution for the new nation. An energetic progressive, Wood emphasized order and efficiency, implementing public works projects, including road building and port improvements. With his medical background, he pushed hard for sanitary improvements on the island, and he made great progress in public health by nearly eliminating mosquito-borne yellow fever, which had scourged the swampy, low-lying areas of Cuba.

Early in 1901, while Wood ruled with autocratic power, Secretary of War Elihu Root articulated the principles of U.S. policy on Cuba that would be presented to Congress as the Platt Amendment. Representing concern about the rising naval power of Germany, the first article of the amendment restricted Cuba from entering treaties with foreign powers that would curtail its independence or—as a possible threat to the U.S.—establish military bases on the island. Nevertheless, the U.S. reserved the right to intervene on the island "for the preservation of Cuban independence," to uphold terms of the Treaty of Paris, and for "the maintenance of a government adequate for the protection of life, property, and individual liberty." To fulfill its protective role on the island and in the Caribbean, the U.S. specified that Cuba would lease or sell land for U.S. Navy coaling stations or U.S. military bases. Guantánamo Bay, near Cuba's eastern tip, at which the U.S. Navy had established a camp in 1898, became a permanent installation as a result of this portion of the amendment. In addition to "protecting" Cuban independence, Guantánamo Bay, partially fulfilled Alfred Thayer Mahan's prescription for national sea power, which called for "coaling stations," or naval bases, at strategic locations around the world. Guantánamo Bay controls the Windward Passage between Cuba and Haiti, one of the prominent routes from the Atlantic Ocean into the Caribbean Sea. After the opening of the Panama Canal in 1914, naval command of the major navigational approaches to the isthmus would become more important, magnifying the role of the Windward Passage and the nearby naval base that sailors call "Gitmo."

The Platt Amendment also codified General Woods's public health efforts on the island. It specified that Cuba would continue plans for urban sanitation to prevent further epidemics of tropical diseases "thereby assuring protection to the people and commerce of Cuba, as well as to the commerce of the Southern ports of the United States and the people residing therein." Even this benevolent provision made it clear that the U.S. considered Cuba an appendage, and that Cuban failure to live up to American standards of disease control would have a deleterious effect on U.S. life and commerce. The provisions of the Platt Amendment were amended to the new Cuban constitution and, after the election of Tomas Estrada Palma—a former Cuban revolutionary and prominent member of the Cuban exile community in New York City—as Cuba's first president, U.S. forces withdrew from Cuba on May 20, 1902. The Platt provisions were further endorsed by a U.S.-Cuban treaty ratified by the Senate in 1904.

It was not long before President Estrada Palma invoked the Platt Amendment and called for U.S. military intervention to combat his enemies, who took to the field against him after a tainted national election in 1905 that kept him in the presidency. By September 1906, ten thousand insurgent troops surrounded Havana, and although President Theodore Roosevelt's secretary of war, future president William Howard Taft, went to the Cuban capital to mediate, no agreement could be reached between the rebels and the government. For the second time in less than a decade, the United States sent military forces to occupy Cuba and ended up taking control of the highest levels of national administration as they had in 1898, displacing Cuban office-holders. The U.S. Army and Navy withdrew in early 1909, leaving the former rebel general José Miguel Gómez as elected president. The Platt Amendment went into effect again in 1912, when the U.S. intervened in a civil clash, and justified continued American involvement in Cuban elections and public order from 1915 to 1922.[1]

The 1920s were less volatile, as President Gerardo Machado consolidated increasingly dictatorial control, then engineered the Cuban constitution to permit his long-term hold on the reins of power. Machado ordered the construction of a giant new capital building with a dome to rival that of the U.S. Capitol in Washington, a project that cost a great deal of money and symbolized the self-aggrandizement of the powerful president. Machado made many enemies as his methods of political control became bloodier in the early 1930s, until a student uprising merged with a conspiracy among noncommissioned officers in the Cuban military to produce the Cuban Revolution of 1933.

The Cuban Revolution of 1933 reached a crescendo in a shoot-out at the Hotel Nacional, headquarters of elite tourism in Havana. When the smoke cleared, a group of sergeants and corporals led by Fulgencio Batista had seized power, which led to the abrogation, or cancellation, of the Platt Amendment. President Franklin Roosevelt was also interested in reducing the level of U.S. intervention in the Caribbean, an approach he dubbed the Good Neighbor Policy, so there was no

The former Hotel Nacional, Havana, 1924. (© Mystic Seaport, Rosenfeld Collection 1984.187.11811F)

military action against the revolution, even though it deposed a government that had worked closely with the United States. Fulgencio Batista was the power behind the Cuban government without serving as president from 1933 to 1944, at which time he left Cuba. Batista returned in 1952, seizing power and becoming president himself. He established an authoritarian regime that became increasingly repressive, while facing growing resistance in the cities and the countryside, finally falling to Fidel Castro in 1959.

In those sixty years after the War of 1898, U.S. investment in Cuban utilities, railroads, sugar-producing machinery, and real estate all increased dramatically. American companies—especially the "Sugar Trust," the American Sugar Refining Company—acquired Cuban sugar lands at a faster pace than ever, stoked by the Cuban Reciprocity Treaty of 1903, which gave the island's sugar a preference in the American sugar market, although it had to contend there with the expanding production of domestic beet sugar. With this guaranteed, artificial, market in the United States, sugar cultivation overwhelmed the Cuban countryside in the first decades of the century, especially in the eastern part of the island. A witness later reported, "I remember in Oriente [an eastern province], the great impenetrable forests that were set aflame, whole jungles that were fired and razed to the ground to make way for the sugar cane. My parents were in despair for that lost wealth of beautiful, fragrant tropical wood—cedar and mahogany and mastic, and magnificent-grained pomegranate—blazing in sacrifice to the frenzy to cover the countryside with sugar cane."[2]

A street in old Havana, 1924. (© Mystic Seaport, Rosenfeld Collection 1984.187.11829F)

The flood of American-owned, Cuban-grown sugar to the New York market drove an entire generation of sugar brigs out of business. These two-masted wooden vessels were nearly identical to the sugar wagons of the past, going all the way back to the 1600s, and they served a trade that was nearly as old, carrying sugar from the British and French West Indies, such as Barbados, Trinidad, and Martinique, to North America. Driven out of New York by Cuban competition, the sturdy little boats shifted their activity to the Canadian market and continued to carry molasses to the lumberjacks of New Brunswick and the fishermen of Newfoundland and Nova Scotia.[3]

Also important for Cuban-American propinquity was the more frequent and convenient steamship service available after the turn of the century. Norton's *Complete Handbook of Havana and Cuba* listed the lines operating there in 1900: the two dominant lines were Ward Steamship Company and Munson Line, but there were also the Peninsular and Occidental Steamship Company, Morgan Line/Southern Pacific, South Coast Line, the Spanish Line, the Spanish firm of *Naviera Herrera*, and assorted coasting steamers serving Havana's periphery. During the 1920s, when North American tourism boomed, twenty steamers and twenty ferries a week connected Havana with New York, New Orleans, Key West, and Jacksonville, Florida.[4]

The United Fruit Company operated its own steamers to transport sugar from the two sugar mills it owned in Cuba. Boston Fruit Company had originally planted bananas on the Cuban land it acquired in the late 1880s. In the 1899 merger that created United Fruit, it brought banana groves so vast they required twenty-eight miles of railroad to move the bananas to the coast. But Cuba was not as well suited to banana cultivation as Central America, so United Fruit went with the flow of agriculture on the island and replaced bananas with sugarcane in 1905. Steel-hulled steamships of United Fruit's "Great White Fleet," their hulls painted white to reflect the tropical sun and protect their fragile cargoes by reducing the heat absorbed by their hulls, continued to call in Havana and Santiago after the change in crops. The famous "banana boats" had pioneered not only the refrigerated transport of their specialty cargo from Central and South America to northern ports, but also the air-conditioned and lavishly catered practice of vacation cruising around the Caribbean. Although

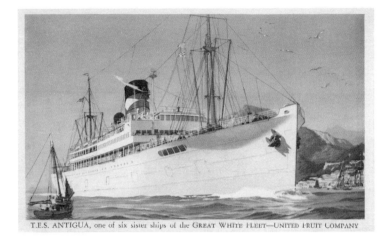

T.E.S. ANTIGUA, one of six sister ships of the GREAT WHITE FLEET—UNITED FRUIT COMPANY

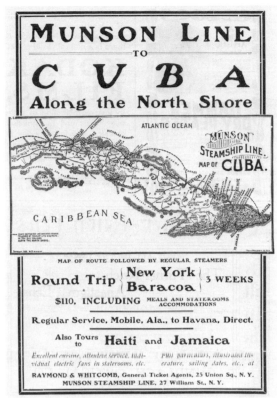

(Top left) the United Fruit Company steamer *Antigua* entered service in 1932. (Roorda/Doyle Collection) (Lower left) A Ward Line mail and passenger steamer departs Havana, ca. 1910. (Mystic Seaport 1952.2262) (Right) The Munson Line provided tourist access to a number of ports along Cuba's north coast. (Roorda/Doyle Collection)

the vessels were better suited to hauling bananas, United Fruit continued to load the sugar from its former banana lands in Cuba, owing to the lock on the shipping market held by the Munson and Ward Lines. Because the Cuban sugar planters had no alternative but to pay the high rates charged by Ward and Munson, they welcomed any attempt at competition such as United Fruit's. While picturesque, the opulent "fruiters" of the "Great White Fleet" hardly dented the Ward/Munson duopoly, but the majestic white ships kept Cuba on their Caribbean cruise itineraries for decades to come. The heyday for these combination cargo and cruise excursions was the mid-1930s, when most other industries were in the doldrums of the Great Depression. Those trying times stimulated the demand for escapist activities, such as going to the movies and cruising around the Caribbean Sea.[5]

In the aftermath of World War I, the U.S. Shipping Board managed the world's largest fleet of new merchant ships, most of which were constructed in

U.S. shipyards between 1917 and 1920 for the transatlantic "bridge of ships" needed to supply Allied efforts during the war. The Jones Act of 1920 authorized sale of these vessels and encouraged, through subsidy and mail contracts, the establishment of strategic routes to maintain the newly revitalized strength of the U.S. merchant marine. During this period, competition for the Cuban carrying trade came from some unexpected directions. The most innovative was the Black Star Line, founded in 1919 by Marcus Garvey, a Jamaican-born New Yorker whose Universal Negro Improvement Association called for nationalist pride from people of African ancestry all over the world, and for business enterprises in many fields to serve their interests and promote ties to Africa. Cuban planters bought stock in Garvey's endeavor and agreed to supply sugar cargoes, but the Black Star Line collapsed in 1922 when its ships, which called at Cuba, were diverted for promotional visits and failed to earn any revenue.[6]

A more powerful competitor entered the lucrative New York-to-Havana service in 1928: the British Cunard Line, the oldest and one of the most prestigious steamship lines in the world. A British diplomat reported that the Cubans welcomed the newcomer, because they "not unnaturally resent the monopolistic attitude of the American Shipping Board," which had ordered sanctions against Cunard, "and its attempt to regard the New York-Havana route as part of the United States coastal trade." At about the same time, Seatrain vessels went into service between Havana and the Gulf of Mexico ports, carrying railroad carloads of cargo and offering an alternative source of food and other products to the island.[7]

In the meantime, the Cuban-flag merchant marine struggled to expand. The Spanish-owned Naviera Herrera converted to Cuban ownership and registry in 1916, emerging as Empresa Naviera de Cuba. Naviera de Cuba continued the same steamship service to the Dominican Republic and Puerto Rico that Herrera had, acquiring new ships into the 1930s. Coastal shipping continued to pose a problem for Cuba, which lacked the merchant marine to supply the needs of the seaside population. The Cuban president was forced to allow the Spanish Line to take part in Cuban domestic commerce, which was widely interpreted as an insult to national pride, prompting legislation in 1928 restricting coastwise trade to Cuban vessels. This provision boosted the fortunes of Naviera de Cuba, which acquired some new steamships to go into the trade, but most of the benefit went to the builders and operators of small wooden ships, whose ranks proliferated in the 1930s.[8]

Irving Berlin's 1920 song "See You in C-U-B-A!" trumpeted the ease and pleasure of a vacation on the neighboring island, now so simple to reach.

Not so far from here, there's a very lively atmosphere.
Everybody's going there this year, and there's a reason—
People always having fun down there, so come along!
I'm on my way to Cuba, that's where I'm going!
Cuba, that's where I'll stay, where wine is flowing,
and where dark-eyed Stellas light their fellas' Panatellas!
Why don't you plan a wonderful trip to Havana?
Hop on a ship, and I'll see you in C-U-B-A![9]

Key West, Florida, was the point of
convergence for three routes to Cuba: the
fifteen-hundred-mile overland railroad route
down the East Coast from New York, the
steamship route across the Gulf of Mexico
from New Orleans, and the steamship route
down the west coast of Florida from Tampa.
In November 1920, Key West would also
become the terminus for the first scheduled
U.S. international airline, Aeromarine West
Indies Airways, which carried passengers and
mail between Key West and Havana daily
in converted U.S. Navy flying boats piloted
by ex-Navy flyers and named, appropriately,
the *Santa Maria* and the *Pinta*. Until the line
folded in 1924, its luxurious eleven-passenger
"boats" offered winter access to Havana
in just an hour from Key West, a service
nicknamed the "Highball Express" by the
thirsty rich who found it a quick way to get to the bars of Havana in those early
days of Prohibition in the U.S.[10]

Havana longshoremen unload Puerto Rican coffee from an
interisland schooner in part of the process that funneled
Caribbean agricultural products to the U.S. (Mystic Seaport
1994.45.5)

The State of Florida was on the Cuban frontier, then as now. This fact
was noted in 1920 by travel writer Harry Franck, who made the journey
through Florida to Key West by train and then by steamship to Havana. "Key
West… is a quaint mixture of American and Latin-American civilization, with
about equal parts of each…. The Spanish tongue, increasingly prevalent in the
streets from St. Augustine southward, is heard here as often as English…. As
in the towns along our Mexican border, the official tongue is bilingual, and
Americans from the North are frankly considered foreigners by the Cubanized
rank and file of voters."

A few months before she was christened *Santa Maria* and began passenger service between Key West and Havana in November 1920, this Aeromarine flying boat was photographed at a yacht race with passengers similar to those she would carry while acting as the "Highball Express" during Prohibition. (© Mystic Seaport, Rosenfeld Collection 1984.187.4263FA)

After visiting a cigar factory, Franck headed for the steamship dock at Mallory Square to board "the ferry, for it is little more than that," to Havana. After customs formalities, the ship was on its way. "Once the door of [the passenger's] breathless cabin is closed behind him, a brief night's sleep, if the inexplicable uproar with which the crew seems to pass its time during the journey permits it, brings him to the metropolis of the West Indies…. Steamers to Havana land the traveler within a block or two of the central railroad station, so that, if the capital has no fascination for him, there lies at hand more than four thousand kilometers [2,500 miles] of track to put him in touch with almost any point of the island."

But Harry Franck stayed to explore Havana first, a visit highlighted by a baseball game he and his wife attended. There they discovered that Cuba was still fighting off Pirates, in this case the professional team from Pittsburgh, who were shut out by the Havana home team at Almendares Field that day!

The Francks explored Cuba from one tip to the other after leaving Havana. The "countrymen in the *bohios*, huts of palm-leaves and thatch which probably still bear a close resemblance to those in which Columbus found the aborigines living," fascinated the couple. They began all the way west, at Pinar del Rio, where tobacco grew six feet high at a *finca*, or estate, where they were hosted. They traveled through the Yumurí Valley to the hermitage on Montserrat, where the view reminded Harry of "pretty views from the abandoned farms of Connecticut." They toured Santa Clara, a good town for "a lazy mood," and continued to Cienfuegos on the coast, named for "the exclamation of a sailor who beheld a hundred Indian fires along the beach." Next came the largest inland city in Cuba, Camagüey, four hundred years old, which "ran away from the northern shore in its early youth to escape the pirates." They reached Santiago de Cuba, second city of the country, on the south coast near the eastern end of the island, and toured its long harbor all the way to the sea. "Morro

Castle, unlike its prototype in Havana, is not visible from the city; nor is the Caribbean itself. As one chug-chugs down the land-locked bay, 'Cuba' shrinks away, and finally disappears entirely in a fold of the fuzzy hills, before the ancient fortress, framed in the bluest of blue seas, comes into sight."

Finally reaching Guantánamo Bay near the eastern end of Cuba, the Francks were fortunate to take passage to Haiti aboard *L'Independence*, a hundred-ton schooner known as *Andrea* when she was a private pleasure craft belonging to the New York Yacht Club, but now the only vessel in the Haitian Navy. No other regular service between Cuba and Haiti existed, except for the craft that brought Haitian sugar workers for the annual Cuban sugar harvest.[11]

This was considered a typical country house in the Province of Havana, ca. 1900. (Mystic Seaport 1997.35.1)

The year 1920, when the Francks toured what they called "the world's sugar bowl," became famous as the "Dance of the Millions" in Cuba. Skyrocketing sugar prices in the aftermath of World War I stimulated trade, as the world went on a collective sugar binge after the deprivations of the war. The sugar market hit historic highs; during that memorable and lucrative year, Cuba supplied fourteen percent of all U.S. imports. The United Fruit Company benefited greatly from this surge in sugar sales. UFCO operated its "Great White Fleet" in service to Cuban sugar plantations and banana plantations in Jamaica and Central America, but it depended on visits to Havana for virtually all of its south-bound freight business. Encouraged by Cuban President José Miguel Gómez, UFCO also began transporting Jamaican workers to its sugar plantations in 1912, an immigrant stream that increased quickly in volume. During 1920, more than twenty-four thousand Jamaicans arrived in Cuba, most of the men to wield machetes in the sugarcane fields, most of the women to clean and cook in wealthy people's houses.[12]

Also in 1920, the era of Prohibition began in the United States. Banning alcohol on the mainland helped to swell the flood of tourists to Cuba, as thirsty Americans went to indulge their taste for rum. One measure of the increased allure of the "wet" islands for many citizens of the "dry" United States was the spike in passenger traffic on the ships of the United Fruit "Great White Fleet," which rose twenty to twenty-five percent when the Volstead Act took effect.

(Top) Havana Yacht Club, 1924. (© Mystic Seaport, Rosenfeld Collection (1984.187.11708F) (Bottom) By the 1920s, Cuba had become part of both the American social scene and the yacht-racing circuit. The Havana Yacht Club, with 1,200 members, built a fleet of Star-class boats in the mid-1920s and thereafter hosted mid-winter racing. Here, with roses strewn across the table, members of the International Star Class celebrate at the Havana Yacht Club following the 1941 series for the Bacardi Cup and the Cup of Cuba. Kiko y Funcasta photo. (Mystic Seaport 1990.155.108)

Havana became a playground for well-to-do visitors and travel writers. The social whirl reached its height every year during the "high season," from the start of horse racing in early December to the closing night at the Spanish Casino in March. As Harry Franck described the scene, "midwinter brings its plethora of cold-fleeing, race-track-following, or prohibition-abhorring visitors from the North." Several prestigious yacht clubs built and patronized by wealthy Cubans and North Americans sprang up on the coast west of Havana, and did "not yield to any similar places in the world for fashionable chic or gaiety." First-time travelers to Havana found a cosmopolitan metropolis: "We discover the Country Club, the nearby beaches, the casinos, the race courses…we may live the same hotel life as in New York, London, Paris—and meet the same people."[13]

The American Colony resident in the environs of Havana grew to about 3,500 in the 1930s, and to 5,000 in the late 1950s. Some of the members of the American Colony had a great deal to do with the development of the city of Havana, especially Frederick Snare, from Pennsylvania. He arrived in Cuba in 1902 at the age of forty, settled in Havana as the U.S. occupation ended, and opened a construction firm. For the next forty years, Snare Company built port works, roads, warehouses, factories, and housing in and around the capital of the new republic. Snare's most cherished project was the Havana Country Club, which his firm built in 1911, complete with an eighteen-hole golf course, imposing clubhouse, and surrounding real estate development of mansions on large lots several miles west of the city. The political significance of Havana social clubs goes back to the 1840s, when the Club de la Habana was a rallying point for Cuban creole planters and U.S. expatriates who favored annexation of the Spanish colony to the United States. Havana Club members supported and sometimes joined filibuster expeditions against Cuba to achieve that end, just as Havana Country Club members later would take part in the Bay of Pigs invasion.[14]

Seaside social clubs dominated the cultural life of the capital. The Havana Yacht Club was difficult for an outsider to penetrate, membership being restricted to the old elite families of

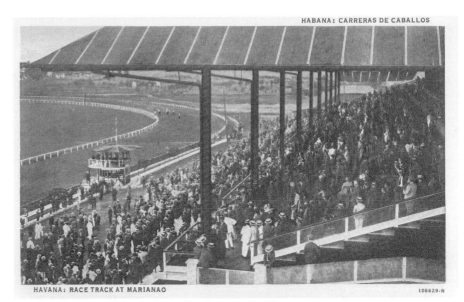

(Top) the Havana Race Track at Marianao, five miles southwest of Havana, was part of the sporting social scene that brought Americans flocking to Cuba in the 1920s. (Roorda/Doyle Collection) (Bottom) Developers like John McEntee Bowman built villas on the American model in the yacht club district to appeal to wealthy Americans. (Roorda/Doyle Collection)

The seductiveness of Havana: Jiggs Cabaret Night-Club. (Roorda/Doyle Collection)

Cuba's "high society." The Biltmore Yacht and Country Club hosted a more cosmopolitan set, including many wealthy winter visitors from the East Coast of the United States. During the high season, the yacht clubs sponsored competitive regattas for international fleets of sailboats and motorboats alike that drew crowds of participants and spectators. The yacht club precincts also included a coastal real estate district, where members could purchase villas for seasonal or year-round enjoyment. The Biltmore development was the brainchild of John McEntee Bowman and Charles Francis Flynn, who also converted a downtown office building to the Sevilla-Biltmore Hotel and operated both the Havana American Jockey Club and Orient Park Racetrack on the outskirts of the city. Bowman managed the entire Biltmore chain of hotels, including the famous properties in New York City and Chicago. There were also many recreational venues for the middle-class people of the western suburbs of Havana, those who had neither the deep pockets nor the blue blood required for the "Big Five" yacht and country clubs. Mixed Cuban and expatriate membership lists were common at such facilities as the Miramar "Club Naútico," or Swim Club, and the Comodoro Yacht Club, which "cost half as much and had a better beach" than the Havana Yacht Club, according to one former diplomat posted in Havana. Whether they were very elite establishments or more socially accessible locales, Havana's seaside clubs all constructed swimming areas enclosed by shark barricades for the protection of the patrons, along with carefully groomed beaches, freshwater pools, outdoor bars, changing cabanas, indoor dining, dancing, and card-playing areas, and storage for sailboats and rowing shells. Swimming, diving, sailing, and rowing competitions punctuated the clubs' annual calendar of events.[15]

Cuban dance crazes thrilled and shocked the North in the 1920s and beyond: mambo, rumba, and salsa. The famous mambo crossed over from the nightspots of Havana to the hot spots of Manhattan, inspiring many versions from a wide range of musicians in both countries. The rumba originated in the frenetic religious celebrations of Santería, then spread from the packed dirt courtyards where these rural gatherings of the faithful took place to the polished wooden dance floors of urban social clubs. Rumba dancers in Cuba often dropped their garments on the floor while moving to its syncopation, which made it the most titillating and scandalous of the imported steps. American rumba hits such as Cole Porter's "*Night and Day*" followed the same beat as the Cuban variety, but northern couples toned down the gyrations that went with it in Cuba when they danced at clubs back home. Salsa became an increasingly hot commercial property with the popularity of such durable expatriate recording artists as Tito Puente and Celia Cruz, who became famous in the 1950s and maintained an ever-widening fan base for decades thereafter. Music and dancing increased American fascination with Cuba, which in turn increased the flow of travelers to the island, especially its largest city, Havana.

Havana was also a popular destination for sailors, merchant mariners and Navy men alike. "*Running Down to Cuba*" was a "halyard chantey" sung by deckhands as they hoisted the sails on their way to the Caribbean, with lyrics that expressed their happy anticipation of returning to the island:

(Top) Unloading a Ford Zephyr, Cienfuegos, ca. 1929. (Mystic Seaport, 1994.62.352) (Bottom) Loading sugar on the Ford steamship *East Indian*, Cienfuegos, ca. 1929. (Mystic Seaport 1994.62.134)

> *Running down to Cuba for a load of sugar!*
> *Weigh me boys, to Cuba.*
> *Make her run, you limejuice squeezers!*
> *Running down to Cuba.*
> *I gotta' girl, she can dance the fandango!*
> *Weigh me boys, to Cuba.*
> *Lips like melon, sweet as a mango!*
> *Running down to Cuba!*[16]

Sailing ships with halyards to haul gradually disappeared, replaced by vessels running on steam or diesel that took over the sea-lanes of the Straits of Florida, but the men who worked on them continued to seek out the same forms of recreation after "running down to Cuba."

Sailors like Rupert Decker found plenty of entertainment in the city of Havana without having to belong to a yacht club or even venture far from the docks. Decker shipped aboard the *East Indian* of the Ford Motor Company fleet between 1928 and 1931, delivering automobiles regularly to the thriving Cuban market. In 1929 alone, Cuba and Mexico together absorbed 9,500 new cars from Ford, which dominated the Latin American motor trade. Rupert Decker was typical of the droves of hard-working, fun-loving seamen who called in Havana down through the years, except that unlike the vast majority of his peers in the maritime world, he sometimes brought along a camera to record his experiences on ships and in port cities. On his visits to the Cuban capital, Decker and a friend would sometimes visit one of the many "dance halls" in the port district, where they enjoyed the companionship of young women before making their return voyage to the United States. Prohibition of alcohol was still the law of his native land during the years that Decker called in Cuba, which never outlawed the rum and beer that sailors sought ashore, a fact that made Havana an even more appealing destination for sailors.[17]

Navy ship "liberty" calls disgorged legions of sailors in Havana and other Cuban port cities during more than a half-century of close military ties between the countries. Havana was a particularly popular and prominent destination, with its large American Colony of compatriots and frenetic night life. Naval contingents visited annually to commemorate the sinking of the USS *Maine* on February 15, 1898, with bluejackets marching in a parade with war veterans, the Havana firemen who carried the dead to the cemetery, and Cuban soldiers. The President of Cuba and high-ranking officers of the U.S. Navy reviewed the procession every year. Though after 1925 the event took place at the Maine Memorial, far from the harbor, most of the action for sailors ashore in Havana was closer to the docks. The shore patrol was vigilant at locales such as Sloppy Joe's Bar, where a detail was stationed for the duration of liberty. The Liaison Committee formed by the Navy, State, and War Departments to coordinate courtesy calls in Latin America called for visiting ships to be equipped with at least one Spanish-speaking officer to translate at meetings with dignitaries, a "good ship's baseball team and rifle team" to compete with local squads, and "most important of all, a good band and orchestra" to play music at parades and parties. The 1930s witnessed extensive "goodwill cruising" by the navy, especially the Special Service Squadron, based in the Caribbean. The Roosevelt administration hoped to use amicable port calls to solidify defense arrangements with neighboring republics through salty hospitality and recreation. One marine colonel taking part in such a pleasant voyage called the experience "Champagning around the Caribbean." The pace of naval visitation only increased during the 1950s. Cuban ports received visits from 375 U.S. Navy vessels during 1956 alone, with 84,000 sailors spilling ashore for a memorable liberty visit.[18]

The Cuban Navy repaid these calls on occasional trips to Florida ports. In 1935, two Cuban ships called at Tampa to help the local Cuban-American community celebrate the jubilee of the tobacco industry in that city. Two months later, a Cuban naval delegation came to Key West in the presidential yacht to participate in the annual commemoration of a Cuban patriotic holiday, the "Grito de Yarra," and was entertained at "the leading night club" in Key West, the Habana Madrid. The Cuban Navy Band toured the United States in 1938, including a visit to Washington, D.C., where the director presented a box of Cuban cigars to President Franklin D. Roosevelt. Sometimes Cuban calls at U.S. ports caused problems, such as when Cuban exiles living in Miami fought with Cuban sailors on shore leave from the visiting gunboat *Patria*. The fight began in a drugstore soda fountain, then became a street riot "in half a dozen places," wrecking the drugstore and a hotel lobby before "a platoon of police" broke it up and "prevented a general uprising of the local Cuban colony." The *Miami Daily Tribune* reported afterward that "injured sailors and civilians bore evidences of the fierceness of the battle," and "pools of blood on the pavements. . . indicated the intensity of the struggle." Visits by Cuban naval vessels and the presidential yacht to Key West became so frequent by 1939 that the local customs inspector suspected they were smuggling rum. After "the complaints of legitimate liquor dealers and of the Florida State Alcohol Board" about Cuban sailors carrying rum ashore to "the large Cuban population" on the little island, the Bureau of Customs asked the State Department to step in to prevent the practice.[19]

Sailor at a Cuban "dance hall," ca. 1929. (Mystic Seaport, 1994.62.75)

The city of Havana had a notorious reputation, especially its waterfront districts, earned over centuries of licentious behavior by visiting sailors and their hosts and hostesses. By 1885, there were more than 200 registered houses of prostitution "with showrooms to the street" in the downtown area. The astounding array of sexual services easily available for a price in Havana tinted its reputation at home and overseas. Havana "is hot, it is 'wet,' it is, in its easy

The American steamship *Philip Publicker* proceeds up Havana Harbor, 1924. Built on the Great Lakes during the World War I shipbuilding boom, this vessel carried Cuban sugar to Philadelphia during the 1920s. (© Mystic Seaport, Rosenfeld Collection, 1984.187.11831F)

tropical way, Wide Open," emoted one magazine writer in 1928, putting into words a libidinous attitude that would persist through the 1950s. During its dubious heyday from the 1920s to the Revolution of 1959, Havana ranked with Amsterdam and Hong Kong among cities famous to mariners for sexual adventure and spectacle. Perhaps the most famous of the live pornography venues was the Shanghai Theater, where sailors on liberty often filled the audience. But as in any "sailortown" precinct, Havana's streets teemed with "rapacious land sharks." Between ten and twelve thousand criminal cases were tried before the Havana High Court every year in the 1890s, making the port city one of the more dangerous on the itineraries of the world's mariners.[20]

Steamship connections to Havana endured despite the onset of the Great Depression in 1929, by which time passengers could bring their own automobiles with them. In the chapter of his 1931 book *Cuba Today* titled "Take Your Car to Cuba," travel writer Hyatt Verrill recommended this strategy to potential visitors, noting that the Havana Automobile Club had lobbied to permit entry of foreign-owned cars without "one cent of expense" from Cuban taxes or fees. Steamship companies made it easy: "If sailing from New York, it is only necessary to drive the car to the Ward Line pier, check it as excess baggage, and pay the charges, and the car will accompany the owner to Havana, where it will be discharged on the dock by the time the passengers' baggage has been passed by customs. If preferred, one may drive southward to Miami or even Key West and there embark one's car on any of the Havana boats. Moreover, if the motorist plans to visit Europe with his car, he can embark the machine on a Pacific Steam Navigation Company's ship at Havana and sail with it direct to England or the Continent."[21]

Competitors in the steamship business vied for passengers among themselves and with the rapidly expanding air service provided by Pan American Airways, which linked Havana and Key West with its first flight in 1927. Steamship advertisements in the Havana press celebrated the ease and convenience of travel on the sea between Cuba and the United States. The Munson Line service from New York via Miami and Nassau featured "excursions on the handsome and popular steamship *Munargo*," which offered "the most advanced modernities for the comfort of passengers" for $110 round-trip to New York, and $25 to Miami. The Ward Line countered that its ships were "Faster! Safer! More efficient!"[22] Claims of safety were of poignant concern in the wake of the line's *Morro Castle* disaster of 1934, when a steamship named for the ancient fortress guarding Havana caught fire on its way from Cuba to New York and burned within sight of the New Jersey shore. Many on board died needlessly due to a lack of lifeboats and to disorder among the crew, leading to stiffer safety standards for passenger vessels in the future.

Along the Havana waterfront, 1924. (© Mystic Seaport, Rosenfeld Collection 1984.187.11832F)

Movies amplified the romantic and titillating image of Havana. The opening scene of *Weekend in Havana* in 1941 showed a wintry Manhattan with snowy streets and huddled commuters hurrying past the window of a steamship agency. The display in the window, a full Cuban orchestra, suddenly comes to life and begins to play a rumba. The orchestra's singer, Carmen Miranda in one of her enormous, hats, trills out the movie's theme song, urging Americans to jump on a steamship to Havana:

> *Would you like to spend a weekend in Havana?*
> *Where the breezes touch the Caribbean shore…*
> *You can be back to the office on Monday,*
> *But you won't be the same anymore![23]*

In fact, American popular culture abounded with enticing references to Cuba, spurring a dramatic increase in tourism to Cuba, and a boost for the infrastructure of tourism. Popular composers George Gershwin and Aaron Copland composed orchestral pieces dedicated to Cuba, and writer Ernest Hemingway, a frequent visitor and later a resident advocate of Cuba's sport fishing, found fiction and nonfiction inspiration there. Common Americans echoed the romantic sentiments of composers and authors, among them a tourist named Adele from Connecticut, who wrote a postcard of the castle-like

Surrounded by locals, an American sport fisherman has his marlin documented by the photographer at Cojímar, ca. 1934. (EH 1831N, JFK Library, A/V Archives, Boston, Massachusetts)

bathing facilities at *La Playa*—"The Beach"— to her friend back home, saying, "I'm sure you would enjoy Havana."[24]

Ernest Hemingway enjoyed both the sport fishing and the socializing so much that in 1938 he bought the home near Havana he called *La Finca Vigía*. The action of his novel *To Have and Have Not* (1934) takes place in the Florida Keys, in the city of Havana, and on the treacherous waters separating them. The central figure in the tale is native Key Wester Harry Morgan, a "Conch" who smuggles Chinese laborers onto the Cuban coast in his fishing boat, which is outfitted as a rum-runner, with a big engine. A vivid example of the "Ugly American," he also behaves brutishly on the streets of the Cuban capital, knocking the hat off the head of an Afro-Cuban man without provocation, then spinning it into the heavy taxi traffic driving past Havana's Central Park, where the hat is run over by a taxi.

Hemingway would win the Nobel Prize for Literature on the strength of *The Old Man and the Sea* (1952), a novella about a Cuban fisherman in the coastal village of Cojímar, near Havana, where the author spent a great deal of time. Hemingway's knowledge of deep-sea fishing, gained from long experience in his fishing boat *Pilar*, comes through in his descriptions of the giant swordfish and of wise Santiago's strategies to conserve his stamina and land his prize catch. In his highly autobiographical novel *Islands in the Stream* (1970), Hemingway presented a portrait of his life in Cuba, including his house near Havana and a fishing boat based on his "old and dirty" *Pilar*.[25]

Steamship service to Cuba fell on hard times with the onset of the Second World War. When the U.S. government suddenly suspended the Seatrain service between Havana and the port cities on the Gulf Coast in mid-1941, shortages of food and other necessities quickly resulted. With a merchant marine consisting only of a few Naviera de Cuba steamers and a large number of wooden schooners, Cuba had a very poor bargaining position with the United States

War Shipping Administration when it came to dividing the inadequate space aboard the available freighters. Cuban products such as sugar, nickel, and manganese were given high priority for export, but imports of basic commodities to Cuba languished on the docks of the United States during the war years. The situation became so urgent that the government created the Cuban Maritime Commission in mid-1942 to avoid reaching the same level of "hunger and misery" the nation had endured during the horrors of Spanish "reconcentration" between 1895 and 1898. The commission marshaled a "miniscule and improvised fleet" of "modest little boats,"

Ernest Hemingway's *Pilar*, a 38-foot Wheeler design from 1934, motors out of Havana with the sport-fishing fleet, ca. 1950. Hemingway added the outrigger spars, which could be lowered to increase her stability. (© Florida State News Bureau, EH 3807P, JFK Library, A/V Archives, Boston, Massachusetts)

most of them wooden, to undertake the needed voyages abroad as the war dragged on for three more years. Ernest Hemingway described "the wooden-hulled ships of the pitiful and grotesque wartime merchant marine" in Havana Harbor, where they "lay against the creosoted pilings of the wooden docks and the scum of the harbor lay along their sides blacker than the creosote of the pilings and foul as an uncleaned sewer."[26] Despite the fleet's unpromising appearance, their efforts succeeded in feeding the Cuban people until peace came in 1945.

The waters around Cuba were particularly dangerous during the Second World War. German submarines attacked merchant shipping with devastating results beginning in early 1942, when the Caribbean became a bloody theater of the Battle of the Atlantic. That long struggle between Allied surface ships and German U-boats began in 1939 in the eastern Atlantic, then spread to the shores of the United States and its Latin American allies after Pearl Harbor. The next six months saw the most destructive naval operations in Caribbean history, with more than 400 ships sunk in the region. The losses were especially severe near Trinidad and Curaçao, where oil refining attracted a steady traffic of petroleum tankers and U-boats to prey on them, but the carnage around Cuba also contributed significantly to the heavy toll in lives and ships.

The U-boats replenished their provisions by "surfacing alongside a Cuban fishing smack [to] buy all the water and food on board," recalled a diplomat in Cuba during the war. Ernest Hemingway became involved in the war against the submarines. In 1943, he outfitted his own deep-sea fishing boat, *Pilar*, to act as an armed decoy to lure submarines to the surface, enlisting many of his colorful friends from Havana to help. The plan was to act as if they were fishermen willing to sell provisions such as fruit and fish, hoping to attract a German U-boat to approach them and open its conning tower, at which time they would throw explosives down the hatch. Hemingway and his crew of international adventurers did not succeed in sinking a U-boat, but their approach was on the right track, and their experiences provided the subject matter for part three of his posthumously published novel *Islands in the Stream*. *Pilar* was converted from a pleasure craft to be a disguised sub-spotter, like many sub-spotters that cruised the coastal waters of North America and the Caribbean during the war. Using yachts and fishing boats as sub-spotters was one of many emergency measures employed to defeat the German threat to shipping. Other tactics included the convoy system, improved radar and sonar, and airplane patrols based in Cuba and other Caribbean island ally nations.

To counter the U-boat war, U.S. shipyards had launched the world's largest merchant marine by the end of World War II. With the return to peacetime trading the U.S. Maritime Commission offered up almost two thousand ships at very low prices. The Cuban Maritime Commission acted to build up the Cuban-flag merchant fleet in order to avoid a repeat of the wartime scarcities the country had recently endured. It ordered two dozen surplus freighters from the United States, but ended up receiving only four standard C1-MA-VI freighters in 1948. Naviera de Cuba, largest of the Cuban shipping firms, operated the four vessels with a government subsidy, mainly on the New York route. But when the company suspended its service to New Orleans in 1950, putting three smaller boats out of work, the crews of the four C1s went on strike until Naviera reinstated the money-losing New Orleans runs. In addition to labor troubles, the growing network of Cuban highways reduced the company's market, as trucks could reach more and more of its remote ports of call. Naviera de Cuba went into bankruptcy, and the four steamers of the Cuban merchant marine deteriorated in the hands of Naviera Vacuba, a firm run by friends of the Cuban dictator Fulgencio Batista. These cronies received operating subsidies from the government while ignoring maintenance to the ships. When the Cuban Revolution of 1959 deposed Batista, and Fidel Castro came to power, the old vessels received complete

This tourist card permitted the entry of Jean Ellen Martin, who visited Havana with her parents on the *City of Havana* in June 1957. (Roorda/Doyle Collection)

refittings and returned to service under direct government operation. It is likely that the Cuban line continued to lose money, with government insiders still reaping benefits from its operations, but that is impossible to document.

When the war ended, the Caribbean cruise industry revived, and Cuba resumed its prominent place on the pleasure itineraries of passenger liners. Holland America Line operated ships such as its flagship *Nieuw Amsterdam* on the route from New York, conducting passengers to Havana in style. A typical visit during these halcyon days for regional tourism began with a morning arrival in the busy harbor of the capital. It was "imperative" for all passengers wanting to go ashore to assemble at 8:00 A.M. sharp on the starboard side of the Promenade Deck, to have their landing cards stamped by Cuban immigration officials. With stamped and signed landing cards in hand, passengers were ready to head for the city. They might also bring along the daily ship's newspaper *The Caribbean Mercury*, which included "useful Spanish phrases" such as "Don't molest me" and "Go away"; instructions on how to hiss for a waiter or taxi driver; and a warning that "a bartender in Cuba puts the bottle on the bar [and] it is customary to serve yourself. The limit is your own judgement." Another source of information for visitors was the free publication *Havana Weekly: The Perfect Pocket Guide*, "approved by the Cuban Tourist Commission." The pioneering travel agency Thomas Cook and Son offered two organized "shore excursion programs" for HAL guests of 1950 to join, if they chose: a morning "City and Country Drive" and an evening "Night Life Trip" lasting until two in the morning. Tourists disembarking from the steamer received invitations to visit a variety of Havana's attractions. Cigar factories beckoned with slick brochures, the Havana Club rum distillery's "Private Bar" offered "frozen, delicious cocktails," and the El Patio Novelty Store, eschewing the customary *siesta* after noon to stay open for northern visitors, gave free perfume to the presenters of promotional cards, in hopes they would buy "Alligator and Snake articles, shoes and Sandals, among Many other Articles." A picture postcard of Marianao Bathing Beach, "the most beautiful spot in Cuba," enticed tourists to the Restaurant De Luxe nearby. For evening entertainment, Jiggs Cabaret Night-Club boasted "the best, fashionable high ball," while the Kursaal Night Club presented "RED-

Ernest and Mary Hemingway and their party are serenaded at La Floridita, the popular Havana nightclub that claimed to be the birthplace of the Daiquiri. (EH 1846N, JFK Library, A/V Archives, Boston, Massachusetts)

HOT RHUMBA, TWO SHOWS NIGHTLY." A bit farther afield, a nightclub in a nunnery two centuries old lured guests to Río Cristal Club Restaurant, where they could take a canoe excursion on the "crystal river" before taking in dinner and a show. Guests returning to the ship early—that is, by 1:30 A.M.—still had time for a buffet supper on the Lido Deck before settling into their staterooms. Groggy passengers who dragged themselves out of their beds for the early morning departure were rewarded by the spectacle of Morro Castle to starboard and the grand, crowded peninsula of Havana to port, as the ship began its return passage up the seaboard to New York.[27]

Naviera García, another Cuban shipping firm to emerge from the wooden ship fleets of World War II, ran six small cargo ships under flags of convenience with Spanish crews in the 1950s, when the Cuban Bank of Foreign Commerce offered the family-owned business incentives to return to Cuban-flag operations. The company ordered four new ships from Germany; then, in 1956, it purchased the name and some assets of the disintegrating Ward Line, becoming the Ward-García Line. With routes to New York, the Gulf ports, and Mexico, Ward-García was a promising venture, but the owners put the line up for sale as the decade drew to a close.

The Cuban Bank of Foreign Commerce also backed Naviera de Navas, which acquired three vessels to carry sugar. After one profitable year, sugar rates plunged and the company went into liquidation. The bank's attempt to purchase the eight ships that the Canadian National Steamships operated in the West Indies also failed, in this case because the Seafarers' International Union struck against the sale and refused to allow the vessels to leave Halifax, Nova Scotia. When the bank sent a Cuban crew there to replace the Canadian sailors and take possession of the ships, American labor unions retaliated. Union members picketed

Cuban-flag vessels, and longshoremen refused to unload them in New York and New Orleans, beginning with the old C1s operated by Naviera Vacuba. The ships stayed in Canada, and the Cuban merchant marine remained weak. The postwar glut in tramp steamship capacity kept rates for freight too low to compete against, so Cuban bottoms carried only three percent of national exports and two percent of imports during the 1950s. The graft and corruption of the Batista regime also led to mismanagement in some of the shipping lines, which operated mainly as funnels for government subsidy money. But like the Cuban merchant marine, the Batista regime itself was on the skids in the late 1950s.[28]

Of all the armed opposition to the Batista regime, the guerrilla fighters in the rugged eastern mountain range called the Sierra Maestra, led by Fidel Castro, proved to be the most potent threat. But the Cuban Revolution of 1959 that brought Castro to power did not begin well for the rebel leader. After attacking the Moncada army barracks on July 26, 1953, the anniversary of José Martí's death, Castro was jailed and then exiled from Cuba to Mexico. Like the exiled Martí in the 1890s, Castro went to New York City to raise money in the Cuban community there. He also waded across the Río Grande/Río Bravo to a Texas hotel, where he met and accepted fifty thousand dollars from a former Cuban president, Carlos Prío Socarrás, in September 1956. Castro intended to buy a boat and launch an invasion of Cuba. He first tried to purchase a World War II surplus PT (patrol torpedo) boat for sale in Dover, Delaware. These sturdy, wooden-hulled vessels had performed well in the Pacific War. PT boats were especially adept at delivering commandos to island assignments, which is exactly what Castro had in mind. But his application for an export license was denied by the State Department, and his 26th of July Movement lost the twenty thousand dollars it had put down on the deal. With another twenty thousand from former president Prío, Castro negotiated for a motor pleasure yacht owned by an American citizen living in Mexico City. A Mexican arms dealer showed Castro the deteriorating vessel at its mooring in the Tuxpan River near the Gulf of Mexico. Castro bought the boat, named *Granma* or "Grandma," for twenty thousand dollars, and paid another twenty thousand for a house nearby to prepare his expedition force. He and about 130 of his followers hurried to make the frail craft ready for the crossing to Cuba. *Granma*, only sixty-two feet long, was large enough for only eighty-two passengers, requiring fifty men to stay behind on November 25, 1956, when Castro and the others jammed on board and went to sea.

Granma departed from the port of Tuxpan de Rodrigues de Cano, Mexico, in the State of Veracruz, on the Bay of Campeche, a hundred miles south of Tampico. The patched-up yacht hit heavy seas and high winds soon after clearing the coast. Its equipment began to fail, and many of the rebels on board became seasick. The little boat's voyage of sixteen hundred stormy miles took seven days, three days longer than Castro had expected, depleting its supplies of food and water by the time it approached the coast of Cuba on December 2. In the meantime, an uprising in Santiago de Cuba that was to have coincided with the arrival of *Granma* took place on schedule, three days earlier, but was crushed by Batista's troops. Worst of all for the invaders, Batista's agents in Mexico had learned of their plans and sent word of *Granma*'s departure to Havana. Forewarned, the Cuban government dispatched troops to the eastern end of the island and placed naval and air forces on increased coastal surveillance to intercept the yacht and its olive-clad passengers.

Granma ran aground in a mangrove swamp. The *fidelistas* found themselves stranded near Niquero and Cabo (Cape) Cruz on the southeastern coast of Cuba, in Oriente Province. They were far from their intended point of rendezvous with their allies, who were supposed to provide food and transportation. Castro and his beleaguered force had to abandon much of their equipment on the yacht and wade for hours through chest-deep water and dense mangrove thickets to reach the beach called Playa de las Coloradas. One of the patrolling airplanes spotted Castro's commandos as they splashed ashore and ran for cover, but they eluded Batista's forces for three days as they hurried toward the mountains of the Sierra Maestra. Then the government troops surrounded the rebels as they rested in a sugarcane field and killed most of them in a surprise attack. Only about a dozen survived to regroup in the mountains, including Castro, his brother Raúl, and the Argentine physician Ernesto "Che" Guevara, who took a bullet in the shoulder during the battle in the cane field. Then, using radio equipment provided by the U.S. Central Intelligence Agency, the insurgents launched Radio Rebelde, or Rebel Radio, to broadcast their message against Batista and to assure their followers that they were still alive.[29]

Granma also escaped destruction in December 1956, and survived the revolution to take an iconic place in the history of the Castro regime. The yacht now reposes in a glass enclosure behind Havana's Museum of the Revolution, which is housed in the old American-built Customs building near the shore. The *Granma* pavilion is guarded by soldiers around the clock and illuminated throughout the night, its white hull gleaming in the fluorescence as the uniformed men march by, as if they were wading to the beach. The area around Cabo Cruz where the motorboat grounded is now officially called Granma Province. The shortage of newsprint in Cuba caused all newspapers but one to cease publication, the exception being the official government daily, named *Granma*. The scarcity of all kinds of paper throughout the last decade forces many people, whatever their political leanings, to use *Granma* in place of toilet

Established on a wide, convoluted bay near the southeastern end of Cuba, the U.S. Naval Station Guantánamo Bay covers nearly 45 square miles. First occupied by U.S. Marines in June 1898, the base grew into an important U.S. Navy coaling and resupply station protecting Atlantic access to the Panama Canal, especially during the world wars, as shown here. After the 1959 revolution, the base was considered a bulwark against Communism. More recently it has housed Cuban and Haitian refugees intercepted by the U.S. Coast Guard. Since 2002 it has been notorious for its use to detain terrorism suspects from Afghanistan and elsewhere. The U.S. has held a perpetual lease on the base since 1903 and in observance of the agreement continues to send an annual check to the Castro government (which goes uncashed). (Roorda/Doyle Collection)

As commemorated on the Cuban one peso note, Fidel Castro and his revolutionary army entered Havana a week after President Batista fled the city on New Year's Day 1959. (Roorda/Doyle Collection)

tissue, a fact joked about by those who look for humor in the difficult daily life of Cuba.

Castro's insurgent forces evoked the Revolution of 1895 by wearing the same kind of hats worn by José Martí's followers, naming themselves the 26th of July Movement after the date of Martí's death, and by espousing the same nationalist message as the fighters of the previous century. Emulating the spirit of 1895 helped the rebels to gain support among the Cuban peasants during 1957. Peasants harbored the small band of survivors and enlisted in their ranks, as depicted in the film *Gua Gua Sí* (1999), which tells the story of a sheltered mountain man who joins the rebel band that his mother is sheltering on the family farm. The worldly guerrillas nickname the new recruit "Gua Gua Sí," because they ask him if he has ever seen a bus, a *gua gua* in Cuban slang, and he eagerly replies "*Guaguasí!*"—he knows all about that, thinking they are referring to a common mountain herb used for folk remedies called *guaguasí*. In fact, he has never seen a motor vehicle of any kind in his life, but within a short time he is riding a captured tank to victory against the Cuban army and entering Havana on a commandeered truck.

Reinforced by peasant fighters, Fidel and Raúl Castro's forces gained strength in the rugged Sierra Maestra for two years after the unlucky voyage of *Granma*. From their mountain bases they targeted American interests on both coasts of Oriente Province, north and south: the Texaco refinery, Moa Bay Mining, and the Cuban Nickel operation at Nicaro. The rebels kidnapped Texaco employees and stole all of the company's jeeps. They bombed a coastal schooner loading gasoline for Moa Bay Mining. They virtually besieged the nickel works at Nicaro in October 1958, until the military transport USS *Kleinsmith* arrived from Guantánamo Bay naval base to evacuate the company's American employees and their dependents. The aircraft carrier *Franklin D. Roosevelt* provided helicopter air cover for the operation, but Cuban Navy vessels arrived at the same time to attack the rebels, disrupting the *Kleinsmith* just as it prepared to embark the evacuees from the plant. After a shoot-out and a round of negotiations between the rebels, the government forces, and the U.S. Navy, the American citizens boarded the transport and made it to Guantánamo Bay.

In the urban and suburban precincts of Havana, the yacht and country clubs frequented by North American expatriates became a focus for the enmity of working people, including the caddies, waiters, cooks, and musicians who staffed the clubs. Their resentment had been simmering for a long time. Golf caddies who had been dismissed from their jobs in the 1920s, because their complexions were too dark, returned to steal golf balls off the course at the Havana Country Club, only to be caught and sent to prison. Strikes by cooks, waiters, and musicians against the yacht and country clubs in 1946 forced the cancellation of holiday parties at Christmas and New Year's Eve, but the "Big Five" social clubs united to break the strike, denying the food-service workers their raises and the musicians their royalties. A siege mentality began to dominate Country Club Park and the other expensive coastal real estate developments in the Miramar and Marianao districts west of the Almendares River, where the wealthiest Cubans and foreigners lived in mansions. The U.S. ambassador, who lived near the Havana Country Club's lush golf course, took to commuting by helicopter to his office at the embassy near downtown, as the Batista regime and civil order disintegrated in tandem.[30]

Fidel Castro's 26th of July Movement gained unstoppable momentum in late 1958, as Fulgencio Batista's cruelty worsened and the Dwight Eisenhower administration kept its distance from his dictatorship, denying him the arms he requested to fight the war against the growing insurrection. Batista fled Havana early on New Year's Day, 1959, the same day Luciano Cuadras Fernández launched a little fishing boat named *Analuisa* down the coast in Mariel. Castro entered Havana less than a week later.

For a while, not much changed in the city, or around the country, after the transition. Castro played golf at the Havana Country Club, took up residence at

The Havana Hilton opened in 1958 along La Rampa, Havana's main street for casinos and prostitution. As a powerful symbol of American influence in Cuba, the 27-story hotel was chosen by Fidel Castro as his revolutionary headquarters, and it still bears the name he gave it: Havana Libre. (Roorda/Doyle Collection)

the new Havana Hilton, and dropped by the movie set of *Our Man in Havana*, a film based on a spy novel by Graham Greene, starring Alec Guinness. Set late in the Batista era, *Our Man in Havana* (novel 1958; film 1959) tells the story of an English expatriate named Mr. Wormold. Wormold is a vacuum-cleaner salesman who becomes a spy, joins the expensive Havana yacht and country club set, and invents fictional reports to send to London. He credits his made-up information to nonexistent "assets" whose names he picks randomly from the members' directory of the Havana Country Club. Foreshadowing the Cuban Missile Crisis of 1962, Wormold informs his superiors that one of his imaginary informers, a Cuban Air Force pilot based on an actual pilot belonging to the club, has spotted a mysterious base under construction in the rugged mountains of eastern Cuba. Greene's prescient novel and screenplay portrayed the brutal tactics of Batista's secret police, and anticipated the continued importance of espionage in Cuba's future.

American steamship companies continued to operate out of Havana, a city of 1.3 million inhabitants, after Castro came to power. The 1960 edition of the *Anglo-American Directory of Cuba* listed agencies for Lykes Brothers, United Fruit Company, Ward-Garéla Line, Moore-McCormack Line, United States Lines, and the Havana Car Ferry Operating Company, which operated the "super ferry" *City of Havana* to Key West.[31] The ferry transported many of the resident Americans out of the country in 1961, when relations between the nations broke down.

Relations between the new regime and the United States grew tense as Castro targeted the country's economic elite, who shared financial interests and yacht club memberships with the wealthiest members of the "American Colony" in Cuba. The sugar industry, foundation of the Cuban economy, was in the hands of these people: Cuban, American, and Cuban-American. Other members of this group ran the steamship lines, distilled the rum, manufactured the cigars, brewed the beer, packed the beef, and ran the casinos and hotels that made Havana famous as a destination for tourists. When news of Batista's fall became common knowledge, the targets of the angry crowds that formed in Havana's streets were parking meters, long identified with official corruption, and casinos, run by a combination of Cuban military muscle and American organized crime. The Sevilla Biltmore Hotel's casino was wrecked by rioters, and the Plaza Hotel burned, with roulette wheels and blackjack tables blazing in the street outside.[32] The Eisenhower administration did not object to the destruction of these institutions, but when Castro began to nationalize sugar plantations, then conflict loomed.

The Cuban National Institute for Agrarian Reform nationalized hundreds of millions of dollars worth of U.S.-owned landed property by the end of the first year of revolutionary government. The Eisenhower administration retaliated with a reduction of the Cuban sugar quota for 1959. The Soviet Union offered Cuba cheap petroleum in early 1960, but U.S. refineries refused to refine the crude, so the Cuban government expropriated the Cuban assets of Standard Oil, Texaco, and Shell in June. The following month, Washington canceled the sugar agreement with Cuba entirely, removing the largest market for Cuban produce and its major source of foreign exchange. In August 1960, the Castro government nationalized several private U.S. enterprises, including banks, sugar mills, and gas stations. This move drew a harsh reprisal in October, when the U.S. government imposed a trade embargo covering all exports to Cuba except medicine. Cuba then expropriated all foreign-owned property and

"Mr. Imperialists, we are not afraid of you!" reads this billboard near the *Maine* memorial and the site of the former U.S. embassy along the Malecon, the seaside Havana boulevard facing the U.S. across 90 miles of water. (AE Doyle photo)

certain Cuban-owned businesses. The consequences were that elite Cubans and American expatriates began to leave the country, tourists stopped coming, and the U.S. government severed relations, extended the economic embargo, and suspended air and ocean travel between the nations.

The close ties binding New York, Florida, and New Orleans to Havana unraveled after three centuries of interaction, leaving a tangle of international tensions. The distrust was heightened in early March 1960, when a French freighter unloading munitions from Belgium exploded at dockside in Havana, killing seventy-five people immediately and wounding another two hundred. Sabotage by anti-Castro agents seemed likely, but was impossible to prove. The mutual hostility produced two important events in American maritime history: the Bay of Pigs invasion in April 1961 and the Cuban Missile Crisis in October 1962.

A year after Castro rode into Havana, his enemies in exile and a team of Central Intelligence Agency agents planned an invasion by sea and air to rally popular resistance and overthrow his government. The operation was one in a long line of invasion attempts going back to the 1840s, some of which had received tacit support from the authorities in Washington, D.C., only to be disavowed when their landings met disaster. Such was the case with the anti-

Castro exile army that left Nicaragua, bound for Cuba's southern coast. The force had received training in Guatemala and Nicaragua, transportation by air and sea, and arms from the CIA during both the Eisenhower and Kennedy administrations. The invasion began with squads of frogmen going ashore to locate the landing area for the main force, which hit the beach called Playa Girón in the Bay of Pigs on April 17, 1961, only to be pinned down by Castro's forces. Soon after the fighting began, the Cuban Air Force sank the invaders' two support vessels, *Marsopa* and *Houston*, stranding the exile army on the swampy coast. With their air support also gone, Castro's foes had no choice but to surrender, which most of them did on April 19. Of the fourteen hundred commandos who invaded Cuba, more than twelve hundred were captured, while the rest died in action.[33] Many of them were former members of organizations such as the Havana Yacht Club and Havana Country Club, who had returned to Cuba under arms in an attempt to reclaim the maritime playground they had lost. Castro had taken over their yacht and country clubs, turning them into a music school, an officers' club, an Olympic training facility, and a hotel, among other uses. The days of the Havana "high season," when the wealthiest American yachters migrated to Cuba to race and relax while Cubans catered to their every need, had come to an end.

Seaborne operations against the Castro regime did not cease after the Bay of Pigs debacle. Cuban exile organizations and various branches of the U.S. government, including the CIA and the Navy, carried out new plans. In April 1962, the Navy conducted war exercises on the island of Vieques off the coast of Puerto Rico, simulating an amphibious landing with forty thousand troops hitting the beach, as they would if the target were Cuba. By then, two hundred anti-Castro exile organizations operated from the United States, some of them carrying out sabotage raids against Cuban infrastructure. One of the commando groups attacked a Cuban Coast Guard patrol boat in May 1962. The CIA's Operation Mongoose attempted a wide variety of assassination schemes against Castro, and invented many other disruptive missions, such as bombing oil storage facilities. The previous counterinsurgency exploits of its commander, Air Force Brigadier General Edward Lansdale, would be publicized in *The Pentagon Papers* (1971), which detailed his activities in Vietnam from 1954 to 1955. Eight years later in Cuba, Lansdale and his associates in the CIA repeated the kinds of sabotage they had carried out in Hanoi and other places in Vietnam. Those previous efforts had aimed to destabilize the government of Ho Chi Minh, but resulted in deeper American involvement in the war in Vietnam. Operation Mongoose tried to disrupt the Castro government and even to assassinate Castro himself, but succeeded only in further embittering relations with Cuba.[34]

The commando raids and U.S. Navy maneuvers together posed the threat of a larger invasion of Cuba, the next time with greater tactical air support from the United States than the Bay of Pigs invaders had received. The prospect of facing a full American onslaught drove Castro into an alliance with the Soviet Union. The Soviet leader, Nikita Khrushchev, seized the opportunity to base nuclear missiles in Cuba, within easy range of the major U.S. cities, partly to balance the threat posed by U.S. installations in Turkey, bordering the Soviet Union. "Che" Guevara traveled to Moscow to seal the agreement, and Soviet ships began to transport the materials required to build missile bases in Cuba.

Originally commissioned in 1943, the heavy cruiser USS *Canberra*, a veteran of the Pacific theater in World War II, was recommissioned in 1956 as the second guided missile heavy cruiser in the U.S. Navy. As seen here, she patrolled off Cuba during the Cuban Missile Crisis of 1962. (Courtesy U.S. Naval Historical Center)

In October 1962, the Kennedy administration learned about the Soviet missiles in Cuba from photographs taken by U-2 spy planes at high altitudes, the only American planes in Cuban airspace in those tense days. The Strategic Air Command attained DEFCON (defense condition) 2 status for the first time—DEFCON 5 is normal peacetime activity, DEFCON 1 is war—during the Cuban Missile Crisis. B-52 jet bombers circulated constantly over the Atlantic, refueling over Spain, ready to divert at any moment to release their nuclear or conventional payloads over Cuba or the Soviet Union. But rather than release an air assault or launch an invasion of Cuban soil, as many of his advisors counseled, President Kennedy, a former Navy officer, took a maritime option.

He looked to the Navy to impose a "quarantine" on Cuba eight hundred miles from its coasts, which might be viewed as the most critical blockade in naval history, in order to halt construction of the missile bases. Appropriately, one of the U.S. Navy ships on blockade was the destroyer *Joseph P. Kennedy Jr.*, named for the president's brother, a casualty of World War II. JFK had a model of the vessel on display in the White House at the time of the crisis. She overhauled and searched the Liberian freighter *Marcula*. The *Marcula* contained no "contraband" useful to the missile site construction and was allowed to continue. The decisive moment came on the morning of October 24, when the Soviet naval vessel *Kimovsk*, which was carrying intermediate-range ballistic missiles, approached the blockade line. Below the *Kimovsk* lurked a Soviet submarine that has yet to be identified publicly. To the great relief of observers everywhere, the Soviet captain received the order to turn back rather than submit to being boarded, averting a cataclysm on the high seas that might have resounded, quite literally, around the world. Instead, Kennedy ordered U.S. missiles out of

Turkey and pledged not to invade Cuba, and Khrushchev withdrew the Soviet missiles.[35]

Neither the United States nor the Soviet Union consulted Castro or the Cuban exiles about the agreement to end the Cuban Missile Crisis, and the mutual antagonism between the different sides in the issue worsened in its wake. The Bay of Pigs captives eventually gained their release in exchange for an indemnification of sixty million dollars from the United States, but their return to Florida only enflamed the hostility between the two countries, as many of them immediately returned to anti-Castro activities of all sorts, including more raids on the island.[36] Some of the Bay of Pigs veterans later formed a covert operations team called the Plumbers, who were hired by E. Howard Hunt. Hunt was a former CIA agent who had been one of the organizers and trainers of the Bay of Pigs invasion forces. He was working for Richard Nixon's reelection committee in 1971 when he contacted his Cuban friends in Miami. The Plumbers accepted a mission to stop the "leaks" of information to the press from inside the Nixon administration, such as the secret Defense Department files known as the Pentagon Papers. The team's bungled break-in of a psychiatric office in search of personal files on Daniel Ellsburg, who leaked the Pentagon Papers, derailed Ellsburg's trial for treason when the burglary was revealed. During the election year of 1972, the Plumbers broke into the Democratic Party's National Committee offices at the Watergate building in Washington, D.C., not once but twice, the second time being caught in the act. The arrest of the Cuban burglars led to the Watergate scandal and the resignation of President Richard Nixon in 1974.

In the meantime, interaction between the Cuban exiles and the Castro regime was mainly limited to two forms: dogged exile commando raids against the island, and Castro government harangues against the people he calls the *gusanos*, or "worms," who left Cuba for Miami. One other connection was a sporadic flow of more exiles from the island to the mainland, some by air, and the rest by sea. Those Cuban immigrants who took to the sea to reach the United States joined a centuries-old tide of newcomers to its shores, and some of them added a new term to the vocabulary of immigration history: "boatlift."

Chapter 5: "Boatlifts": Immigration on the High Seas

A tempestuous noise of thunder and lightning heard…
(A confused noise within:) "Mercy on us!"—
"We split, we split!"—"Farewell my wife and children!"
  —"Farewell, brother"—
"We split, we split, we split!"

The cries of terrified sailors and passengers caught in a violent storm at sea set the tone for William Shakespeare's play, *The Tempest* (1611), which he wrote after hearing news of the wreck of the *Sea Venture* on the previously unexplored island of Bermuda in 1609. The *Sea Venture* was one of the ships of the Dale Expedition, which sailed to relieve the starving colonists at Jamestown, Virginia. The ship was carrying new immigrants and fresh supplies when it was caught in a storm that drove it aground on Bermuda, "otherwise called the Isle of Devils," as the first published account of the wreck phrased it.[1] The opening lines of Shakespeare's drama express the distress of immigrants on the oceans down through the centuries, especially those who attempt their crossings in small wooden boats and run into heavy weather.

Comparing the dimensions of the *Analuisa* to the immigrant craft that took part in the first "Great Migration" to America in the 1600s points to the similar experiences of the most hard-pressed immigrants, then and now. The Dale Expedition evoked by Shakespeare followed in the wake of the first three Jamestown vessels, which arrived in 1607 to establish the first permanent English settlement in North America. Sources differ, but it seems that the *Susan Constant* was no bigger than seventy-six feet long, 120 tons; *Godspeed* was forty-eight feet, 40 tons; and *Discovery* was perhaps as small as thirty-eight feet long, only 20 tons! The famous *Mayflower* of 1620 carried 102 dedicated men and women from Southampton, England, to Plymouth, Massachusetts, which was about one foot in ship's length for each person on board.[2]

Accommodations in the dark steerage of a transatlantic immigrant ship consisted of a rude cubicle for each family. (*Illustrated London News*, May 10, 1851; G.W. Blunt White Library, Mystic Seaport)

In the year 1635, twenty ships cleared from London bound for Virginia, and another seventeen left for New England, with more than three thousand colonists on board. A total of sixteen ships departed for the Caribbean island colonies, half of them for Barbados, the others for St. Kitts, Bermuda, and Providence Island near Central America, carrying a total of almost two thousand people. The size of only ten of those vessels is known today. The largest of them was 300 tons, capable of carrying 200 cramped passengers, but the smallest of them was the *Batchelor*, only 25 tons. Vessels to New England tended to be smaller, averaging fewer than 70 passengers per ship that year, while vessels to the Chesapeake region averaged 100 people aboard, and those to Barbados carried more than 120 on each voyage from London.[3]

By the time English people began their colonizing efforts in Virginia and Plymouth, Spanish people had been arriving in Cuba for a full century. Whether voyaging to the English mainland or Spanish Cuba, conditions of the ocean passage during the early centuries of immigration were grim. Passengers traveling aboard cramped and dangerous wooden vessels died of many causes en route: disease, drowning, disaster. They fell prey to attackers of all sorts: official navies, semiofficial privateers licensed to capture an enemy nation's ships, and unofficial pirates who captured any ships that appeared valuable. But in the face of all these risks, Europeans poured across the ocean in ever-greater numbers during the colonial years. Africans unwillingly joined the streams of human circulation around the Atlantic World, many of them ending their horrific travels in Cuba and the colonies along the North American coast. In both places, the populations soon manifested a blend of genes: native, European, and African.

They became "Creole," or "home-grown," a new people created by the forces of the sea, the medium of their mixing.

Far more Africans crossed the Atlantic during the British colonial period than did members of other ethnic groups, perhaps three or four times as many.[4] The first African immigrants to the British mainland colonies arrived in Virginia in 1619, having come from the Caribbean aboard a Dutch ship. By 1740, England dominated the traffic in human cargo, with a fleet of slave ships mainly based in Liverpool and Bristol, England, and Providence, Rhode Island. Two million Africans sailed away on British ships in the 1700s alone, during which time the thirteen United States gained independence from the empire, but continued their slave trading. Sullivan's Island in Charleston Harbor received a large percentage of the 450 to 600 thousand Africans who landed in what became the United States, while the population of the colony-turned-state of South Carolina contained a majority of people of African descent.

Rescued before they were landed in Cuba in 1857, these African boys demonstrate how they were forced to squat in the hold of a slave ship during the "Middle Passage" transatlantic crossing, a horrendous ordeal endured by millions of Africans during the more than 350 years of the Atlantic slave trade. (*Illustrated London News*, June 21, 1857; G.W. Blunt White Library, Mystic Seaport)

Great Britain and the United States both abolished the African slave trade in 1807-08, but a great deal of slave smuggling eluded the Royal Navy's efforts to enforce the ban on stealing people, while the United States Navy made only sporadic efforts between 1820 and 1862 to stop the horrors of the Middle Passage or even the short-range traffic in humans from Cuba. The creation of the ineffectual African Squadron in 1843 did little to improve the level of official vigilance, and was in fact probably worse than useless, because it provided slavers with a convenient way to avoid search and seizure by the Royal Navy—flying the American flag![5]

There was very high mortality among the unwilling passengers aboard slave ships, as there was among the crews of those despised vessels, which earned a wicked reputation among mariners.[6] Herman Melville characterized the common view of "black birders"—men who participated in the slave trade—in *Redburn* (1849), his novel about crossing the Atlantic before the mast on a packet ship in 1839. One member of the crew of the fictional *Highlander*, which was closely based on Melville's real-life experience sailing from New York to Liverpool on the *St. Laurence*, was Jackson, portrayed as having had long experience in the repugnant industry. "He had served in Portuguese slavers on the coast of Africa; and with a diabolical relish used to tell of the middle-passage, where the slaves were stowed, heel and point, like logs, and the suffocated and dead were unmanacled, and weeded out from the living every morning, before washing down the decks; how he had been in a slaving schooner, which being chased by an English cruiser off Cape Verde, received three shots in her hull, which raked through and through a whole file of slaves, that were chained." Melville suggested that Jackson's character reflected this despicable contact with the evil trade: "Nothing was left of this Jackson but the foul lees and dregs of a man... . He seemed full of hatred and gall against every thing and every body in the world."[7]

Melville's *Redburn* also evokes the experience of Irish and German immigrants during the great wave of migration from northern Europe that preceded the Civil War. Both nationalities had long been a part of the American scene. Irish indentured servants had helped to populate the Chesapeake colonies, such as Catholic Maryland, since the mid-1600s. Germans accepted William Penn's invitation to settle in his colonial experiment around Philadelphia, beginning in the late 1600s. In the 1700s, particularly large numbers of both groups entered what had become thirteen colonies just prior to their declaration of independence. Beginning around 1820, several factors resulted in the surge of newcomers from Erin and Deutschland in which Melville played a part. Political unrest, agricultural failure, and economic breakdown displaced many inhabitants of the emerald island and the many continental jurisdictions that would later come together to form Germany. The Irish flocked to Liverpool looking for a way out, and Prussians, Rheinlanders, Bavarians, Silesians, and members of many other Germanic ethnicities fled wars in their homelands to places such as the port in France called Le Havre, which means "the harbor." The city harbored both the refugees and the ships they took from there to the wide-open spaces of America. The Irish potato famine of 1846 and the wave of revolutions across Europe in 1848 spurred the rate of arrival to its antebellum height in the 1850s. More than five million people came from Europe during the forty years before the attack on Fort Sumter in 1861, two million of them from Ireland, and two million more from Germany.

Regular passenger service across the Atlantic, also beginning around 1820, facilitated maritime immigration from Europe. Whereas ships had formerly operated unpredictably, sailing only when their holds were full, the packet liners transformed the business of shipping goods and people on the sea by guaranteeing a regular schedule of service. They linked the swelling port cities of New York, New Orleans, and Boston, the top three immigrant ports in the United States, with the major ports of Europe: Liverpool, Glasgow, London, Le Havre, Bremen, and Hamburg. Twenty-seven transatlantic packet lines operated during the 1850s, sixteen of them serving New York, which received about four out of every five immigrants to the United States during those decades before Civil War hostilities. Beginning in 1855, these huddled masses found refuge when they came ashore at Castle Clinton on the Battery of Manhattan Island, where various immigrant aid societies conducted a kind of outreach program for them. Prior to that, fresh immigrants had been on their own, prey to the same landsharks that victimized sailors in the slum districts adjacent to the docks along the East River, such as crooked boardinghouse operators.

The first and most famous of the American packet lines that revolutionized shipping was the Black Ball Line of New York to Liverpool packets, which sold steerage berths for $20.00, while cabin passengers paid $140.00. The line aided "chain migration" by making it simple to send passage money from family members in the United States to their relatives back in Europe. This is still a very typical pattern for American immigration to follow, one in which the first family members who arrive earn money to help their loved ones reunite with them in their new home. Cuban families continue to follow this difficult path across the water today.

The most durable of the passenger transportation companies is the Cunard Line of England, founded in 1841, which offers the last remaining transatlantic passenger service with the new luxury liner *Queen Mary II* on cruises between New York and Southampton. The immigrant boom of the mid-1800s that produced the venerable Cunard Line occurred in tandem with the rise of the cotton economy in the United States. Cotton, raised by enslaved African-Americans in the South, fuelled the Industrial Revolution in the factories of Europe and the North, where many Irish and Germans ended up working after their arrival. Cotton filled the holds of the packet ships on their eastward passage while, on the westward trip, immigrants were "stowed away like bales of cotton, and packed like slaves in a slave-ship," as Herman Melville described them in *Redburn*. The small packet he served aboard carried 500 "friendless emigrants… confined in a place that, during storm time, must be closed against both light and air." Even in fine weather, the "between decks" where the passengers lived were suffocating spaces, with triple-tiered bunks that "looked more like dog-kennels than anything else; especially as the place was so gloomy and dark; no light coming down except through the fore and after hatchways, both of which were covered with little houses called 'booby hatches.'"[8]

Most packet liners were sailing craft, but steam-powered ships gained in importance as immigrant conveyances just before the Civil War. There were only 5,000 steamer voyages completed on the Atlantic in 1856, but by the time South Carolina seceded in 1860, there were 34,000. During that same brief span of turbulent years the number of sailing voyages on the routes linking Europe and America declined by almost half, from 136,000 to 74,000. Ten years later, few immigrants traveled under sail; almost all of the new wave of immigrants made the trip in passenger liners under steam. But for a time, the turmoil of the Civil War reduced the rate of immigration drastically. Those who came sometimes found themselves drafted into service, as recounted in the haunting ballad played by Irish mariners, "By the Hush." In the song, an Irish immigrant tells of leaving his farm and his tearful beloved to come to America, then being conscripted into the Union army right off the dock in New York, and losing his leg in battle. Warning other Irishmen not leave home, the narrator wishes he'd never come to a country immersed in violence.

Just off the boat and waiting to make connections with family already in the U.S., these European emigrants line up at an Ellis Island phone booth in 1924. (© Mystic Seaport, Rosenfeld Collection 1984.187.19684F)

Here's to you, boys! Take my advice—to America I'd have you not be coming! For there's nothing here but war, and the murdering cannon's roar, and I wish I was back home in dear old Erin! [9]

The Irish and Germans resumed the rapid pace of their exodus to the United States after the Civil War ended, but under much improved conditions during their transit. Steamship lines processed passengers with much greater comfort, dignity, and efficiency than their predecessors under canvas had been able to do during their extended "golden age." The great shipping lines of that storied era of steam transportation introduced their foreign passengers to America via the famous facilities of Ellis Island in New York Port, which opened in 1892. The big steamships docked at the Hudson River piers, then ferried immigrants back across the harbor to the arrival hall at Ellis Island aboard diminutive steamers. In addition to many natives of "old immigrant" countries such as Ireland, England, and Germany, millions of "new immigrants" came from Eastern and Southern Europe to file through the halls of Castle Clinton and later Ellis Island and get a new start in the United States. Three million immigrants came in the 1870s, five million in the 1880s, and almost nine million in the first decade of the 1900s. An anti–immigration law curtailed the rate of arrival in 1924, but the National Origins Act, as it was called, left some loopholes in an otherwise strict quota system. They permitted some continued entry for Northern Europeans and "chain" migrants who were joining family members already established in the United States. During the big years for Ellis Island, 1892 to 1924, there was a very low turned-away rate for newcomers when they

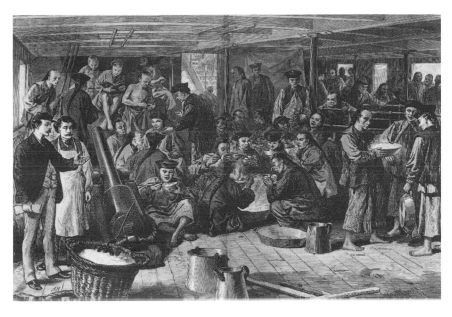

Chinese migrants made the long Pacific crossing to America intending to prosper and return home, not to settle. Most never realized their dream, and their growing presence in the U.S. labor force heightened racial tensions and anti-Chinese sentiments from the 1880s to the 1940s. (*Harper's Weekly*, May 20, 1876; G.W. Blunt White Library, Mystic Seaport)

disembarked from all those little white ferryboats. Only about two percent were sent back, mainly refused admission due to disease or poverty—immigrants had to be healthy and have a modest sum of cash to begin life in America.

At Angel Island in San Francisco Bay, the "Asian Ellis Island," ten in every hundred people were told they had to make the sad return voyage. Not only was the risk of rejection five times higher at Angel Island than at Ellis Island, the voyage across the Pacific Ocean took three times longer than an Atlantic crossing, and was more expensive. Many natives of Zhong Guo (China) and Nippon (Japan) completed their passages aboard specially built steamers such as the Pacific Mail Steamship Company's *City of Peking* and *City of Tokio*, the largest ships in the world when they came off the ways at the Roach Shipyard in Philadelphia in 1874. For many young Chinese men, California, called *Gam Saan* or "Golden Mountain" in the Cantonese language, was a place to try to make a fortune mining, or building railroads, or performing other kinds of labor before returning to their families in China. But conditions were rarely conducive to accumulating a mountain of gold, and many continued to labor in the West, never returning home. After a nativist backlash against Asian laborers, Congress passed an exclusionary act in 1882, making further entry very difficult.

From whatever direction they came, and for however long they planned to stay, waterborne emigrants to America faced many miles of trackless ocean. (© Mystic Seaport, Rosenfeld Collection 1984.187.86528FA)

Similar restrictions were imposed against Japanese nationals in 1907, expressed in the "Gentlemen's Agreement" between the Japanese government and the administration of President Theodore Roosevelt.

Being shipwrecked has been a peril faced by every immigrant at sea. From the 1609 wreck of the *Sea Venture* dramatized by Shakespeare, to the very recent drowning of Cuban rafters and Chinese freighter passengers, maritime immigration to America has been punctuated by disasters that claimed the lives of countless aspiring travelers. Some lost vessels have been fragile craft, but even the "unsinkable" *Titanic* took hundreds of would-be Americans to a deep grave when it struck an iceberg on its maiden voyage in 1912.

A rash of shipwrecks doomed the Collins Line, the most ambitious American attempt to rival the dominance of the Cunard Line in transatlantic steam navigation. While Samuel Cunard's enterprise tallied a remarkably unblemished record of safe deliveries of its passengers, the Collins Line lost two large ships in a short time. The liner *Arctic* was built in 1850 in New York, a 285-foot-long paddle-wheeler that boasted a speed of twelve knots and set a speed record for a passage to Liverpool in 1852. The ship had well-ventilated accommodations for two hundred first-class passengers and eighty passengers in second class. But after only four years in service, the *Arctic* sank after a collision with the French steamship *Vesta* near Cape Race, Newfoundland, with the loss of around three hundred lives. The well-publicized loss of the *Arctic*, coupled with the disappearance of her sister ship *Pacific*, spelled disaster for the Collins Line. The macabre setting of the *Arctic*'s demise, in a fog on a rolling gray ocean, and the mysterious loss of the *Pacific*, with their staggering death tolls, cast a pall on the company from which it never emerged.

One of the most powerful accounts of the desperate aftermath of a shipwreck in the Gulf Stream is Stephen Crane's vitally evocative short story, "The Open Boat." The author, famous for the classic Civil War novel *The Red Badge of Courage*, based his gripping tale on his own harrowing experience as a survivor of the wreck of the tugboat *Commodore* off the coast of Florida in January 1897. Crane had been hired as a war correspondent to cover the revolution in Cuba for the *New York Press*, and he was en route from Jacksonville to Havana with a gun-running expedition, having signed on as an able bodied seaman in a crew of twenty-three men. Leaving Jacksonville on New Year's Eve with fifteen tons of arms and ammunition, the 123-foot *Commodore* ran aground and had to be towed off a mud bar on New Year's Day. On the open ocean in heavy seas, the vessel began taking on water, but the engineer was unable to get the pumps to work. Despite a bucket brigade formed by the Cuban revolutionaries on board, the rapidly rising water extinguished the steam engine in the wee hours of January 2, 1897. As the *Commodore* sank, taking seven men down with her, Crane found himself in a ten-foot dinghy fighting for his life against the brutal elements, twelve miles off the coast of Daytona.[10] In his fictionalized version of the events, Crane described the plight of the four men in the open boat trying to make landfall through stormy seas: the injured captain, the cook, an oiler from the engine room of the doomed steamer, and a "correspondent" who was Crane himself. Surviving the subsequent ordeal allowed Crane to capture in words the intense feelings of pain and helplessness of people trying to stay alive in a cockleshell of a vessel, on the immense and daunting expanse of the angry ocean—not unlike those who embarked from Cuba in the *Analuisa*. The first sentences of the story set the depressing scene: "None of them knew the color of the sky. Their eyes glanced level and were fastened upon the waves that swept toward them. These waves were of the hue of slate, save for the tops, which were of foaming sea white, and all of the men knew the color of the sea."

The constant motion of the boat, surging, nauseating and utterly fatiguing, was like a rodeo ride lasting for hours and hours.

A seat in this boat was not unlike a seat upon a bucking broncho, and by the same token a broncho is not much smaller. The craft pranced and reared and plunged like an animal. As each wave came, and she rose for it, she seemed like a horse making at a fence outrageously high. The manner of her scramble over these walls of water is a mystic thing, and, moreover, at the top of them were ordinarily these problems in white water, the foam racing down from the summit of each wave requiring a new leap, and a leap from the air. Then, after scornfully bumping a crest, she would slide and race and splash down a long incline, and arrive bobbing and nodding in front of the next menace.

A singular disadvantage of the sea lies in the fact that after successfully surmounting one wave you discover that there is another behind it just as important and just as nervously anxious to do something effective in the way of swamping boats.

After a grueling day and night struggling to stay afloat, the quartet closed with the land, only to be ignored by people on the beach, who thought the men in the boat were merely fishing. When they tried to come ashore, the furious breakers crashing in along the dunes turned them away. Spending another agonizing night lashed by wind and saltwater spray just outside the breakers, and menaced by a large, persistent shark, Crane swore he would never again row for pleasure, and he asked himself again and again, "If I am going to be drowned, why, in the name of the seven mad gods who rule the seas, was I allowed to come thus far and contemplate sand and trees?" Finally deciding to make a try for dry land before succumbing to hunger and fatigue, the men in the open boat were buffeted by combers that capsized their craft, forcing them to swim for it. Three of the four were lucky enough to make it, but Billie the engine-room oiler drowned in the undertow just a few yards from safety. Stephen Crane, aided by a brave rescuer on the strand, lived to tell the tale, and to express the altered sense of reality shared by people who survive a shipwreck. "When it came night, the white waves paced to and fro in the moonlight, and the wind brought the sound of the great sea's voice to the men on the shore, and they felt they could then be interpreters."[11]

But Crane never fully recovered from the horrors of his time in the open boat. Weakened by the experience, he contracted tuberculosis. Although he soon after made it to Cuba to cover the war, staying aboard the filibustering steamship *Three Friends*, he died in 1900. Stephen Crane's last words were agitated ravings in his sleep, as he was tormented by a nightmare of trying to change rowing positions in an open boat on the ocean without capsizing.

Despite the inherent risks of travel on the high seas, immigrants continued to take their chances, coming to America from near and far. But fewer and fewer arrived on American-flag ships. From the Civil War to World War I, the British Cunard and White Star lines, the German Hamburg-America and North German Lloyd lines, the Dutch Holland America Line, and the French Line carried the bulk of the Atlantic's passenger and emigrant trades.

About the farthest that the immigrants of today come is from China. The Chinese immigrants of the 1800s mainly originated in the provinces called Guangdong, near Hong Kong on the Pearl River Delta, and Fujian, on the Formosa Straits, which separates the mainland from the island that now is called Taiwan. More recent Chinese immigrants also hail from those regions,

Generally considered economic rather than political refugees, Haitian migrants who undertook the 800-mile passage to the U.S. in their home-built sailboats were usually interdicted by the U.S. Coast Guard and returned to Haiti. (Courtesy U.S. Coast Guard)

joined by many people who come from Jiangsu province near the thriving port of Shanghai, and from northern China, around the Yellow Sea. Some of those who make the move from the People's Republic of China to Chinatown neighborhoods in New York and San Francisco, among other cities, arrive clandestinely in freighters and containerships. Early morning visitors to New York's Fire Island beach were shocked to see the wreck of the *Golden Venture* unfold before their eyes in June 1993. With a cargo of more than 200 Chinese immigrants who had already endured a four-month passage via Africa, the rusting vessel ran aground while making its quiet approach to the Port of New York. Some of the passengers swam to safety and incarceration, while others drowned in the surf. Of those who survived, most were deported back to China, while another group of forty-eight waited in jail for three years and eight months before gaining provisional freedom.[12] The pathetic end of the *Golden Venture* made the headlines, but for every such smuggling voyage that comes to grief, there are probably many others that end by delivering their human contraband safely and silently to the United States.

The nation of Haiti, Cuba's neighbor to the east across the Windward Passage, has also been a source of recent immigration by sea to the United States. The Haitian exodus began in 1972, when a boatload of sixty-five refugees landed in Miami. During the long dictatorship of François "Papa Doc" Duvalier, Haitian citizens had been effectively prevented from fleeing the regime's brutality and injustice, but under the rule of his son Jean-Claude, known as "Baby Doc," thousands of desperate Haitians took to the sea to get away. The crossing to the U.S. from Haiti, which occupies the western third of the island of Hispaniola, which it shares with the Dominican Republic, is a grueling 800 miles long. The dangers of making the passage, such as the risk of sinking, and of death by thirst or exposure, are compounded by the length of the trip and by the primitive watercraft employed. The refugees usually crowded aboard wooden boats with square hulls that are pieced together with scavenged scraps of material in makeshift shipyards along the coast, propelled by patchwork sails assembled from burlap bags and old clothing.

An average of ten thousand unfortunate souls made the voyage every year during the decade of the 1970s, with untold numbers lost at sea before sighting Florida. The height of the Haitian wave of newcomers came in 1980, at the same time as the famous Mariel "boatlift from Cuba, with more than twenty-five thousand arrivals. One important difference between the Cuban and Haitian immigrants was the status accorded to them by the American immigration authorities, who considered those from Cuba to be political refugees who were escaping the tyranny of the Castro regime, while those from Haiti were considered economic refugees, forced out by poverty. In fact, abuse at the hands of the vicious Haitian secret police motivated many, if not most, of them to leave, but nevertheless, those who were apprehended en route were returned home to face further violence.

The fall of the Baby Doc government in a revolution in 1986 did nothing to reduce the level of political intimidation or alleviate the dismal circumstances of life in the poorest country in the hemisphere, causing a fresh surge in departures to the United States and the Bahamas, neither of which granted political refugee status to Haitians. The chaos and bloodshed surrounding the military coup that removed the elected president Jean-Bertrand Aristide in 1991 boosted the rate of emigration from Haiti again, forcing the administration of President Bill Clinton to respond to conflicting points of criticism. On one hand, residents of south Florida opposed further additions to the burgeoning Haitian population in Miami. On the other hand, human rights advocates decried the inhumane practice of sending victims of political terror back to the scene of their mistreatment, where further attacks could be expected.

The compromise implemented by the U.S. government was to employ the Coast Guard to interdict the frail Haitian immigrant craft at sea and take the passengers on board, where they were interviewed as part of a screening process to determine which of them were political refugees and which had left for financial reasons. Few of the Haitians subjected to this litmus test were allowed to continue on the way to freedom, while most were deposited back on the eroded soil of the native land. When the United States sent troops into Haiti in 1994 to depose the military regime and return Aristide to power, one result of the occupation was to cut off Haitian migration at its source. Since then, as the country succumbed again to civil war and was battered by the catastrophic hurricanes named Mitch and Jeanne, only a handful of Haitian vessels have been able to escape and sail successfully to the United States.

Among the shortest, but most perilous, immigrant voyages is the one from the island of Cuba. It is impossible to know when the first Cuban

Babalua/San Lázaro and Oshun/Caridad del Cobre remain potent symbols in Cuba. (AE Doyle photo)

immigrants came to the British North American colonies. Perhaps the mulatto Cuban soldiers taken prisoner during the War of Jenkins' Ear, those formerly free men who later participated in the New York Conspiracy of 1741, were the first. Or the first Cuban immigrants may have come to America even earlier; perhaps they were Creole slaves born on the island and transported unwillingly to new homes and more hardships on the mainland. Certainly many Cuban slaves arrived there later, smuggled easily to southern ports before and after the abolition of the slave trade to the United States in 1808, all the way until the Civil War.

Whatever the origin of Cuban immigration, the number of people who relocated freely to the United States increased in the mid-1800s, with the migration of cigar makers to Florida. The number increased during the Ten Years War in the 1870s and the unsettled decade of the 1890s. More Cuban immigrants came to the United States in the early 1900s, after the War of 1898 forged new links between Cuba and its northern neighbor. The new city of Miami became a destination for many Cuban immigrant families in the 1920s and during the years of the international Great Depression in the 1930s.

Millions of Americans felt an intimate insight into the Cuban American community as a result of Desi Arnaz and Lucille Ball's portrayal of a 1950s Cuban-American couple in *I Love Lucy*. The immense influence of this popular comedy brought Cuban dance rhythms and folk music into homes all over the country, such as the song "Babalua," dedicated to the Santería god of health, who is also represented by Saint Lazarus. Cubans everywhere revere Babalua/ San Lázaro, much as they do Oshun/Caridad del Cobre, especially people who hope for cures of their own or their loved ones' health problems. Some Cuban rafters make promises to Saint Lazarus at his shrine in Rincón near Havana before setting out, vowing to shave their heads for a period of years or go on their knees to a Lazarus shrine in Miami after their safe passage, to show gratitude. Immigrants like Juan Alfaro, whose principal motive in leaving is to seek medical care, are particularly likely to make a promise to Saint Lazarus/ Babalua. During the same years when U.S. audiences learned about Cuban

An outboard skiff and some inner tubes got these Cuban migrants close enough to the U.S. be rescued by a Coast Guard cutter. (990917-M-7777A-015, courtesy U.S. Coast Guard)

The U.S. Coast Guard rescued the passengers from this raft built from an old fuel tank. (Charles Smith photo, 990917-C-5200S-016, courtesy U.S. Coast Guard)

culture from a man named Desiderio Arnaz, the harsh conditions of the Batista regime produced a steady flow of exiles to the United States, although at that time rafts were unnecessary. Approximately eighty thousand Cubans arrived in the U.S. from 1952, when a coup brought Batista back to power, until the fall of his dictatorship on the first day of 1959.

In the two years after Castro seized power from Batista, he placed increasing pressure on the wealthiest Cubans to leave the country, nationalizing their businesses and taking over their social clubs. When these "golden exiles" left behind their mansions in the elite precincts of Vedado and Marianao to come to the United States, the government appropriated the deeds to their property and gave the keys to supporters of the revolution. From Castro's entry into Havana, in early 1959, until October 1962, when direct flights between Cuba and the United States ended, about 200,000 "golden exiles" made their exit from the increasingly difficult situation.

Flights from Cuba to the United States via third countries such as Spain and Mexico continued after direct connections ceased, allowing another fifty thousand people to leave the island between late 1962 and 1965. Anti-Communist Catholics introduced "Operation Pedro Pan" to escort children out of Cuba to foster families in the United States, where they would wait until their parents could join them. Fourteen thousand Cuban children left their homes during the life of the program, often enduring long separations from their loved ones. It was especially difficult for men between the ages of fourteen and forty-five to get government permission to leave Cuba, because they were subject to the draft.[13] Although most of these well-heeled immigrants left by airplane or took the ferry to Key West, a few in desperate circumstances made the crossing to Florida in small boats or rafts. They became the first *balseros*, or rafters, of the many who would attempt the trip, trusting their lives to over-burdened skiffs, inner-tubes, or empty steel drums.

The rafters of the 1960s set the precedent for the untold numbers to follow. A single article in the *Key West Citizen*, "Southernmost Newspaper In The U.S.A.," can capture the dreadful uncertainty pervading the forty-year history of Cuban raft voyages across the Gulf Stream. In September 1969, the Coast Guard found a "handmade raft, lashed together with string, wire and wood" floating ten miles out in the ocean, empty but for three sets of identification for Cuban men. According to the Coast Guardsman who inspected it after it came ashore in Key West, the raft showed fine workmanship requiring months of effort. "Working cleverly with the thin but flexible lengths of wood, the Cubans formed a hollow hull for the raft inside of which they placed three tractor inner tubes, and lashed them in place." A small outboard motor was wired onto the stern. On this occasion, the Coast Guard surmised that a Soviet freighter had picked up the three men, because the boat was floating well, the weather was fine, and there was no sign of a problem on board. Just the week before, twelve men in an eighteen-foot boat had been picked up by a Coast Guard cutter near Key West. But no one knew anything about the three men who had left their official papers on a primitive-looking bundle of sticks floating in the open sea. Although not beyond the realm of possibility, thinking they had been rescued by a Soviet vessel and taken back to Cuba was wishful thinking. None of the likeliest scenarios of what happened to the three missing men were as optimistic, because the facts show that seriously dehydrated and sun-burned individuals often lose their senses and go overboard to escape their thirst and the blazing sky, only to drown.[14]

By many estimates, most of those who try to cross the Straits of Florida in marginally seaworthy small craft and buoyant contrivances perish in the attempt.[15] Marine scientists at the University of Miami's Rosenstiel School of Marine and Atmospheric Science ran computer projections of oceanographic factors to predict the path of five hundred imaginary rafts set adrift from the Cuban coast around Havana. Even under optimum wind and current conditions, which are uncommon in that turbulent region, only two of the hypothetical voyages made it to Key West after four days. After six days, six percent were predicted to make it to land, and up to twenty-five percent of them would come ashore within eight days, according to their calculations. But most people are only capable of surviving five days of privations at sea, as they run out of water and succumb to the relentless exposure to the elements.

The first wave of Cuban refugees fled in the Camarioca boatlift of 1965. About 5,000 seasick Cubans made it to Florida in a motley fleet of pleasure boats. (26-G-10-13-65, courtesy National Archives)

The director of the Transit Home for Cuban Refugees in Key West estimated from his experience, not from computer models, that only one percent of rafts without propulsion make it to Florida, perhaps forty percent of all attempts. Worried relatives in Cuba used to telephone the Transit Home which closed its doors in 1994, with vague requests for information on relatives who had taken to the water. Hundreds of their messages were pinned up on what the staff of the Transit Home called the "Wall of Sorrows," because they rarely had good news to report back. Many balsersos are captured by the Cuban Coast Guard before they can cross the capricious ocean currents near the island that hold flotsam close to shore. There are happy exceptions, of course, like the man who pushed off on his own in a four-foot raft, then was picked up by the British royal yacht HMS *Britannia*! The Cuban Transit Home hosted more than five thousand refugees, comprising an amazing variety of people fortunate enough to beat the odds and arrive in Key West: a woman eight months pregnant; another sixty-six years old, traveling with her paraplegic son; and several infants. Most of the survivors of the harrowing passage have been young men. A few of the refugees have brought their dogs and cats, "afraid that if they leave them, the neighbors will eat them," claimed one staff member. One man used a flipper to swim until rescued. A paralyzed man rowed with paddles lashed to his body, which he threw back and forth to move water.[16]

Thousands of Cubans did not have the means to buy airline tickets, but wanted to get to the United States any way they could, especially those with family members already living there. Their opportunity came in September 1965, when the first of three major "boatlifts," or periods of departure from Cuba, took place. These boatlifts also occurred in 1980 and 1994, with sporadic bursts of traffic in between, bringing a new wave of maritime immigration to the United States. Between 1960 and 1995, nearly ten percent of the population of Cuba, more than a million people, made the journey to America. Perhaps a quarter million of them came by sea, most of them in one of the three big boatlifts.[17]

The first boatlift occurred after Castro announced that Cubans with relatives in the U.S. could leave the country, provided that an American vessel pick them up at the port of Camarioca, near Varadero Beach and the town of Cárdenas, about twenty miles east of Havana. The resulting exodus took place in the middle of the hurricane season, mainly aboard Florida pleasure craft, ending after five thousand people had made the nauseating trip. The boatlift was replaced by an airlift arranged between the two countries to provide safe passage for several thousand people with relatives in the United States every month, resulting in a total of seventeen thousand Cubans leaving by sea and by air during 1965. The airlift lasted until 1973, bringing more than a quarter million immigrants from Cuba and greatly reducing the number of boaters and rafters in the Straits of Florida.

The Mariel boatlift, between April and September 1980, brought the heaviest period of migration from Cuba of all time, about 125,000 people. The event began on April 1, when a group of six asylum-seekers crashed through the fence of the Embassy of Peru, in the elite Miramar district of western Havana, in a borrowed bus. One of the Cuban soldiers guarding the embassy was killed in the incident, prompting Fidel Castro to remove all of the security forces from around the property. News that the Peruvian embassy was left unguarded spread rapidly among Cubans looking for a chance to leave Cuba. In a short time, the embassy compound was full of people who had climbed over the fence onto the grounds to petition for asylum, a total of almost 11,000 of them before the Peruvians stopped the human flow into the over-crowded area. Castro's offer for dissidents to quit the country began with the crowd at the Embassy of Peru. In addition, Cuban prisons held a numerous and wide variety of "criminals," including prisoners of conscience, victims of sexual discrimination, prostitutes, and individuals with psychological illnesses, whom the government wanted to send out of the country. The invitation to depart extended to the many Cubans who had been jailed for various reasons in the past, been released from incarceration, and lost their jobs, homes, and ration cards. Eventually, exit permission included many individuals who had no previous record of criminal or political offenses, people who simply wanted to leave.

The suspension of direct airline flights to the United States seven years earlier had increased the pent-up demand for a way out of Cuba when the Mariel boatlift took place. The 1970s had also been hard times economically for the country, with the government depending heavily on subsidies from the Soviet Union to sell its sugar and buy its oil, and shortages in many basic commodities, so many Cubans hoped for a fresh start in the United States. The government barred many others from taking the option of expatriation. The authorities excluded skilled professionals, such as doctors and engineers, and unmarried men of military service age.

As he had done fifteen years earlier in the case of the Camarioca boatlift, Castro announced that those with the desire to leave, and who had the government's permission to go, could be picked up by anyone willing to come from Florida to pick them up, this time at the port of Mariel, fifty miles west of Havana. Boats arriving for that purpose had to come with a list of passengers they intended to transport. The hitch was that no more than sixty percent of the people on that list would actually be allowed to board; the other places would be taken by individuals placed there by the government, which caused a great deal of confusion and heartache. The opening of Mariel brought more than two thousand cabin cruisers, pleasure yachts, and fishing boats mainly from Florida, beginning with a flotilla of forty-two assorted vessels that left Miami on April 19. The subsequent evacuation took place during the calmest months of the year, rather than during hurricane season, when the Camarioca boatlift had taken place. The "freedom flotilla" made Key West, Florida, into an immigration boom town. The relatives of Cubans eligible for departure rushed to the island to charter or purchase every available vessel, enticing sport-fishing boats away from the hunt, and offering such fantastic sums for the service that even drug-smuggling boats returned to port to take advantage of the lucrative trade in refugees. Prices for provisions and fuel skyrocketed, as more and more boats made runs to Mariel, returning with scores of immigrants crammed above and below deck. Greyhound buses waited to take some of them to the next stage of their travels, with the destination sign behind their windshields reading "America."[18]

Back in Cuba, "repudiation committees" abused many of those Cubans who asked permission to leave, usually at the moment they had to resign from their places of employment, with their former co-workers formed up to harass and often assault the would-be emigrants. Stories of the brutal treatment involved in these "acts of repudiation" motivated some of the boatlift voyages, such as that of *God's Mercy*, a former World War II submarine chaser and Massachusetts whale-watcher purchased by Episcopal priests in New Orleans to retrieve loved ones of their parishioners.[19]

The immigrants from Mariel overwhelmed the facilities in Miami to process immigrants, so thousands of newcomers were herded into the Orange Bowl football stadium, which became their temporary home while the government sorted them out. These survivors of the Mariel boatlift have suffered from a particularly negative image in popular depictions and perceptions of them in both Cuba and the United States. *Marielitos* sounds like a fond nickname—"little ones from Mariel"—but it is actually a derisive reference. The fact that one thousand of the Mariel immigrants were inmates of Cuban prisons and asylums gave them all a bad reputation in many of the U.S. communities where they later settled. In Mariel, the boatlift of 1980 was embarrassing to many residents of the city. A quarter century later, they still denounced the emigrants as "the riffraff, the prostitutes, the crazy ones."[20]

The 1983 film *Scarface*, directed by Brian DePalma and starring Al Pacino, put a Cuban spin on the 1932 gangster movie of the same name. The earlier film had starred Paul Muni in the lead role, with supporting actors Boris Karloff, of horror-movie fame, and George Raft, who later became closely associated in real life with one of the most notoriously gang-operated casinos in Havana, the Capri Hotel. (Raft personally defended the casino from being vandalized by a mob during the first hours after Batista fled Cuba, on New Year's Day, 1959, when the rest of the corruption-tainted casinos were stormed and sacked. "In his Hollywood, gangster-like style, Raft snarled, 'Yer not comin' in my casino.'")[21] The 1983 *Scarface* opens with actual footage of densely packed boats leaving Cuba, and depicts the horrifically violent criminal career of "Tony Montana," a Mariel immigrant in Miami, including a knifepoint murder in the chaotic detention facility. *Scarface* did well at the box office, spreading the pernicious stereotype of Cubans as gangsters to a wide audience of Americans.

A lighter cinema treatment of the ordeals of the Mariel immigrants was the 1995 film *The Pérez Family*. The movie depicted a loveable but bizarre Cuban "family," really an assemblage of unrelated outcasts posing as a family to fool the customs authorities, who build a new life together. Director Mira Nair took a comic approach to refugee life first in the crowded Orange Bowl, then in the daunting city of Miami. The cast included the great vocalist Celia Cruz as a wise woman and a kind of oracle, but the leading role, played by Marisa Tomei, is a prostitute, which perpetuated the negative stereotypes clinging to "the Mariels." Neither *Scarface* nor *The Pérez Family* did the Mariel immigrants any favors. Both of the movies portrayed them mainly as social misfits, and prepared the way for the unfavorable reception accorded the next wave of Cuban arrivals in 1994.

Other events taking place on television screens, rather than in movie theaters, also stained the reputation of the Mariel immigrants. Governor Bill Clinton of Arkansas lost his bid for re-election in 1980 partly because of the riot earlier that year by Mariel detainees housed at Fort Chaffee, which resulted in one immigrant dead, forty of his compatriots wounded, and fifteen injured Arkansas State Police officers. Clinton returned to be governor in Little Rock after winning re-election in 1984, then went on to the White House in 1993, only to deal with another Cuban boatlift the very next year.

One of thousands of American boats enlisted to ferry Cubans to Key West between April and October 1980, the aptly named shrimp boat *Americana* approaches the U.S. with a full load of Cubans allowed by Castro to leave through the port of Mariel. During the six months of the Mariel boatlift, at least 125,000 Cubans crossed the Straits of Florida in this way. (© *Miami Herald*)

More than twenty-five hundred boatlift participants with felony convictions in their Cuban past, or who had committed crimes in the United States since 1980, found themselves caught in a state of international legal limbo. Some of them had been forced to leave by the Cuban government, others had chosen to leave and had been red-flagged by the Immigration and Naturalization Service as individuals disqualified from entry into the United States, but most had committed a crime since Mariel. The INS would not release them except to deport them back to Cuba, but Cuba would not accept them back, so they were stuck, even after the end of the prison sentences imposed by American courts. They languished in maximum-security cellblocks all around the country for years after their arrival, wards of the Federal Bureau of Prisons. With no resolution to their "temporary detention" in sight, some of these frustrated inmates took part in prison riots in several states across the Union.

A group of Mariel immigrants behind bars at Oakdale federal prison in Louisiana, and another group housed at the Atlanta penitentiary in Georgia, rioted and took more than one hundred hostages in December 1987. The Cuban government had agreed to repatriate some of the felons, honoring a 1984 agreement, prompting the prisoners to seize hostages and demand that they not be sent back to Cuba. The eleven-day stand-off with the authorities that ensued set the record for the longest in U.S. prison history, but it ended peacefully, with no harm to the hostages, and the prisoners received a hearing and a guarantee not to be deported. A similar hostage stand-off in Talladega, Alabama, in April 1991 lasted almost as long, but it did not end as quietly. Instead, the prison authorities launched an assault to break the impasse, causing injuries on both sides.

Since 1988, Cuba has repatriated more than fourteen hundred convicted felons, or those judged to be criminally insane, who were deported during the chaotic course of the Mariel exodus. But twenty years after arriving in the U.S., there are still seventeen hundred and fifty individuals from the Mariel boatlift in the custody of the Immigration and Naturalization Service, incarcerated around the country for crimes carried out in the United States. This prison population continues to tarnish the reputation of all Mariels, but statistical evidence shows that the rate of criminality among the Mariels is only a small fraction of the rate in the general American population.[22]

During the Mariel boatlift, the Immigration and Naturalization Service did not maintain such occupational categories as "artist," "cinematographer," "dancer," "musician," "novelist," "painter," or "playwright," to classify the newcomers. Nevertheless, several hundred people who fit these descriptions came into the country at that time. Some of them had careers working with official bodies, such as the National Folkloric Culture Institute founded by the Castro government in 1964, while others were critical outsiders, deemed "insane" and "delinquent" by the authorities. Whatever their background, these creative souls made Mariel into "a cultural injection," "a super-motor" for culture in the exile community. The "Mariel generation" includes writers (Andrés Reynaldo, Manuel Serpa, and Roberto Valero); visual artists (Carlos Alfonso and Juan Boza); choreographers (Juanita Baro); musicians (Amado Rafael); and filmmakers (Carlos Arditti). Their work tends to reclaim the African roots of Cuba and to protest Castro. Mariel artists express their resentment of the dictatorship that betrayed them in all of their respective media, but writer and painter Juan Abreu did it perhaps most graphically and eloquently, with his design for a post card called "Portrait of Fidel Castro." The post card shows a man's buttocks surrounded by "a sea of microphones."[23]

The rate of known Cuban crossings dwindled to only forty-four in 1987 and fifty-seven in 1988, then rose to more than twenty-five hundred in 1992. The "Keys News" edition of the *Miami Herald* ran poignant notices asking for information on drowned people washing up among the islands, complete with descriptions of their likely age and the clothes they had on. So many unidentified bodies were washing up on Key West that a local detective compiled a book of photographs to show the many people who inquired about missing loved ones. Some deaths came slowly, such as those caused by dehydration and exposure, while others were over in an instant, such as being run over by a seagoing barge. Some new arrivals avoided the perils of rafting by paying high prices to be smuggled into Key West aboard large sport-fishing motorboats, thirty feet long and equipped with powerful engines. The smugglers charged an amount equal to a year and a half's wages in Cuban pesos per person for the service, delivering groups of about a dozen passengers in predawn runs into the Florida Keys, where they deposited their human cargo in shallow water to wade ashore, or in one case dropped them off on a jetty in front of the "Southernmost Hotel!" Others hijacked vessels, such as "the Cuban Bruce Lee," who used his expertise in martial arts to take control of a fishing boat. The karate champion and nine others, including an infant, disembarked on one of the Florida Keys, leaving the fishing boat's captain "a little bruised" and in the custody of the Immigration and Naturalization Service along with his mate, both of them accused of smuggling the immigrants! They asked to have their boat back and be allowed to return to Cuba, as the perpetrator admitted that he had forced the two to make the crossing. In another case, three men jumped off of a Cuban fishing boat into an inflatable life raft while the captain fired shots at them with a rifle, badly scaring a vacationing family on a charter fishing boat nearby. The charter boat captain kept his vessel out of gunshot range until the Cuban boat motored away, then radioed the Coast Guard to pick up the men, who escaped the incident unhurt and soon were on their way to the Cuban Transit Home.[24]

At the same time, some Cubans who had already relocated to the United States decided they had made a mistake, and they became desperate to return. Two of them, who had just rafted over the year before, murdered a charter-boat captain while stealing his vessel for a passage back to Cuba. The captain had settled in Key West after serving there as an Army missile specialist during the Cuban Missile Crisis.[25]

Cubans embarking on the risky voyage across the Gulf Stream were often caught by police on the beach while trying to launch their boat or raft, and many others are seized at sea by Cuban Coast Guard patrols. Cuban Coast Guard cutters sometimes pursue boats that initially elude their shoreline blockade, often coming within fifteen miles of Key West. In one case, two American fishing trawlers spotted a Cuban "gunboat" and called the United States Coast Guard. A U.S. Coast Guard cutter arrived on the scene and followed its Cuban counterpart until it left the area, which was well within international waters. Even though the incident made the front page of the Key West newspaper, it was nothing new for the American Coast Guardsmen, who saw Cuban patrols "on a regular basis." "They're always out there," one of them told a reporter, adding that it was the Cubans' right to patrol offshore waters, but they did not usually come so close. Eighteen Cuban refugees in four small boats, none of them longer than twenty feet, showed up in the vicinity in the next few days, spurring speculation that the Cuban gunboat had been searching for them.[26]

Those who are apprehended in the attempt to float away from Cuba face a standard prison sentence of three years on a charge of "illegal exit," but some have served more than six years for the conviction. They are often incarcerated as political prisoners at Havana's Combinado del Este prison. A smuggled letter from a group being held there for the crime of attempted departure stated that "ten or twelve" more joined them every day, during the spike in raft crossings that began in 1989, when the rate of attempts quadrupled that of the previous two years.

But as the number of "daring refugee voyages" from Cuba to Florida increased, the level of public attention and sympathy in the United States waned. Because of "sheer mathematics," their "news value" declined with each new report of an arrival from the sea. "It is a Miami cliché," wrote a reporter for the *Miami Herald* in 1989, "tormented Cubans escaping their homeland and appearing in between leisure boats and wind surfers in their rough-hewn vessels. 'Sailing to Freedom,' the headlines say." That was only in 1989, five years before memories of the Mariel boatlift were stirred by the events of August 1994. The proprietor of a gift shop on Grassy Key literally seized on the "cliché" of Cuban refugee boats, displaying an ingenious wooden catamaran that had washed up nearby in the front yard of his business, along with a giant fiberglass shark head, hoping to draw in customers from U.S. Highway 1. Even though the arrival of Cubans was no longer a novelty, media coverage returned to the subject whenever the Castro regime allowed the tide of rafts to rise again. People left because the Cuban ship of state was on the rocks, as cartoonist Jeff McNelly symbolized the situation in August 1994. In his cartoon, Castro sits worrying in the aft cabin of a stranded, dismasted galleon, while shadowy figures dismantle the hull to make rafts and float away.[27]

The wave of Cuban immigration that rose in 1994 was not organized by the Cuban government and carried out by American watercraft, as the 1980 Mariel boatlift had been. Instead, it came about because individual Cubans, motivated by economic desperation, decided to embark on their own. The pattern of "chain migration" continued, however, involving many who had relatives in the United States who could assist in their resettlement. Three or four thousand Cubans were permitted to leave the island with official permission aboard direct flights to the United States, which resumed when the Mariel boatlift ended in September 1980. An agreement reached by the administration of President Ronald Reagan in 1984 gave the United States authority to issue 27,645 visas per year to Cubans. But during the early 1990s, the United States consular office in Havana granted only about 3,000 per year.[28] Many people wanted to come but either could not get a visa or could not afford the cost of airplane tickets, or both, so they took their chances in whatever small craft they could construct or find, including makeshift rafts and small open coastal fishing boats. All of them hoped to cross the Straits of Florida before exhausting the scant amount of water they could carry.

The rate of clandestine embarkation from Cuba increased each year, beginning in 1989, but the diaspora reached its climax in August 1994, when

Arriving at Key West from Mariel in 1980, Tomasa Enriqueto and her 75-year-old mother Machada Ruiz wait for clearance to go ashore in their new land. (© *Miami Herald*/ Chapman)

the Cuban government suspended its efforts to prevent people from leaving in boats. This decision came after gunmen seized a ferryboat in Havana Harbor and tried to cross to Florida in it. Cuban naval vessels rammed and sank the ferry, drowning many of the pirates as well as those passengers who had opted on the spur of the dramatic moment to go to the United States. Castro had often criticized what he saw as a double standard in American policy, which condemned airplane hijackers who wanted to go to Cuba, but welcomed Cuban boat hijackers as political refugees. His revenge was to open the gates to emigration, as he had when the Peruvian embassy extended asylum to all comers in 1980, precipitating the Mariel boatlift.

Thousands of hopeful Cubans flocked to the beaches and ports on the northwest coast of the island to launch just about anything that would float toward Florida. In all, thirty-six thousand Cubans completed their passages to Florida during 1994. Estimates of the death toll among those taking part in that flotilla run as high as fifty percent. Of those who survived, many were swooped up "like fireflies" by U.S. Coast Guard cutters like the *Baranof*. Sixteen of the 110-foot cutters, half the entire national fleet of the workhorse boats, patrolled the Straits of Florida during the crisis, joined by eighteen other Coast Guard vessels, including a group of old buoy tenders commissioned a half-century earlier. Ten U.S. Navy ships also served in "the most intense rescue operation in fifty years," in the words of Coast Guard Commander Jim Howe. Between them, the forty-four Coast Guard and Navy vessels plucked thousands of Cuban boaters and rafters from the water. the *Miami Herald* ran a banner headline, "2,269," announcing the "record number picked up in [the] human tidal wave" in the single day of Monday, August 22. The record only lasted twenty-four hours, because the very next day more than three thousand came, part of a total of eight thousand people in four days. The commander of the cutter *Nantucket* said the refugees were arriving on "anything that floats," including contraptions made of the kind of foam used to pad televisions inside boxes for shipping, and others constructed of bamboo![29]

Then the weather changed, turning tranquil seas into whitecaps, and sunny skies were obscured by rain squalls that brought lightning and wind gusts of more than forty miles per hour. Fewer than four hundred were rescued on the stormy Straits of Florida on Friday, August 26. Like everyone rescued during the previous week, American ships deposited them at Guantánamo Bay Naval Base, because a change in American immigration policy had taken place, ordered by

President Bill Clinton. For the first time since breaking relations with the Fidel Castro regime, the United States government considered refugees from Cuba to be economically motivated, not political exiles.

Seventy-two-year-old retired merchant seaman H.T. Pontin of Ramrod Key, Florida, went out on his fifty-three-foot sailboat on August 22 to look for refugees in need of assistance. He encountered six empty small craft, then found a raft with six exhausted men who had been on the water for five long days. They accepted the sailor's offer to come aboard, then posed with cold drinks and beaming, grateful faces as he took their photograph. But later, the Coast Guard boarded Pontin's boat and took the six men into custody, marking the end of their failed voyage to America. They were on their way first to Key West to be turned over to the INS, then to Krome Detention Center in Miami, then on to a tent city at Guantánamo Bay Naval Base back in Cuba, where they would spend an indeterminate amount of time waiting for the next twist of foreign policy to determine their futures. Before they left, the Coast Guard boarding party handed the captain of the sailboat who had just saved the six men a federal circular. It was a warning to "Good Samaritan" boaters that if they helped Cubans on the high seas, they would face prosecution for smuggling. Ten thousand of the circulars were distributed in South Florida, stating that anyone caught helping the emigrants to reach land could have their boat seized by the government, be slapped with a $100,000 fine, be sentenced to a year in prison, or all of the above. If convicted of receiving payment for assisting a refugee, a boater could be fined $250,000 and sent to jail for five years. The fortunes made by Key West charter boats during the Mariel boatlift were a thing of the past! Pontin later watched the Coast Guard remove another group of Cubans from a fishing boat. The Coast Guard left the Cuban vessel drifting there as they motored away with its former occupants, so the old merchant mariner took the skiff in tow. Like coming to the rescue of people in trouble on the ocean, removing a navigational hazard (and respecting a carefully constructed wooden launch), must have seemed to him like the right thing to do.[30]

Abandoned boats and rafts became a mounting menace as the summer of 1994 drew to a close. Towboat Captain Bill Hicks of Miami cleared 122 rafts from Biscayne National Park in twenty-two days. Park rangers at Cape Canaveral National Seashore, far to the north of Miami, picked up forty more rafts along the beach. Twenty pleasure boats were damaged after colliding with abandoned rafts, one of them having its propeller shaft ripped out of the hull when it became entangled with an inner tube. The largest boating hazards were rafts constructed solidly of steel drums, welded together with steel rebar supports and decked with wood, which could sink a sizable vessel in a collision. The smallest contrivances, made of lawn chairs lashed together with blocks of

127

Heading for the beach at Cojímar in 1994, balseros prepare to launch a catamaran for their passage to the U.S. (© *Miami Herald*/ Al Diaz)

foam, posed less danger, but they brought to mind a pitiful picture of desperate, probably doomed, people at sea.[31]

Others looked for a bright side to the countless boats and rafts floating eerily empty off the Florida coast. "As rafts drift in the Gulf Stream, baitfish gather under them the way they do under most floating debris," wrote the *Miami Herald* fishing columnist at the height of the 1994 exodus. "It isn't long until dolphin fish [also called dorado or mahi mahi] come up to the rafts in search of bait fish," he continued, reporting that one charter fisherman found "schools of twenty to thirty" of the valued sport fish around rafts, and caught some that were up to twenty pounds in size. Of course, dolphin fish are not the only large predators attracted by schools of bait fish; sharks often hover around rafts! The macabre down-side of looking for Cuban rafts to sport-fish, the columnist noted, was spotting one without the tell-tale official orange Coast Guard PFD (Personal Flotation Device) tied to its highest point, which indicated that the authorities had already been there and that the raft or boat was abandoned. Unmarked rafts either had people still in them, dead or alive, healthy or sick, or were mysteriously empty, which was usually not a good sign. Corpses were tragic and depressing. Living refugees required a call to the Coast Guard and a delay. Sick ones presented a sad sight, with severely dehydrated and sun-burned bodies, which are never pretty. Of course, the former passengers of empty rafts and boats could be dead, but they could also be among the happy few scooped up by a cruise liner. One group of outdoor journalists rescued a pair of hard-pressed Cuban refugees, five days out at sea and out of water, then caught a twenty-five-pound dorado while they waited for the Coast Guard to arrive.[32]

The Clinton administration reached a settlement with the Castro government on September 9, 1994, agreeing to accept twenty thousand Cuban immigrants annually, officially and by air, in exchange for Cuban government enforcement of the ban on immigration by sea. Beginning in October, the people intercepted in the Straits of Florida who were taken to Guantánamo Bay began to receive paroles to the United States, and none of them were deported without legal representation. Although it sometimes took several months, most of the Cubans held at the naval base since August 1994 were permitted to enter the country, although anyone who had a criminal record joined the felons from the Mariel exodus in legal limbo in federal prisons.

A Spanish documentary tracing the lives of a group of 1994 immigrants, *Los Balseros*, was released in 2002 with the English title *The Cuban Rafters*. The film drew the largest crowds at the Havana International Film Festival, an extremely well-attended annual city wide event that draws audiences from all over the world. The theater showing the movie was besieged by Cubans interested in the sold out film. Even though they could not get tickets, they came because the screening of the movie was itself something of an event. The documentary's gritty portrayal of the rafters' lives follows them from Havana in 1994, through their voyage, several months of incarceration at Guantánamo Bay Naval Base, and the years after their release in 1995, when they were permitted to enter the United States and settled in places like Miami, Connecticut, and the Bronx. The seven immigrants profiled in *Los Balseros* endured a variety of hardships in both countries, before and after their dangerous ocean passage by raft. At the Havana Film Festival, directors Carles Bosch and Josep Domenech said their film was "a true story about a people torn between two worlds."[33]

The 1994 Cuban immigrant exodus had not ended for everyone, however. At least 900 of those who had seized the opportunity to leave that summer set out from the south coast of the island and could make it only as far as the Cayman Islands, a colony of Great Britain. They remained there, living in a tent city, unable to return to Cuba or continue to the United States. The following February, at least 160 of them hired boats to deliver them through the Yucatán Channel to the west coast of the Florida peninsula, which rarely sees Cuban immigrants along its beaches. Sixty of them arrived in two vessels, twenty-four and thirty-two feet long, which dropped them close to Venice, Florida, as the sun came up behind Manasota Key. Early morning beachcombers on Casperson Beach, armed with wire baskets on poles to find the prehistoric shark teeth famous in the area, found swimmers splashing ashore from the Gulf of Mexico, chattering cold and stung by jellyfish. One of the first to reach dry land asked a walker, "Is this America?" Being assured it was, he thanked God. Another approached the shark-tooth gatherer gesturing for the nearest telephone. One of them knocked on the door of a house to ask for help. In all, about two dozen intrepid Cuban souls assembled along the beach. By the afternoon, they were on their way by bus to a local community center, then on to Krome Detention Center to wait for an immigration hearing. The boat that brought them had disappeared, but later a fishing boat registered in Grand Cayman was detained in Tampa, and its crew of five Hondurans, Jamaicans, and Cayman Islanders were arrested for smuggling immigrants.[34]

In the meantime, the other people in the group tried to row to shore in two fiberglass launches, but the Coast Guard cutter *Point Countess* intercepted them and took them into custody a mile from shore. They said the sailboat they were aboard had sunk. They spent a day aboard the 82-foot Coast Guard cutter before being transferred to another cutter, the *Monhegan*, which took them to the 378-foot Coast Guard ship *Gallatin*. There they met more than one hundred other Cubans who had tried to make the trip from Grand Cayman Island in three boats, but had been foiled by Coast Guard patrols. The largest of the vessels was a 47-foot motorboat named *Osprey* that was captured by the cutter *Decisive*; the names of the vessels involved in this game of cat and mouse recall the pirate and privateer past of the waters separating Florida and Cuba. The *Gallatin* remained in an undisclosed location on the high seas while United States State Department representatives negotiated the fate of the Cubans with British colonial officials responsible for the Cayman Islands. They would eventually be sent to Guantánamo Bay to join thousands of their countrymen still being held at the naval base since August 1994.[35]

While the diplomats discussed the future of 123 Cubans living under tarps on the decks of the *Gallatin*, an editorial back in Venice, Florida, captured the antagonistic shift that public opinion toward Cuban refugees had taken in recent months. The essay recalled with sympathy the five "working-class fishermen" that had that been "stranded in Gulf waters back in July" 1994 and brought into the local Coast Guard station. They had been "willing to risk their lives for a better world." But the recent arrivals had "nice clothes and clean-cut appearance," which "fueled fires of indignation for some residents who want to see U.S. borders closed."

Relations between Cuba and the United States did not improve in such a climate. The Cuban Adjustment Act, passed in 1995, provided that any Cuban with a visa or a parole who stayed in the United States for a year and a day would be eligible for permanent residency and a "green card." Also as a result of the 1995 legislation, those Cubans who made it to American soil would receive paroles, permitting them to stay in the country and apply for the green card a year and a day later. Cubans who were intercepted at sea, even if they got close to shore before being apprehended by the Coast Guard, would still be sent back to Cuba. This came to be called the "feet wet/feet dry" policy.

Other pieces of legislation affecting Cuban-American relations were the Torricelli Act and the Helms-Burton Act, which tightened the provisions of the U.S. economic embargo. The Cuban government denounces this anti-trade policy as "The Blockade" in the official graffiti painted by the Communist youth organization. It has contributed to the hardships endured every day by average Cubans, such as the scarcity of soap, gasoline, paper, and many other quotidian "necessities" of the average American. The stricter rules passed by Congress not only maintained the prohibition on trade from the United States, but also pressured other countries that do business with Cuba to adhere to the American embargo, imposing penalties on those who refused.

To make matters worse, on February 24, 1996, two Cuban MiG fighter jets, flown by two brothers in the Cuban Air Force, Lorenzo Alberto and Francisco Pérez-Pérez, shot down two small private airplanes, flown by four of the Hermanos al Rescate, "Brothers to the Rescue." The incident was foreshadowed by a *Time* magazine article on the pilots' organization published two years before, which had reported that "Cuban MiG jets sometimes buzz them." With such incidents in mind, one pilot said, "You have to be a bit adventurous and nutty to do it, but there's nothing like saving a life." Founded in 1991, the Brothers' sorties had already rescued 1,286 people at the time the article appeared in March 1994, before the crescendo of immigration that took place in August of that year. Flying with three or four planes at a time, the two dozen pilots kept a close eye on the waters separating their old home from their new one, decorating their airplanes like fighters, with decals to represent rafts retrieved, instead of bombers shot down. The oldest refugee ever found by these humanitarian flyers was seventy-seven years old, the youngest only five days! The four pilots died while conducting one of their search-and-rescue missions for Cuban rafters in the Florida Straits. The Cuban exile community charged that they were innocent victims who only wanted to prevent the deaths of imperiled refugees. The Cuban government charged that the Hermanos had also been dropping anti-Castro leaflets over Havana, violating Cuban air space, and claimed they had been amply warned in advance to stay away from the island—including being buzzed by MiGs, as reported nationally two years earlier. In late 1997, the families of the murdered pilots won a federal judgment against the Republic of Cuba, and four years later the U.S. government awarded them fifty-eight million dollars from frozen Cuban assets. On August 22, 2003, a United States court indicted the two Cuban pilots and the former Cuban Air Force chief, General Rubén Martínez Puente, for the killings. As of this writing, the tragic event is still being litigated in court, as anti-Castro organizations seek the extradition of the pilots who pulled the trigger, and the Cuban regime maintains that its pilots were defending the Republic of Cuba. In the meantime, Brothers to the Rescue and another group of pilots called Rafters' Rescue Legion continue to patrol the waters around Cuba. The Rescue Legion does its flying out of Key West and Puerto Rico. With two Piper Aztecs devoted to the search, these volunteers, some of them veterans of the Bay of Pigs invasion, saved more than 600 refugees as of 1994.[36]

The occasional success story buoyed the optimism of would-be rafters in Cuba, and also inspired positive feelings about Cuban immigrants among the general population of the United States. The adventurous tale of baseball brothers Livan and Orlando "El Duque" Hernández, stalwarts of the Cuban national team, did a great deal to increase the visibility of Cuban rafters. Little brother Livan was the first to leave Cuba, choosing a terrestrial route when he defected in Mexico in 1995. As a starting pitcher for the Florida Marlins, based in Miami, Livan received the Most Valuable Player award for the 1997 World Series, after winning two of the team's four victories in taking the championship. Livan's big brother Orlando, "The Duke," was arguably the greatest pitcher in Cuban history, who made the national squad one of the best in the world over years of tournament competition. After Livan defected, Orlando was banned from Cuban baseball on all levels. But on the day after Christmas 1997, he and seven others left Cuba by sea, making it to Anguilla Cay off the coast, where they spent three nervous days before being picked up by the U.S. Coast Guard. Orlando became a citizen of Costa Rica, then joined the Major League ranks to earn his own World Series ring with the 1998 New York Yankees, who won the championship held for a year by Miami's own Florida Marlins.

The Cuban world in Miami is a very insular one. Its center is in Little Havana, but it extends into Hialeah and west of the city along US 41, known as "Alligator Alley." Miami has twenty-three sites on Florida's Cuban Heritage Trail, second only to Key West. The heart of "Little Havana, USA" is Eighth Street, or Calle Ocho, scene of frequent street festivals marking Cuban holidays and musical concerts of salsa and merengue. In addition to the "Plaza of Cuban Patriots," parks nearby bear the names of the leaders of the Cuban Revolution of 1895: José Martí and Máximo Gômez. There are museums devoted to Cuban Arts and Culture, cigar manufacture, Cuban Baseball Players, and the Bay of Pigs invasion. Among Havana Pequeña's many religious institutions is a shrine to Cuba's patron saint and protector of people imperiled at sea, Caridad del Cobre, Our Lady of Charity. Sites such as the Freedom Tower and the Liberty Column in Bayfront Park and Little Havana refer to the hoped-for end to the Castro era, which locals make reference to in the phrase "Next year in Havana!"

Miami has the highest percentage of foreign-born residents among all American cities, the 2000 national census revealed. Along with Miami's polyglot variety of ethnicities has come some friction among them, and sometimes violence. The worst clashes have taken place in the Overtown and Liberty City areas bordering on Little Havana, where African-American residents have sometimes resented the success of their Cuban neighbors and the actions of white police officers. Overtown was once known as "Colored Town," founded in 1890 by the Flagler railroad company as segregated housing for its black workers. The community was bisected by a federal interstate highway project in the 1960s, which displaced half of the residents in Overtown, forcing many of them to relocate to Liberty City in the face of racial hostility from its white homeowners. In December 1979, an African-American motorcyclist named Arthur McDuffie was beaten to death by white policemen in the Overtown neighborhood. When an all-white jury acquitted the officers in Tampa on May 17, 1980, the verdict spurred three days of riots in Overtown, which boiled over into Liberty City. More rioting over the McDuffie case followed in 1984, again in Overtown and Liberty City.[37] These sections of Miami are next to the large Haitian community called "Little Haiti," which used to be an African-American enclave known as "Lemon City," and are also quite close to Little Havana. The number of Haitians in the city, like the Cuban population, grew as a result of seaborne immigration in the 1970s. Also in common with their Cuban neighbors, many of the Haitian newcomers fled political repression and economic failure in their homeland, where the father-son dictatorship of "Papa Doc" and "Baby Doc" Duvalier remained in power from 1960 to 1996. One big difference between the Cuban and Haitian immigrants, up until 1994, was that Cubans were considered political refugees and given preferential treatment in their resettlement process, while Haitians were considered economic refugees, so they were much more liable to being deported.

The Cuban-American community in Little Havana found itself in the spotlight for weeks after Elián González, not quite six years old, was found at sea on Thanksgiving Day, November 25, 1999. The circumstances of the little boy's life and his tragic voyage testify to the pain inflicted on families by the tense geopolitics of migration, which divides siblings, parents, and married couples over the question of whether to stay in Cuba or try to make it to the United States. The González family first began to split up thirty years before Elián became a household word in both countries. His great-aunt Caridad, second oldest of nine children, became the first in the clan to leave their hometown of Cárdenas, a coastal city near the resort of Varadero, east of Havana and directly south of the Florida Keys, when she took a plane to Miami during the Camarioca exodus of 1965. Caridad's brother Delfín had been in prison since 1962, serving a ten-year sentence for subversion against the Castro government, a judgment that had driven a wedge deep into the family. Some of the siblings resolved to get out of Cuba, while others took jobs working for the state, including Elián's grandparents, a police inspector and a court clerk. Released from prison, great-uncle Delfín obtained an American visa and followed his sister Caridad to Miami in 1979. Within five years, three more of their siblings

Elian Gonzalez became a focus for the Cuban community in Miami in 2000 when the Clinton administration favored the boy's repatriation with his father in Cuba. (© *Miami Herald*)

and their father Luís González, Elián's great-grandfather, joined the American branch of the family. Two of the brothers came through Costa Rica after long waits in legal limbo, while their families stayed back in Cárdenas for months until they could establish residency.

Elián's parents married in 1984, then both found jobs working on nearby Varadero Beach. His father Juan Miguel took admissions at the seaside mansion of the founder of the Havana Club rum distillery, which had been made into a park after the Cuban Revolution, and his mother Elisa put in long hours as a maid at a tourist hotel. Together they made a very good living by the standards of contemporary Cuba, even being able to afford a 1956 Nash Rambler car, but their relationship became strained after twelve years of marriage and increasingly difficult financial times. Elisa and Juan split up in February 1997, when Elián, whose name they created from the first three letters of her name and the last two of his, was just three years old. His parents shared custody of the child, but they each soon found another partner with whom to share their lives; his father remarried and had another son with his new wife, while his mother took Elián to live with her new boyfriend, Rafa. On November 22, 1999, Elián was absent from school without an explanation—Elisa and Rafa had taken the boy and "left on some kind of boat," recalled his great-uncle Lázaro, who would spend weeks in the media spotlight from his front yard in Little Havana, as the controversy over Elián González subsequently unfolded.[38]

Their voyage was very nearly another of the anonymous disasters that make it so difficult to estimate the death toll of Cuban emigrants adrift in the Straits of Florida. Their makeshift raft foundered in the waves and his mother, her boyfriend, and all but one other passenger drowned. Elián spent two days at sea in an inner tube, possibly kept alive by porpoises or dolphins that may have boosted the five-year-old's head above the surface when he started to slip beneath the salt water, a plausible scenario based on the child's own dream-like memories of his ordeal. A mural depicting these lifesaving sea mammals and the merciful intercession of Caridad del Cobre today graces a wall in Havana Pequeña. Fishermen spotted the boy and retrieved him from the waves, and soon he was on his way to a hospital in Fort Lauderdale, where the first press coverage of his miraculous survival originated. While his Florida relatives hoped that a permanent reunion of the whole family in Florida would result from the traumatic event, his father, grandfather, and great-grandmother, along with other family members still in Cuba, wanted him to return home to Cárdenas. The ensuing dispute involved not just the two sides of the family, divided by the open water between Florida and Cuba, but also their respective governments, which were even further distanced from one another by the harsh rhetoric and ideological deadlock of the Cold War. Within the United States, there was little common ground between those who thought the boy should remain in the land of prosperity and democracy with his relatives, a goal his mother had died for, and those who believed his proper place was with his father, from whom the adorable child essentially had been stolen.

In the Cuban neighborhoods of Miami, the overwhelming consensus was in favor of keeping Elián in the United States, rather than sending him back to the privations and suppression of Castro's Cuba, and the people of Little Havana rallied around the little house of Lázaro González to prevent his young nephew from being removed. Lázaro's daughter Marisleysis doted on her photogenic cousin and took a starring role herself in the extensively televised effort to make their modest abode and the area around Calle Ocho into Elián's new home. News crews filmed the cousins playing on a swing set in the tiny yard of the residence and sorting through an avalanche of new toys sent by well-wishers. A television series began on the Spanish-language channel Univision in February 2000 that eerily mirrored Elián's saga, called *El Niño que Vino del Mar* or "The Boy Who Came From the Sea," about a mystery child found alone in a small boat.

But the Clinton administration sided with Elián's father, who plaintively asked for his son's repatriation. Unable to cleave the tot in two, as in the Biblical story of Solomon and the disputed infant, authorities seemed to allow no room for compromise. Finally, in spite of the phalanx of local support, federal government agents seized Elián from Lázaro González's besieged bungalow in a dramatic predawn raid. The climax of the SWAT-team-like operation was captured in a widely published photograph of an immigration officer, complete with helmet, body armor, and goggles, looking like a scary bogeyman-soldier, pointing his rifle at a horrified Elián, who had been hiding in a closet. The frightened child's sudden, forced departure left the Cuban-American community in Miami in a state of clamorous outrage, led by his distraught cousin Marisleysis. Elián, whisked away to an estate in Maryland, was soon reunited there with his father, who had been flown into the country in the company of Cuban government officials. After a lengthy diplomatic wrangle and public relations circus, Elián eventually returned to Cuba with his father.

At the height of the acrimony in May 2000, the Cuban government bussed tens of thousands of Communist youth organization protesters to Mariel, where Fidel's brother, Defense Minister Raúl Castro, harangued the Torricelli and Helms-Burton legislation and demanded Elián's return.[39]

The case of Elián González pointed to a loophole in the immigration policy established by the Clinton administration. This "humanitarian exception" to the rules barring the entry of Cubans by sea allowed anyone in critical need of medical care to be transported to a hospital on the mainland, rather than being returned to Cuba. Once on shore, the patients came under the "feet dry" provision of the Cuban Adjustment Act, making them eligible for a year of parole followed by United States resident status. This humanitarian wrinkle in the Cuban Adjustment Act received publicity from the rescue of Elián González and by the admission into the United States of another group of "feet dry" Cubans at the same time. Just as the Elián González drama unfolded in Florida, fourteen more of the boy's compatriots were rescued from their little boat after drifting without water for more than a week. They were dangerously dehydrated, so the Coast Guard took them to the hospital in Miami, where they quickly recovered. All of them were released to the care of happy relatives living in the city.[40]

Knowing the situation they faced, some determined emigrants who were on the verge of being apprehended and returned to Cuba chose to induce illness in themselves to compel the Coast Guard to take them to receive medical assistance. Some of them drank gasoline or cut themselves with machetes. In March 2003, nine Cubans intercepted near Islamadora in the Florida Keys quickly took some sort of pills as the Coast Guard closed in, so by they time they were taken into custody they were sick. After they were transported to Marathon Key for observation, the effects of the pills wore off in a few hours, and the Cubans walked out of the hospital with a new lease on life in the United States.[41]

Another state-owned Cuban ferryboat was hijacked from its route across Havana Harbor on April 2, 2003. This incident began much like the ferryboat hijacking of August 1994, which precipitated the exodus by sea in which the *Analuisa* took a part. It ended where the voyage of the *Analuisa* began, at the dock in Mariel. About ten hijackers seized the ferry during its Wednesday commute between the Havana waterfront and the town of Regla, with about thirty passengers on board. The hijackers ordered the ferryboat captain to take them to Florida, but the ferry ran low of fuel thirty miles out to sea, still sixty miles from Key West, and began to drift. Cuban authorities and the FBI located the ferry and negotiated with the hijackers, who demanded to have the boat refueled so they could complete their passage to the United States. Before long, the rough seas of the Straits of Florida threatened to capsize the ungainly vessel, which had

been designed only for motoring back and forth across flat water with a cargo of people and their bicycles. Fearing for their lives, the hijackers allowed a Cuban Coast Guard cutter to take them in tow to the shelter of Mariel Bay, where it moored thirty feet from the dock for further negotiations. Fidel Castro came to Mariel to be on hand for the solution to the crisis, which was a sudden raid by Cuban government commandos on Thursday afternoon. Everyone on board jumped overboard as the soldiers stormed the ferry and took control without firing their weapons.[42]

In this seagoing pickup truck, Luis Grass made his first attempt to escape Cuba in July 2003. When the Coast Guard sank his truck and returned his family to Cuba, he tried again in a converted Buick sedan in February 2004. Turned away again, the resourceful "autonaut" and his family were finally released to Costa Rica in December 2004. (Greg Ewald photo, 030717-C 000A 001 (FTt), courtesy U.S. Coast Guard)

Certainly one of the most inventive and most determined would-be emigrants is Luís Grass Rodríguez, who has converted two different vintage automobiles into seagoing vessels to cross the Straits of Florida. In July 2003, he and eleven companions, including his wife and little boy, set out in a 1951 Chevrolet pickup truck he had turned into a motorboat. He had attached fifty-five-gallon drums beneath the chassis for increased buoyancy, sealed the body of the vehicle to make it watertight, and harnessed the original engine to a propeller. The ingenious contrivance made it to within forty miles of Florida before the U.S. Coast Guard spotted it, removed its passengers, and sank the truck-boat as a navigational hazard. Luís Grass and his companions were deported back to Havana, where he started working on a second daring experiment in nautical architecture, this time beginning with a 1959 Buick sedan. Again employing the original V-8 engine to run a propeller, the new vessel could go through the water at eight miles an hour. In addition to the old car's ostentatious fins on its "stern," the floating Buick sported a prow that Luís added to its "bow" and painted lime green to match the color of the vehicle. After it set out in February 2004, news of the Buick's brave voyage hit TV stations in Miami before the Coast Guard knew anything about it, apparently tipped off by relatives or acquaintances of Luís Grass and his ten passengers, again including his spouse and four-year-old. Pictures of the durable craft were broadcast on the evening news, showing it plowing through the waves with Luís and a friend rooting on the roof of the car, and others seated inside looking out the open windows as if they were on a drive in the countryside. Again, as the classic auto neared Key West, the Coast

Guard intercepted it to remove and deport its passengers back to Cuba, then blew up the car. Their amazing attempt to drive across the strait elicited great sympathy in Miami, where the Spanish-language press dubbed them "autonauts." Widespread public opinion held that they should be treated as an exception to the wet feet/dry feet rule of immigration, and allowed into the country. Instead, the eleven were sent back to Cuba.

The Grass family joined the growing ranks of Cubans who have tried and failed more than once to make it to the United States. Some of these have been apprehended and returned three times, such is their determination to leave Cuba. What a Florida relative of Luís Grass said about him applies to the other frustrated emigrants, as well: "My cousin isn't crazy. He wants to be free. That's how crazy he is."[43]

Cuban fishing boats—rowing and sailing antecedents of the boat in Ernest Hemingway's *Old Man and the Sea* and of the *Analuisa*—lie along the rocky shore near the mouth of Havana Harbor in 1924. (© Mystic Seaport, Rosenfeld Collection 1984.187.111802F)

Chapter 6: The Voyages of *Analuisa*:
Fishing Boat, Immigration Vessel, Museum Exhibit

Analuisa's home port is Mariel, fifty miles west of Havana. Mariel Bay is the closest harbor to the Cuban metropolis and is the busiest port on the north coast, aside from the capital. It is also close to Florida. The first solo flight from the United States to Cuba was completed from Key West to Mariel in 1913 by daredevil Cuban aviation pioneer Agustín Parla. The scenic excursion by rail or car along the coast from Havana to picturesque Mariel became a standard feature of the Cuban tourist itinerary. The sights included the Cuban Naval Academy, located on a hill overlooking cloverleaf-shaped Mariel Bay and a fishing village located on a point in the middle of the bay, called "La Puntilla." Some visitors to Mariel drove down to La Puntilla in their big Fords to admire the view. The children of the fishing families ran out to greet them and have their picture taken near the pretty waterfront they called home. Nearby Havana provided the market for fish caught by the men of Mariel.[1]

Cubans have been described as "people with their backs to the sea," partly because fish were never part of the traditional diet of the island. The Taino Arawak people had seafood barbecues on the beach; Spanish immigrants retained a taste for the *bacalao* (salted cod) of their homeland; and Cuban slaves were often forced to subsist on rancid salted cod imported from New England; but pork, beef, and the sturdy creole chicken were preferred to fish by most people. As a Cuban TV chef commented on the subject, "most Cubans think fish is only to be eaten as a last resort!" In the 1950s, Cubans consumed only about ten pounds of fish per person annually, and most of that was considered to be high-quality seafood, with prices to match, species such as lobster, crab, snapper, and grouper. But the Cuban Revolution of 1959 changed all of that, as Castro's

Children gather in the street at Mariel for photographer Fred Hill in the 1930s. (Fred Hill Collection #1503, The Mariners' Museum, Newport News, Virginia)

government began to ration increasingly scarce food supplies in 1962, and began to look for alternate sources of nutrition for the Cuban people. One area for growth was the fishing industry, which received official encouragement in the 1960s and 1970s. The annual Cuban catch increased eight-fold in the first three decades after the revolution, with many irrigated freshwater fish farms constructed during the same period. By the end of the 1970s, Cubans were eating roughly thirty-three pounds of fish per capita each year, three times as much as in the 1950s, much of it raised inland and retailed as frozen fish sticks. Inland food stores equipped with freezers introduced fish in various frozen varieties to the diet of people who had never previously had access to seafood of any kind. Fish was so abundant by the end of the 1970s that it became legally available outside the rationing system, one of the first commodities to be distributed freely. But the species that were most prevalent in the 1950s became rare on Cuban tables, because most of that prized catch went overseas to earn foreign exchange, the same way Cuban tobacco and rum are exported and very infrequently enjoyed by the Cubans themselves.[2]

Mariel did not prosper as a result of the greater prominence of fish in Cuban cuisine. Although a city of 41,000 inhabitants at the time *Analuisa* embarked for the United States in 1994, Mariel was in many ways still an insular, self-sufficient fishing village, at least in the La Puntilla neighborhood. The people there experienced a crisis in their local fishery that put most of the little boats out of work, forcing fishermen into unemployment or jobs on land, and motivating some of them to board their fishing boats and leave their homes for the United States. The fishing industry fell on hard times, but Mariel still had a naval installation, a power plant, a scrap-metal works, an oil storage facility, and the largest cement factory in Cuba, managed by a Mexican corporation, where many of the former fishermen went to find work. Even so, by 1995 the city seemed deserted and deteriorated, with many vacant houses and streets of crumbling pavement, empty except for occasional vintage sedans rumbling by or reposing curbside like beached whales, huge and finned.

The Academy of Nautical Sports near the fishing docks continued to train Olympic-level athletes in rowing, sailing, canoeing, and windsurfing, helping to preserve the town's connection to the water. But even the water sports

The Old Man and the Sea personified, an ancient Cuban fisherman and his crew have landed an enormous marlin in their small sailing skiff, ca. 1934. (EH 1846N, JFK Library, A/V Archives, Boston, Massachusetts)

school became associated with wild attempts to cross the ocean to the United States, as is the entire town of Mariel. Twenty years after the Mariel boatlift of 1980, a resident asked a visiting reporter, "Do you know that sometimes one of those windsurfers just keeps going? They say that from here to Key West it is 18 hours if you go that way. People have done it. It is true!" A bronze monument beside the water's edge commemorates the first solo flight high above the waves from Key West, but there is no memorial to the voyages across those same perilous waters attempted by so many of the town's former citizens.[3]

Now, after many years of chain migration to Florida, Mariel has become a transnational community divided by the last chasm of the Cold War. It has often been the case that entire communities migrated across the water over the course of years, and this is now true of Mariel, Cuba. As in fishing communities around the world, the same families worked the sea for generations in Mariel, living in La Puntilla's thatched houses, operating a fleet of boats they built themselves. The Cuadras family was among these fishing folk, who handed down the skills of boat construction and coastal fishing from father to son. Luciano Cuadras, son of a fisherman, and Analuisa Fernández, daughter of another fishing family, married and had two children. Their daughter Trinidad had five children: Amarilys, Pedro, Luís, Antonio, and Carlos. Their son Luciano Cuadras Fernández never married. He was born in 1930 in Banamaguá, and grew up in Mariel, where he started building small boats as a boy. His first boat was a little one his grandfather helped him to build when he was a teenager. All of the Cuadras family boats were painted orange and white and were named for women in the family, including *Julita Rubirosa*, a fishing launch bigger than *Analuisa*, built by his father and grandfather in the 1950s. Luciano watched and learned from his relatives and from others in Mariel, building at least a dozen boats over the years, including *Daiyamí* and *Oria*. Most of the boats were built for fishing, and he usually worked on them alone, which is the way he preferred it, although he permitted two or three younger men to learn from him, as well.

Swordfishing skiffs on the beach at Cojímar, 1934. The next generation of such boats, like the *Analuisa*, would have a small engine to drive the wedge-shaped hull. (EH 8208P, JFK Library, A/V Archives, Boston, Massachusetts)

Cuban fishermen land a large in their sailing skiff, ca. 1934. (EH , JFK Library, A/V Archives, Boston, Massachusetts)

Cuban fishing boats evolved just as Cuban fishing did. Commonly launched off the beach, the early boats in the Havana area resembled ship's boats, heavily built with sharp bows and high gunwales, and with fine lines for either rowing or sailing. In smaller ports like Cojímar or Mariel, a cruder form of boat developed, with flat bottom and flat, slightly flaring sides. It was like a wedge on edge, similar to the "flat-iron skiff" of North America. Some were fine sailers. By the early 1950s, small motors became available for fishermen. *Analuisa* is representative of the new style of fishing boat: still featuring the flat bottom and slightly flaring sides of earlier boats, but built wider and with a broad transom board at the stern. The engine was placed in a box amidship, with the propeller shaft angled down to pierce the bottom just forward of the transom and the large rudder. A narrow foredeck and side decks helped keep out spray or provide footing while fishing in coastal waters. These simple, home-built boats were steered with a tiller and often were fitted with an awning to shelter the crew from sun and shower.

Luciano built *Analuisa* in 1958 and named her for his mother. The design of the boat was his own; he "invented the lines in [his] head," and they were different from other Mariel craft. The sturdy launch was also heavier than most around the bay, and was the first in the family to have power. The one-cylinder, nine-horsepower Briggs and Stratton engine was similar to those that powered lawn mowers in the U.S. But this sturdy little engine ended the years of rowing that previous Cuadras men had endured while fishing, and it simplified the jobs of netting and handlining.

While auxiliary power was transforming the lives of Mariel fishermen, other events were transforming Cuba. On New Year's Day, 1959, the dictator Fulgencio Batista fled the country, giving way to the revolutionary forces that had been fighting in the

Luciano Cuadras Fernandez poses in his Mariel yard near *Ileana*, the boat he finished in 1995.
(Eric Paul Roorda photo)

mountainous eastern region of Cuba since 1956. On that same day, Luciano Cuadras Fernández launched *Analuisa*.

With the decline in fishing in his hometown, Luciano began to work in 1962 as a carpenter at a shipyard on the Almendares River in western Havana, building large ships until his retirement in 1990. Throughout nearly three decades as a commercial shipbuilder, however, Luciano continued to work on small fishing boats in his spare time. He encountered increasing shortages in the materials necessary for construction of new boats and maintenance of existing boats. To surmount his supply problems, Luciano made his own nails out of copper wire with a nail machine and recycled as much as possible of old boats to build new ones. He also kept old boats afloat for as long as possible, with particular attention going to *Analuisa*, which he completely overhauled and replanked in 1982, after more than twenty years in the water. After another decade of service as a family boat for recreational fishing *Analuisa* was rebuilt again, in 1993.

Because of this history of rejuvenation by Luciano Cuadras, *Analuisa* is an excellent example of the geist of watercraft preservation, which demands that every well-maintained vessel, like every human body, will over time be composed of entirely different physical material than it comprised at the start (new wood and metal, new cells), but it will still be the same entity: the same boat, the same person. The second time Luciano rebuilt *Analuisa*, very little of the physical material of the boat he originally launched in 1959 remained in the vessel. It only had the same 1956 Briggs and Stratton engine, and the same iron mooring ring, which had been used in other family boats before, and was as old as Luciano himself! Everything else in the boat was new. Luciano had "taken the lines" of the old *Analuisa* and constructed a precise copy, yet it retained the same name, and everyone in the family refers to "*Analuisa*" as a single boat. For instance, Luciano's grandnieces do not distinguish between the boat they grew up playing in and the rebuilt boat they emigrated in; "It's the same boat," said Miralys in an interview conducted alongside her great-uncle Luciano.

With an identical profile to the 1959 boat, the 1993 version of *Analuisa* is made of pine and Nicaraguan mahogany that Luciano received on the sly from his former work site, where he still went for lunch daily after retiring. He seasoned the wood well in the wind in his backyard, separating the pieces to allow for free airflow, and fitted them together with tight joints that did not need much cotton caulking. Like the wood, his tools came from the Havana shipyard, which allowed him to buy them when he left, and which he repaired whenever they broke, because new tools, like everything else, are in short supply in Cuba. He always used only hand tools to build his boats, even after electric tools became available in the last decade, because he had to get his wood from the black market, so he had to build the boats secretly. Electric tools would give him away, with the possible punishment being confiscation of both his tools and his boat.

The government inspector from the Cuban Boat Registry office did not notice the difference in the reconstructed *Analuisa*. Visiting in June 1992, February 1993, and February 1994, the official certified the vessel using the same registration information as before, which noted the date of construction as 1959. The "Certificate of Navigation of the Republic of Cuba" limited *Analuisa* to operations for recreation within Area III of the coast around Mariel, and rated it to safely carry only three crew members, with zero passengers. The inspector listed the full complement of safety equipment carried by *Analuisa* at the time of her departure: three orange *chalecos salvavidas* (personal flotation devices) and a box of sand in case of fire.

Luciano rebuilt *Analuisa* to fish during his retirement, but he never had the chance to wet a line or set a net in her again. When his nephew and niece and seventeen others boarded the boat in August 1994 to make the voyage to Florida, he did not even consider it to be finished, because benches, and a gunwale board to keep the water out, were still lacking. He had not been aware of his relatives' intentions before their sudden departure, even though several of the boats he built previously had been taken away to the United States by relatives, neighbors, and friends. Nor would *Analuisa* be the last of his boats to go. Even *Majadero*, the only one of all the Cuadras craft that was not named for a woman, but instead was called "fool" because it could not steer straight, brought more people from Mariel to the United States in 1997.[4]

The Cuadras family had not been affected by the Camarioca boatlift in 1965—which was open mainly to those who already had relatives in the United States—because they did not have the first link in the chain migration it encouraged. But like the other families of Mariel, they faced twin traumas thereafter: national economic woes like scarcities and inflation, and the depletion of fish species such as snapper and swordfish. So when the next opportunity to leave the country arose in 1980, right there in the port of Mariel, the first member of the Cuadras clan left for Florida. Luciano's nephew Pedro, the oldest of his sister Trinidad's five children, was among those who found a spot on a departing cabin cruiser during the famous Mariel boatlift.

The next to youngest of Luciano's nephews and Analuisa's grandchildren, José Antonio, called Tony, planned his attempt to make the crossing for two years. He finally set out aboard *Katia*, a new fishing boat owned by a friend he often fished with, in April 1991. The boat slipped out of Mariel Bay at night with seventeen passengers, bound for Key West. Tony's nephew Pedro Jr., called Pedrito, whose father had been a "Mariel" eleven years earlier, accompanied him. Fitted with a new eighty-horsepower engine, the vessel made good time across the Straits of Florida, until her anxious passengers could see the Key West Lighthouse. Then the diesel line broke. *Katia* was adrift on the Gulf Stream for five days. The only other vessels they saw were two cruise liners, on the first and second day, which they were unable to hail. A third cruise liner, the *Royal Prince* of the Royal Caribbean Line, appeared on the fifth day and rescued them. Despite a close call, none of the emigrants perished. After arriving in Miami, Tony Cuadras spent three days going through formalities at the Krome Detention Center run by the Immigration and Naturalization Service, then he and Pedrito happily reunited with the boy's father Pedro, Tony's big brother.

Carlos, the youngest child of the five Cuadras siblings, followed his older brothers Pedro and Tony to Florida in September 1991. He made the crossing in one of his uncle Luciano's boats, *Oria*, together with nine other passengers. Luciano's *Oria*, a traditional Mariel fishing boat about twenty feet long with a small inboard engine, proved more reliable for his nephew Carlos than the newer *Katia*, with its enormous engine, which had failed his nephew Tony. But in both cases, knowledge of the sea and access to sturdy fishing boats had helped the brothers to leave Mariel. But the brothers' departure left no more of the

Cuadras family fishing professionally; Luciano had retired from the shipyard, three of his nephews had sailed away, and the fourth had taken a job at the local power plant. Meanwhile, the depletion of the fisheries and the food shortages in Mariel worsened every year, causing more and more of the fishing families to sacrifice their vessels to emigration attempts.

When another opportunity to leave suddenly materialized in Mariel in August 1994, the two remaining children of the Cuadras family left: Luciano's niece Amarilys, first-born, and his nephew Luís, middle child of the five, thirty-five years old at the time. In contrast to their brother Tony, who plotted for two years before slipping out of Cuba, Amarilys and Luís spent less than a year mulling over the decision to attempt a crossing to Florida.

Amarilys anxiously debated the question with her husband Victor, while he began the preparations for departure in late 1993. Victor helped Luciano work on *Analuisa*, devoting most of his attention to the engine, which had not been operated for three years. As the summer of 1994 wore on, the decision to leave began to solidify in their minds, and their daughter Miralys decided with her new husband Julio to join them. Miralys foresaw her future in Cuba being limited to motherhood, and she decided she wanted to do more with her life. Julio had been a national champion canoeist and an instructor at the Academy of Nautical Sports, but after a knee injury he saw no future in the sport as a career. Victor enlisted his son-in-law Julio's help to get the boat seaworthy, and they spent the last few nights before departure working together on the project. They hurried to get everything ready as quietly as they could, telling almost no one of their intentions, and watching the weather for smooth seas and clear skies.

In the meantime, Luís Cuadras had traveled inland to Las Villas to bring his wife Maribel back from her parents' farm, then returned with her to Mariel on August 14 to find the town thronged with people trying to take advantage of Castro's offer to leave Cuba unopposed. The next morning Luís woke up and said to Maribel, "Let's go to Miami. Today." She was reluctant, unlike her husband, because she had never been to sea and had no relatives living in the United States. But with her consent, Luís also went to work on *Analuisa*. The newly repaired engine toppled off its blocks onto the pavement of Luciano's patio when they tested it, breaking one of the four anchor screws used to secure it in place in the boat. Luciano told his nephew, "That's a problem!" But Luís resolved to leave "with three, four, or two screws!" They returned the old engine to its place in the wooden engine box, ending its long period of storage in the house, and reseated the propeller shaft.

With Castro's green light and a window of sunny conditions, they had to act quickly. They packed food, water, medicine, the compass, and the three life preservers. Many boats had been stolen in Mariel at the time, so Luís also brought the deed for the boat to prove that he owned it in case the authorities stopped them. Finally he repainted the orange trim as well as the black numbers on the side by which the government officially identified the boat. The prefixes for the numbers, Lta and Flo, stood for Lista and Folio, the list and book in the government files where *Analuisa*'s registration could be located.

Julio told his parents, who lived on the east side of Havana, that he would be back in three days; that he and Miralys, who were living with them at the time, would just be visiting her parents in Mariel. Miralys packed a small backpack from her in-laws' residence, containing everything she would take along with her on the boat. Julio's parents did not find out that he had left until his father went to Mariel several days later, because no one was answering the phone. He found the house sealed by the government, which is the practice for houses left empty by emigrants, to prevent break-ins.[5]

By the time *Analuisa* was ready to go on the evening of August 15, the docks at La Puntilla were crowded with out-of-towners asking to accompany them, offering money for a place on board. But nineteen people were going in the twenty-foot boat, most of them members of the Cuadras and Fernández families, and there was no room for more. In addition to the families of Luís and his sister Amarilys, each with a spouse and two children, there were also a cousin and two friends with their families coming along. Miralys's puppy Sisi, which she refused to leave behind, completed the list of passengers. The scene around the docks "was quite tumultuous," recalled Luís, so to protect the boat from would-be hijackers, Victor and Julio took *Analuisa* to the middle of Mariel Bay at about six or seven that night, then returned to pick up the others after midnight. "There were people on the dock, in the water," remembered Julio, who had to use a knife to fend off desperate strangers as *Analuisa* left Mariel for the last time, since they had agreed they could not take anyone else on board the dangerously crowded *Analuisa*. Luís did not even tell his children that they were leaving home. His wife Maribel, who had no chance to tell her own parents the news, told Yadira and Luís Jr. that they were going fishing, but it was late, so the ten-year-old girl was suspicious. When she heard they were really going to the United States, Yadira was glad to "go to another place." She and her little brother took a pill and went to sleep.

Soon after their departure, the last of the boats Luciano Cuadras built in his life, *Daiyamí*, left the port. Towing another small boat behind, *Daiyamí* carried forty passengers from Mariel to Florida.

Luís had spent a great deal of time on *Analuisa* in his life, fishing and going to the beach, and he believed the boat was strong enough to make the passage. But the motor remained a question; it failed on the way out of the bay, and everyone on board was worried because the government said unseaworthy vessels would

In 1995 a few fishing boats still rode at their moorings off La Puntilla, the fishing village at Mariel. (Eric Paul Roorda photo)

be turned back. Another cause of concern was the fact that some of those on board were government workers, and if they were caught trying to leave, word would be out that they were against the government, and they would be "marked" if they had to return, facing loss of livelihood and possible physical violence. After managing to get the motor fired up again, they were afraid to turn it off. The two Cuban Coast Guard patrol boats they later encountered as they left took no action to detain them, and they were on their way.

Analuisa motored out of Mariel Bay and into the rising waves of the Florida Straits, with dark clouds rolling in overhead. The women and children pressed into the bow of the boat beneath the shelter of a tarp, and everyone in the overcrowded craft prepared for the worst as the storm approached. Luckily for them, no deluge ensued to swamp *Analuisa*, nor did the wind rise to capsize her, though the waves made many of them seasick. After a short rain shower, they joked to keep things light during the cramped night, but then the passengers watched the sun come up and found they were still in sight of Cuba, on seas as "flat as a bed," and so grew quiet. A freighter going past failed to respond to their frantic signals. Julio sat on the engine box, "cooking himself" and bailing with a plastic container, because the boat leaked from having been out of the water for so long. As the morning wore on, they seemed to be in the middle of nowhere, and ships passed them by without stopping. As the tension increased, they began to argue. Luís and Victor had the compass and the experience, however, so those two remained in a position of command as the anxiety on board *Analuisa* increased. Everyone got thirsty, but there was no water remaining ecept a little for the children. They steered to account for the east-bound current of the Gulf Stream, as the little engine propelled them toward their destination under sunny skies, until there was water "north, south, east and west."

When they checked the fuel tank and found it almost empty, they conferred about the risk of turning off the engine while refilling the tank. Worried that it might not start up again, they chose to risk fire or explosion rather than aimless drifting. As the engine continued its loud drone and vibration, they braced themselves and carefully poured the gasoline into the tank, so close to the hot engine. All must have exhaled with relief when the cap went back on the fuel tank. But relief was only momentary. Luís had never experienced the feeling of helplessness brought on by the surging Gulf Stream, and he realized that he probably would not have risked his own life and the lives of his wife and children, had he known what it was like. The waves began to run higher, bringing more seasickness to those on board. During the next several hours of terror and tension, they argued about what to do next. Some proposed steering to a buoy and hoping for help. Others were determined to continue on against the current.

At five minutes to six on the evening of August 16, they sighted the cruise ship *Ecstasy* of the Carnival Cruise Line. As Amarilys remembered the moment, first they "saw a smokestack, and then something like a huge building. It was a cruise liner, and it was miraculous to us, but I was a little afraid. I'd never seen such a huge ship, and *Analuisa* was *chiquitica* [so small]." They began waving clothes in a successful effort to signal the luxury liner. *Analuisa* had made sixty miles in fifteen hours, but they had been set to the east by the current, so they were still seventy miles from Key West. Exactly as the *Royal Prince* had done when it rescued Tony Cuadras and his party in April 1991, the 855-foot *Ecstasy* shielded the tiny vessel in her lee to transfer the passengers. Little Yadira and Luís Jr. woke up to see the awesome cruise liner towering over their little boat, and their mother began to cry from fright at having to climb the long ladder up the side of the ship. Making the scary ascent was better than remaining on the Gulf Stream without water, though, so off they went, one by one, to safety. Julio came last, carrying Sisi the dog. With the Cubans safely on board, the ship continued on to Cozumel, Mexico, leaving *Analuisa* bobbing empty in her wake. There was a storm that night, making the unexpected Cuban guests glad to be aboard the *Ecstasy* and settled comfortably into staterooms, rather than in their open boat under the elements, even if they did get seasick in the shower! Amarilys recalled, "We were taken care of on that ship, really. When we left, they gave us some things, like the photo [of the ship] on the wall of our house. And who knows what might have happened if they hadn't picked us up, we could have died!"

But going to Mexico was another potential problem for the *Analuisa* refugees, because they knew others from Mariel who had been deported back to Cuba after reaching Mexico. The ship's captain assuaged the Cubans' fears, telling them that he considered the ship to be American soil, and assuring them that they would not be turned over to Mexican immigration officials. After spending a day at the resort of Cozumel, during which the nineteen of them stayed aboard the ship, they cruised to Florida with the *Ecstasy*, arriving August 18. On the return trip, the *Ecstasy* picked up another group of Cuban refugees,

The Cuadras family poses with *Analuisa* at Mystic Seaport, 2000. (Bill Grant photo)

six people from Pinar del Rio: four men with a woman and her baby. The rescued immigrants disembarked first in Key West with U.S. Coast Guard officers, then continued to Miami to Krome Detention Center, where they expected to stay for a short time before being let out to join the Florida branch of the family. But while they were still being processed in Key West, President Bill Clinton delivered a speech that changed the immigration rules. In response to Florida opposition to uncontrolled Cuban immigration, he revoked Cuban political refugee status. Thereafter, all "boat people" intercepted at sea were taken to camps in Guantánamo Bay Naval Base or the Panama Canal Zone rather than to Miami, and all Cubans who had already managed to land in Florida were ordered to Krome Detention Center rather than to their relatives' homes. The *Analuisa* people would get to know Krome better than they expected or desired.

Meanwhile, back in Mariel, their neighbor Juan José Alfaro sized up the chance that had suddenly been presented to motor to America in a fishing boat. Like the Cuadras family, members of the younger generation of the Alfaro family have taken to the seas one by one to reach the United States. Their mother Caridad watched seven of her eight children sail away: three in the 1970s, two in the Mariel boatlift of 1980, and two in the rush of August 1994. Five of the Alfaro siblings continued to fish commercially, operating a boat of their own out of Key West. Juan himself had stopped trying to make a living from the sea and was driving a bulldozer for pay, fishing only for leisure. He never had intended to leave Cuba or his young son, who lived with his former wife. But with the exodus taking place from Mariel that August, he decided to go to Key West to visit his brothers and sister and to seek treatment for his worsening heart problem, hopeful he could return to Cuba later to see his son.

Juan Alfaro first tried to leave with a group that included his brother in someone else's boat on August 13, but the Cuban Coast Guard intercepted them and forced their return. Two days later, Juan decided to start out with three friends in his own boat, *Carmencita*, using the gas that he had saved for recreational fishing. His brother made different plans this time, and did not come along with Juan. *Carmencita* had recurring engine trouble, beginning only fifteen or twenty miles from Mariel. Then the four men in the boat ran out of food, water, and fuel, until they were distraught and prayerful. When Juan and his companions saw *Analuisa*, they were overcome with emotion at their serendipitous deliverance. They jumped aboard, saw the supplies that had been left behind, then touched the motor and found it to be still warm. They tinkered with the spark plug, and the engine ignited. They motored for a long time, losing track of the hours, still lost on the open ocean, then stopped the motor to conserve gasoline. They started up again sometime after midnight, because Juan began to experience severe chest pains. As Juan tried to sleep, one of his friends said he saw light in the sky, which turned out to be Key West. At about eight in the morning of August 18, a U.S. Coast Guard vessel encountered them some three hundred yards off the coast. A Spanish-speaking Guardsman asked them many questions, and after the exchange of some information, he turned out to be a friend of Juan's sister. She and her brothers were in the fishing business together in Key West, where she occupied a house close to the Cuban Transit Home, an excellent location to welcome new arrivals from Mariel and to catch up on news from home. She had told her Coast Guard friend that her brothers were on their way, so he was expecting them, although the two brothers had ended up taking different boats across the Straits. When the Coast Guard vessel with the family friend aboard intercepted Juan and his friends, it towed them ashore and took them to Miami, leaving *Analuisa* on the beach, having delivered a total of twenty-three desperate passengers to safety.

Not long after Juan and his friends came ashore in Key West, the *Ecstasy* passed by with the first nineteen *Analuisa* passengers at the rails. Victor Milian could scarcely believe his eyes when he saw the distinctive orange and white launch reposing on the sand as the cruise liner prepared to dock. The others in his party did not believe he had seen their cherished boat landed safely in Florida before them, but once they tapped into the information grapevine at Krome Detention Center, the miraculous tale of *Analuisa*'s voyage became known to them. They later reunited and celebrated with their Mariel neighbor Juan

A *Miami Herald* photographer caught Luís Cuadras Fernández, his wife Maribel Hernández Montenegro, and their children Yadira, 9, and Luís, 5, during a brief reunion at the Krome Detention Center. Luís Cuadras Fernández spent six weeks in detention, while his wife and children were released after four weeks. (© *Miami Herald*/Candace Barbot)

Alfaro, who, like them, owed his life to the capable *Analuisa*.

Krome Detention Center in Miami served the function of a Cuban Ellis Island or Angel Island, as the *Analuisa* people soon discovered for themselves. Complications arising from the shift in U.S. immigration policy kept them behind barbed wire for one to three months, depending on their age and their marital and parental status. The policy of releasing Cuban detainees dictated that pregnant women went free first, followed in order by mothers and their children, then fathers, and finally couples without children and unmarried people. Maribel Cuadras and her daughter Yadira, ten years old, languished at Krome for a month, kept separate from her husband Luís and her son Luís Jr., six years old. The older Luís remained for an additional two weeks in detention after his wife and children received their discharge. Miralys Milian and Julio González, married but childless, spent three and a half months in the overcrowded conditions of the grim facility. There were one thousand women and five hundred children on the female side at that time, and the men, who outnumbered them, had to live outside, exposed to the sun, with mosquitoes tormenting them. The Cuban inmates hurt themselves on the barbed wire trying to talk through the fences. For the *Analuisa* immigrants, their time at Krome has been their worst experience in the United States. Since none of them had any criminal past whatsoever, they were surprised and disheartened to be dressed in orange jumpsuits and treated like prisoners under grueling conditions for so long.

A photograph of the unhappy family of Luís Cuadras appeared on the front page of the *Miami Herald* on August 27, with a story relating their plight and that of many other recent arrivals from Cuba. The image shows the exhausted parents and their two children during a brief reunion when ten-year-old Yadira was ill with a high fever. Her father had not been permitted to see the sick child since their arrival, so in the photo her arms are draped around his neck poignantly, while her mother stoically holds her little brother. The photograph, with its compelling *sacra familia* composition, appeared again in the paper the following week, briefly making the Cuadras family the poster children for the abuses of Krome. The photo helped to prompt reforms in the way refugees are treated in Miami.[6] When the family was released, brother Tony came from his new home in Orlando to pick them up, with television stations on hand to cover the story. Luís took one week off to "relax, vacation," then found a job the first day he looked.

Life has gone fairly well for the *Analuisa* immigrants since their arrival in the United States. As might be expected, however, there have been rough spots in the process of adjusting to American society and culture. The increased dangers of car transportation have taken a high toll. One Cuadras family friend who came in *Analuisa* died in a car crash not long after his arrival. Amarilys, Victor, their daughter Miralys, son-in-law Julio, son Leo, and new American-born grandchild Julio Jr., were also involved in an automobile accident when a drunk driver going the wrong way on a highway access ramp hit them, injuring everyone except the baby in his car seat. All of them recovered fully from their injuries except Victor, who continues to walk with a limp and a cane. But the legal settlement after the wreck brought the Milian family sufficient financial means to buy a nice house in Tampa and invest in a dry-cleaning business of their own. There is a large statue of Caridad del Cobre in the kitchen. Miralys, whose strong language ability allowed her to become fluent in English soon after their arrival in Florida, fulfilled her aspiration of working outside the home, taking a job in an office. Her husband Julio, who left his parents behind in Cuba and has difficulty with English, experienced the hardest time adjusting. He has some regrets about his sudden departure, saying "I had to leave my mother and father, my homeland. This country received us, but it doesn't know us. The language is different, but still… the dictatorship was too much, life was hard. It was liberty or death. We were going to find one or the other." Miralys's brother Leonardo Jr. chose to serve his adopted country in the U.S. Marine Corps.

Six years after her voyage on *Analuisa*, teenaged Yadira told an interviewer in halting English, "We're living next to Florida, in Disney World, five minutes to Disney World." While this place of residence might seem idyllic for a young person, she has also had a difficult time getting used to her new home, and she often misses her old one. "As a child in Cuba, you're free, you can go anywhere you want. Here, you can't go to the disco because you're too young. I want to go back there, it's so much fun."[7]

Although Yadira's father Luís quickly found work customizing vans, and picked up a good deal of English at his place of employment, her mother Maribel had little opportunity to learn the language, and she longed to see the family she had left behind on their farm in the Cuban countryside. She has since been able to host her mother in Florida. Her son Luís Jr., who was only six at the time of the crossing, seemed to have the best chance to assimilate quickly, being the youngest of the refugees and therefore likeliest to gain command of English and to fit in with other children his age. But even little Luís had a difficult time, as his family moved from Orlando to Miami and then back to the Orlando area, and he changed schools with each relocation. His autobiography, written as part of a class project in his new school in Miami three years after the voyage of *Analuisa*, testifies to the personal drama bound up in every act of immigration, especially when serious risks accompany the immigrant on the journey.

The Life of a Little Boy Named Luís Cuadras

It was nighttime when we sneaked out of Cuba. We got into a little boat that had been made by my father and uncle. It had a little motor and a sail that helped us when the motor broke down. My mom cried all the time and I remember thinking how lucky we were that there were no sharks in the water!

Just when we got to the middle of the ocean, a big boat rescued us. We were very lucky, because by that time we had run out of gas and food. In the big boat I slept in a bed, and I was very happy because I hadn't been able to sleep on the floor of the little boat. The wood was too hard for my head! When I woke up I took three baths! In Cuba there are no bathrooms, and we had to wash ourselves with a bucket. We all went to a beautiful restaurant and ate fish dinner. I was very happy!

After arriving to the United States, I went to a place that looked like a jail. It was called the "Krome Detention Center." Families were separated there, and I had to go with my dad, while my mom and my sister went to the other side of the building. In the morning I would always ask the policemen if I could play with the toys there. You never knew what they would say, because sometimes they would be in a bad mood. I didn't go to school there, and all I did was take naps and play.

When I was free and left the detention center, I went to live with Tony and Olga. There I started school and learned English. I felt shy and afraid. I was only six.

Everyone who came aboard *Analuisa* had to face difficult transitions, from little Luis, the youngest passenger, to Juan Alfaro, the oldest. Juan Alfaro joined his sister and brothers in Key West and sought treatment for his heart condition. But his coronary ailment was serious enough to prevent his return to the strenuous career of commercial fishing with his siblings, as he had hoped and planned. A buoyant and humorous man by nature, a trace of sorrow nevertheless enters his eyes years later, when remembering Cuba and the son he left there to come to America.

The derelict *Analuisa* lay in the impoundment yard at the Key West Coast Guard station, awaiting destruction, when Mystic Seaport requested an example of a refugee boat. She was selected by the Coast Guard for her "third world" look.

Though the Cuadras siblings all left their country to begin different lives, *Analuisa* continued to touch their existence. The little boat which had been around for as long as they could remember, kept coming back even after being abandoned in the Straits of Florida. First, they saw her in Key West when the *Ecstasy* arrived there, and they wondered how she had gotten there. Later at Krome Detention Center they heard how their neighbor Juan Alfaro, together with his three companions in the stalled *Carmencita*, had been saved by *Analuisa*'s appearance.

The members of the Cuadras and Alfaro families living in Florida see each other now and again, but in August 1994 they assumed they'd seen the last of the fishing boat they both used to make part of the trip from Cuba to the United States, since it is Coast Guard procedure to destroy the immigrant craft that come into their possession.

But instead of being destroyed, *Analuisa* survived by chance to come to Mystic Seaport. Recognizing that the lack of a vessel to represent the history of immigration at sea was a gap in the Mystic Seaport fleet, several members of the Museum staff saw the August 1994 diaspora of Cubans as an opportunity to obtain and preserve one of the hundreds of boats involved in that particular boatlift. As a result, the vice president for watercraft at Mystic Seaport, Dana

Hewson, telephoned the Coast Guard station in Key West to ask if they could save one of the Cuban boats in their impoundment yard from destruction.

U.S.Coast Guard Chief Warrant Officer Dave Gilkerson at Key West agreed to cooperate with the unusual request from Mystic Seaport. He described the selection of durable vessels, as opposed to the numerous improvised rafts, currently sitting in the fenced-off area behind the station. Vice President Dana Hewson's notes of the conversation show that *Analuisa* already stood out in the crowd: "Best: 20' wooden hull inb[oar]d open fishing boat. 3rd World-looking." The other contenders included a fiberglass fishing boat that was "very grungy looking" and a twenty-six-foot cabin cruiser. The Coast Guard kept no records of the boats, nothing on the people that came in them or the dates of their arrival, Gilkerson said. Moreover, his superiors were "on [his] case big time to get rid of them," since all the vessels were "slated for disposal." Speed was of the essence, so rapid removal of the artifact became an important provision of Coast Guard cooperation with Mystic Seaport. Chief Petty Officer Gilkerson called Mystic back on October 17 to ask, "when are you getting the Boat in Key West? Need to get rid of it." Again the next day came a telephone message from the anxious CPO, which hints at other elements involved in the urgency than simply clearing out the impoundment lot, as dictated by USCG standard operating procedures: "Wants it gone by Friday—if possible. Political celebrity—LOCAL problems." Did the lingering presence of *Analuisa,* two months after the end of the 1994 "boatlift," bring back unpleasant memories for the citizens of the resort community?

A truck with a boat trailer from Mystic Seaport drove down the coast to Key West to bring *Analuisa* back to the Museum, arriving on October 20. The Coast Guard signed over the boat as a gift to the Museum: "21' open wooden boat, used by Cuban Refugees" is the full description on the receipt. Despite the lack of official records, CPO Gilkerson indicated in a phone call that *Analuisa* was first at the Hogar de Transito para Refugios Cubanos (Cuban Transit Home) before it came to the Coast Guard station.

On the day *Analuisa* arrived at Mystic Seaport, November 10, Hewson composed a memo to other members of the museum staff: "THE BOAT HAS ARRIVED TODAY... The fact that it exists is because people arrived in the Keys on board this boat. Most if not all boats were destroyed after people were taken off if intercepted at sea." Hewson wrote back to Gilkerson, expressing concisely the reason for acquiring *Analuisa* in the first place: "We feel that the boat is a symbol of the desire to come to our shores to build a better life, which has been a constant since our land was first settled."

Accessioning a piece of such recent history turned out to be "a Pandora's box of curatorial challenges," according to Marifrances Trivelli, who went to catalog the contents of *Analuisa* after the vessel's arrival from Florida. Her memo on that occasion offers a picture of the boat's sorry state, in the wake of her adventures: "1. Gasoline and oil are leaking all over the boat… 2. There are several shirts and overalls which are interesting in that the laundry labels are printed in Russian, but they are covered with large bugs, the likes of which I have not seen in New England… 3. Goods news, I did accession the canopy, drinking cups, and rusty tools."[8]

After nearly 50 years of embargo, American-built Ford Zephyrs from prerevolutionary days still serve Havana passengers, as they did the author in 1995. (AE Doyle photo)

The problem for Mystic Seaport was the vacuum of information about *Analuisa*. The name of the boat, its home port of Mariel, and the registration numbers were the only bits of solid data available to begin the search for the vessel's past. The Coast Guard had no records or would not release the records they had, and if anyone at the Cuban Transit Home knew the story of how Juan Alfaro had joined his sister next door after trading *Carmencita* for *Analuisa*, they were not saying. Advertisements in Miami Spanish-language newspapers asking for information on *Analuisa* brought no responses. The best option, then, would be to go to Mariel itself to ask if anyone knew anything about an orange and white fishing boat named *Analuisa*.

That turned out to be a simple task when I undertook it with my wife A.E. Doyle and daughter Alida in December 1995. We hired a 1959 Ford Zephyr and with a tank full of black market gasoline headed down the coast to look into the background of *Analuisa*. In addition to our driver, Guido, we were accompanied by our friends Norge and Rebeca, who helped us to translate. As soon as we arrived in Mariel, we asked directions to the fishing boats and were directed to the La Puntilla area of the city. Having found a flotilla of launches resembling *Analuisa*, we asked a little boy if he knew a boat by that name. He smiled and pointed, so we went as he indicated, until encountering two young men, who answered our question with greater detail. *Analuisa* was a boat built by a man named Luciano, who lived in a nearby house, in the direction the little boy had pointed. Within a few minutes we had found Luciano Cuadras. He was

Luciano Cuadras Fernandes was reunited with his boat, *Analuisa*, during a special visit to Mystic Seaport in 2001.

helping a young friend to build a boat quietly in his backyard, but he took time to tell us the story of his *Analuisa*, and to give us the addresses of his nephew and niece in Florida. His mother Analuisa had died and the last of his sister's children were gone, so he lived alone, but he had no desire to leave his home to follow his niece and nephews. He knew about how Juan Alfaro and his friends had found his boat abandoned in the middle of the Straits, and told us where to find Juan's mother, Caridad. We went to meet her, too, and she told us how to get in touch with her son Juan. She missed him and her other children touchingly, and rather tragically. The immigration experience is bittersweet for everyone affected by it.

A year after the last voyage of *Analuisa*, Luís Cuadras received a letter telling him his uncle's boat with his grandmother's name was now at Mystic Seaport, where the vessel would be preserved, exhibited, and appreciated. The death of Analuisa Fernández that year had left fond memories of a woman who was like a mother to everyone in the La Puntilla neighborhood of Mariel. Now the boat that bore her name, which had survived in such an unlikely sequence of events, would continue to exist as a lasting memorial to Analuisa. The reaction of her grandson Luís to the unexpected news was fitting, whether it is taken to mean the boat herself, the spirit of her namesake, or the courage of immigrants through the centuries: "She's alive! Analuisa is alive!"

When *Analuisa* went on public exhibit in the year 2000, many of those who had embarked on her came from Florida to see her displayed prominently in the exhibit *Voyages: Stories of America and the Sea*.[9] It was the first time in more than five years that they had seen the little boat they had given up as a sacrifice to reaching their goal, and their reunion with *Analuisa* was understandably emotional, almost reverential. Luciano also later received permission to make the trip from Mariel to visit *Analuisa* at Mystic Seaport. He and his niece Miralys brought a statue of Caridad del Cobre to include in the exhibit, to help tell the story of the boat and her people. In an interview on that occasion, he said he was proud that several of the boats he had built in his life safely delivered many people, including most of his relatives, to the United States. He also expressed professional satisfaction that *Analuisa* had come to rest in a museum full of beautifully crafted wooden boats: "Everything is there. My creation is there."

Since 1994, visits to Cuba by members of the extended Cuadras family have not been uncommon, although not everyone who came in *Analuisa* has had the chance or the funds to return to see their loved ones in Mariel. Strong family ties endure despite the estranged political relationship that exists between the two nations, both of which now have a claim on the loyalties of these recent immigrants. Such has the case ever been for those who leave their home countries to make a new start in the United States. That new start brought scarcely imagined material benefits to the people who left Mariel in *Analuisa*, as they watch their big-screen televisions and go shopping at stores that never knew the meaning of the word "ration book." But at the same time, the Cuadras family's bountiful new home in the United States has allowed them to drift apart. Back in Cuba, they lived within a few blocks of each other, they shared the same problems and joys, and they met life with the same kind of stoic humor. Now, the siblings have lost touch with one another as they follow their separate lives in different cities in Florida. Acrimony over unspoken private family matters prevents the brothers and their sister from renewing their close ties in their new home. Meanwhile, Luciano Cuadras lived back in Mariel until his death in July 2004. He must have stopped now and again to take a long, wistful look toward the sea, where boats he built sailed away, carrying most of his family to distant shores.

The voyage of *Analuisa* to America was one of countless passages made over centuries of maritime immigration to these shores, all with their measure of emotion, danger, and serendipity. *Analuisa* evokes the experience of all immigration on the sea, which was a literal rite of passage for millions of new Americans. Even an experienced boater like Luís Cuadras was deeply moved by the expanse of water separating his old life from his new. He vowed never to make the trip in reverse, and believes he would not have tried it in the first place, had he known what the voyage would be like. Whether the millions of immigrants who came before him traveled on a square-rigger, on a steamship, or in a twenty-foot open boat, they were changed by the spectacle of being out of sight of land. The transition they made in leaving their homes was marked by the sublime blankness of the sea. Luís felt overwhelmed during the long hours on the high seas, "when you see water, water, water, water!" and nothing else, as anxieties rise and hopes dim with doubt. Luís and his friends and family aboard *Analuisa* were fortunate indeed when the wide, lonely ring of the Gulf Stream horizon was broken by the approach of the cruise ship that saved them. Likewise, Juan Alfaro and his friends avoided a far worse fate when *Analuisa* made her lucky appearance. But the desperate journeys of many others before and since did not end happily, and with conditions getting worse instead of better on the island, it is likely that many more immigrants to come will add to the sad toll of those who have died between Cuba and America on the sea.

Endnotes

Chapter 1

1. Except where noted, all information concerning the voyage of the *Analuisa* and the lives of her passengers contained in this book is drawn from correspondence and interviews with the following individuals: Luciano Cuadras Fernández, Caridad Alvarez Sánchez, and Ariel Hernández Alfaro in Mariel, Cuba, December 17, 1995; Luís Cuadras Fernández, José Antonio Cuadras Fernández, and Maribel Hernández Montenegro in Orlando, Florida, December 28, 1996; Amarilys Pita Cuadras, Leonardo "Victor" Milian, Miralys Milian, Julio González, and Julito González in Tampa, Florida, December 26, 1999; Leo Milian, Juan José Alfaro, and others above in Mystic, Connecticut, September 2000.

2. Philip Caputo quoted in John Dorschner, "Cuban Roulette: Miami Marine Scientists Have Bad News For the Thousands Fleeing Cuba in Flimsy Rafts: It's the Most Dangerous Trip in the World," *Tropic* magazine, *Miami Herald*, July 4, 1993; Richard J. King, "The Straits of Florida: Where Oceanography Makes History," *Sea History* 107 (Spring/Summer 2004): 22-25.

Chapter 2

1. José Almoina Mateos, *La biblioteca erasmista de Diego Méndez* (Santo Domingo: UASD, 1945).

2. A fine overview of the native cultures of Cuba is Irving Rouse, *The Tainos: Rise & Decline of the People Who Greeted Columbus* (New Haven: Yale University Press, 1992).

3. F.A. Kirkpatrick, *The Spanish Conquistadores* (1934; London: The Cresset Library, 1988), 46, 88.

4. A critical revision of Columbus, timed for the 500th anniversary of his first voyage, is Kirkpatrick Sale, *The Conquest of Paradise: Christopher Columbus and the Columbian Legacy* (New York: Plume, 1991).

5. Herbert S. Klein, *African Slavery in Latin America and the Caribbean* (New York: Oxford University Press, 1986), 150-51.

6. Antonio Vázquez de Espinosa, quoted in Charles Gibson, *Spain in America* (New York: Harper and Row, 1966), 123.

7. Eric Williams, *From Columbus to Castro: The History of the Caribbean* (New York: Vintage Books, 1984), 50-51. Williams was prime minister of Trinidad and Tobago from the country's independence in 1962 until his death in 1981.

8. Wim Klooster, *Illicit Riches* (Leiden, Netherlands: KITLV Press), 26.

9. John Ogilby, *America* (London: author, 1671), 336.

10. Klooster, *Illicit Riches*, 52, 77, 189.

11. Peter Linebaugh and Marcus Rediker, "The Outcasts of the Nations of the Earth," in *The Many-Headed Hydra: Sailors, Slaves, Commoners and the Hidden History of the Revolutionary Atlantic, 1740-95* (Boston: Beacon Press, 2000): 174-210.

12. Williams, *From Columbus to Castro*, 94.

13. Louis A. Pérez Jr., *Cuba and the United States: Ties of Singular Intimacy* (Athens: University of Georgia Press, 1990), 4, 6; Franklin W. Knight, *The Caribbean: Genesis of a Fragmented Nationalism*, 2nd ed. (New York: Oxford University Press, 1990), 45, 115, 126.

14. Jesse Lemisch, "Jack Tar in the Streets: Merchant Seamen in the Politics of Revolutionary America," *William and Mary Quarterly* 25 (1968): 377.

15. Pérez, *Cuba and the United States*, 13.

16. Hugh Thomas, *The Slave Trade* (New York: Simon & Schuster, 1997), 532-35.

17. Anna Lisa Thomas, "The Turtle Feast: Salem, Massachusetts, Encounters the World" (paper, Munson Institute of American Maritime Studies, Mystic Seaport, 2004).

18. Luis Martínez-Fernández, *Torn between Empires: Economy, Society, and Patterns of Political Thought in the Hispanic Caribbean, 1840-1878* (Athens: University of Georgia Press, 1994), 58-88.

19. Sherry Johnson, *The Social Transformation of Eighteenth-Century Cuba* (Gainesville: University Press of Florida, 2001).

20. Fernando Ortiz, *Cuban Counterpoint: Tobacco and Sugar*, Harriet de Onis, trans., (New York: Alfred A. Knopf, 1947), excerpted in Ilan Stavans, ed., *Latin American Essays* (New York: Oxford University Press, 1997), 70-74.

21. Cirilo Villaverde, *Cecilia Valdés* (1839), in Willis Knapp Jones, trans. and ed., *Spanish-American Literature in Translation*, vol. 1 (New York: Frederick Ungar, 1966), 127-32.

Chapter 3

1. Franklin W. Knight, *The Caribbean: Genesis of a Fragmented Nationalism*, 2nd ed. (New York: Oxford University Press, 1990), 170-71; Hugh Thomas, *The Slave Trade* (New York: Simon & Schuster, 1997), 532-35.

2. Robert E. May, *The Southern Dream of Caribbean Empire, 1854-1861* (Athens: University of Georgia Press, 1989), 24, 29.

3. Luis Martínez-Fernández, *Torn between Empires: Economy, Society, and Patterns of Political Thought in the Hispanic Caribbean, 1840-1878* (Athens: University of Georgia Press, 1994), 60-64.

4. George Washington Lee Collection, Coll. 23, box 1/19, G.W. Blunt White Library, Mystic Seaport (hereafter cited as GWBWL); Silas Beebe Collection, Coll. 40, box 1/6 and 7, GWBWL.

5. Hiram Clift, journal, sloop *Gallant*, November 19, 25, December 25, 1824, March 5-11, 1825, Clift Family Papers, Coll. 65, vol. 11, GWBWL.

6. David F. Long, "The Navy under the Board of Navy Commmissioners, 1815-1842", in Kenneth J. Hagan, ed., *In Peace and War: Interpretations of American Naval History, 1776-1984*, 2nd ed. (Westport, CT: Greenwood Press, 1984), 69-70; Clift, journal, sloop Gallant, December 9, 1824, March 20, 1825, GWBWL.

7. Martínez-Fernández, *Torn between Empires*, 67; figures compiled by Benjamin W. Labaree; Louis A. Pérez Jr., *Cuba and the United States: Ties of Singular Intimacy* (Athens: University of Georgia Press, 1990), 14-15.

8. Martínez-Fernández, *Torn between Empires*, 76-78; Pérez, *Cuba and the United States*, 44; Robert G. Albion, *The Rise of New York Port* (1939; reprint, Boston: Northeastern University Press, 1984), 395.

9. Carl Seaburg and Stanley Paterson, *The Ice King: Frederic Tudor and His Circle* (Boston and Mystic: Massachusetts Historical Society and Mystic Seaport, 2003).

10. Sidney W. Mintz, *Sweetness and Power: The Place of Sugar in Modern History* (New York: Penguin Books, 1985), 160-61; Albion, *Rise of New York Port*, 184; Knight, *The Caribbean*, 231; Martínez-Fernández, *Torn between Empires*, 70, 72, 87; William Earle Papers, Coll. 28, box 1/1, GWBWL.

11. Thomas, *Slave Trade*, 604-05, 636-37.

12. Klein, *African Slavery*, 151; see George Coggeshall, *Voyages to Various Parts of the World Made between the Years 1802 and 1841* (New York, 1852), 170-85, which describes the delivery of the schooner *Swan* to Havana; cited in Pérez, *Cuba and the United States*, 35; one historian's estimate of Americans comprising 90 percent of the crews on Cuban slavers is cited by Pérez, *Cuba and the United States*, 35.

13. W. Jeffrey Bolster, *Black Jacks: African American Seamen in the Age of Sail* (Cambridge, MA: Harvard University Press, 1997), 199, 206.

14. Thomas, *Slave Trade*, 606-07.

15. Howard Jones, *Mutiny on the Amistad: The Saga of a Slave Revolt and Its Impact on American Abolition, Law, and Diplomacy* (New York: Oxford University Press, 1987); "The *Amistad* Incident: Four Perspectives," *The Connecticut Scholar*, No. 10 (Middletown, CT: Connecticut Humanities Council, 1992); Martínez-Fernández, *Torn between Empires*, 102.

16. Knight, *The Caribbean*, 186; list of *Cimarrones*, Cárdenas, Cuba, GWBWL.

17. Pérez, *Cuba and the United States*, 25; Martínez-Fernández, *Torn between Empires*, 58-88; Samuel Eliot Morison, *The Maritime History of Massachusetts* (1921; reprint, Boston: Northeastern University Press, 1979), 396.

18. Robert H. Holden and Eric Zolov, eds., *Latin America and the U.S.: A Documentary History* (Oxford and New York: Oxford University Press, 2000), 9.

19. Robert E. May, *The Southern Dream of a Caribbean Empire, 1854-1861* (Athens: University of Georgia Press, 1989), 43-44, 58-59.

20. Holden and Zolov, eds., *Latin America and the U.S.*, 36-38.

21. Julia Ward Howe, *A Trip to Cuba* (Boston: Ticknor and Fields, 1860), 28-29.

22. Martínez-Fernández, *Torn between Empires*, 81; Pérez, *Cuba and the United States*, 14.

23. Pérez, *Cuba and the United States*, 26; George R. Leighton, "Louisville, Kentucky: An American Museum Piece," *Harper's* (September 1937): 400; René De La Pedraja, *Oil and Coffee: Latin American Merchant Shipping from the Imperial Era to the 1950s* (Westport, CT: Greenwood Press, 1998), 143.

24. William Earle Collection, Coll. 28, box 1/1, GWBWL. Captain William Walker should not be confused with filibuster William Walker, frequent invader of Nicaragua in the 1850s; Pérez, *Cuba and the United States*, 19.

25. *Illustrated London News*, April 10, 1847.

26. Richard Henry Dana Jr., *To Cuba and Back: A Vacation Voyage* (Boston: Ticknor and Fields, 1860), 10-11, 227-28, 20-30, 217-19, 276.

27. Francisco López Segrena, "Cuba: Dependence, Plantation Economy, and Social Classes, 1762-1902," in Manueal Moreno Fraginals, Frank Moya Pons, and Stanley L. Engerman, eds., *Between Slavery and Free Labor: The Spanish-Speaking Caribbean in the Nineteenth Century* (Baltimore: The Johns Hopkins University Press, 1985), 83-84.

28. Martíncz-Fernández, *Torn between Empires*, 170-77; Eliza McHatton-Ripley, *From Flag to Flag: A Woman's Adventures and Experiences in the South During the War, in Mexico, and in Cuba* (New York: D. Appleton and Company, 1889), 104-33.

29. Carol W. Kimball, "The Spanish Gunboats," *The Log of Mystic Seaport* (Winter 1980): 117-22.

30. Jeanie Mort Walker, *Life of Captain Fry, Cuban Martyr* (Hartford, CT: J.B. Burr, 1875); Hagan, ed., *In Peace and War*, 69-70.

31. Louis Pérez Jr., *Cuba and the United States: Ties of Singular Intimacy* (Athens: University of Georgia Press, 1990), 66, 96-97; Mirta Ojito, "Old Cuban Neighborhood Acquires New Accents, Still Spanish," The *New York Times*, January 28, 2000; Allen Freeman, "A Sense of Belonging," *Smithsonian*, March/April 1994, 28-34.

32. Rebecca J. Scott, "Explaining Abolition: Contradiction, Adaptation and Challenge in Cuban Slave Society, 1860-1886," in Fraginals et al., eds., *Between Slavery and Free Labor*, 25-53.

33. Statistics compiled from U.S. Register of the Treasury, Bureau of the Census, *Foreign Commerce and Navigation*, annual volumes, 1870 to 1890; De La Pedraja, *Oil and Coffee*, 143.

34. Quoted in Knight, *The Caribbean*, 79.

35. Quoted in Gilberto Toste Ballart, *Guantánamo U.S.A. al desnudo*, 2nd ed. (La Habana: Editora Politica, 1990), 25.

36. John Edward Weems, *The Fate of the Maine* (New York: Henry Holt, 1958), list of crew, 184-96.

37. Hyman Rickover, *How the Battleship Maine Was Destroyed* (Washington, DC: Department of the Navy, 1976), 27-41.

38. John L. Offner, *An Unwanted War: The Diplomacy of the United States and Spain Over Cuba, 1895-1898* (Chapel Hill: University of North Carolina Press, 1992), 24, 96-100, 112, 124-26, 136, 261. A second investigation of the *Maine* disaster took place in 1911, when a cofferdam was constructed around the wreck and the water was pumped out. That look at the evidence was inconclusive, ruling out neither the external nor the internal explosion theories. When the investigation concluded in 1912, U.S. naval authorities towed the wreck of the battleship out to sea and let it sink again, five miles off the coast. A decade later, a large memorial to the *Maine* was erected on the coastal avenue called *Malecón* opposite the resting place of the wreck, becoming the center of attraction for reunions of veterans and commemorations of the brief Spanish American War. A third inquiry into the cause of the *Maine* explosion, led by Admiral Hyman Rickover in 1975, concluded that the original investigation had been faulty, and that an internal explosion accounted for the damage to the *Maine*'s buckled frames, Rickover, *How the Battleship Maine Was Destroyed*, 107-28.

39. Rickover, *How the Battleship Maine Was Destroyed*, 72; Jennifer Johnson and Marifrances Trivelli, "Images of the Spanish-American War," *The Log of Mystic Seaport* 50:1 (Summer 1998): 20; John D. Alden, *The American Steel Navy*, rev. ed. (Annapolis: Naval Institute Press, 1989).

40. Joshua Slocum, *Sailing Alone Around the World* (1900; reprint, New York: Dover Publications, 1956), 264-66.

41. James Baughman, *The Mallorys of Mystic: Six Generations in American Maritime Enterprise* (Mystic: Mystic Seaport, 1972).

42. A.C.M. Amoy, *Signal 250!: The Sea Fight Off Santiago* (New York: David McKay, 1964), 4-12.

43. Louis A. Perez Jr., *Cuba Between Empires, 1878-1902* (Pittsburgh, PA: University of Pittsburgh Press, 1983), 199-210.

44. Rickover, *How the Battleship Maine Was Destroyed*, 17.

Chapter 4

1. Louis A. Pérez Jr., *Cuba Under the Platt Amendment, 1902-1934* (Pittsburgh, PA: University of Pittsburgh Press, 1986).

2. Louis A. Pérez Jr., *Lords of the Mountain: Social Banditry and Peasant Protest in Cuba, 1878-1918* (Pittsburgh, PA: University of Pittsburgh Press, 1989), 157.

3. Eric Roorda, "One Hundred Voyages of the Brig *Gem*," *The Log of Mystic Seaport* 46:1 (Summer 1994): 2-9.

4. Pérez, *Cuba and the United States*, frontispiece, 113-48; Albert J. Norton, *Norton's Complete Hand-Book of Havana and Cuba* (Chicago and New York: Rand, McNally and Company, 1900), 182-85.

5. Frederick Upham Adams, *Conquest of the Tropics* (Garden City, NY: Doubleday, Page and Co., 1914), 110-11; A.E. Doyle, "Banana Boats: A Missing Link in the Rise of Cruise Vacationing, 1881-1956" (paper, Munson Institute of American Maritime History, Mystic Seaport, 2004).

6. Sources on the Black Star Line include, most comprehensively, Robert A. Hill, ed., *The Marcus Garvey and Universal Negro Improvement Association Papers* (Berkeley: University of California Press, 1983), especially volumes 1, 2, and 4; Hugh Mulzac's *A Star to Steer By* (New York: International Publishers, 1963) is the autobiography of one of the line's officers; for a condensed treatment, see Marifrances Trivelli and Dwayne E. Williams, "Sailing, Shipping, and Symbolism: Marcus Garvey and the Black Star Steamship Line, 1916-1922," in Glenn S. Gordinier, ed., *Perspectives on Race, Ethnicity, and Power in Maritime America: Papers from the Conference Held at Mystic Seaport, September 2000* (Mystic: Mystic Seaport, 2005).

7. René De La Pedraja, *Oil and Coffee: Latin American Merchant Shipping from the Imperial Era to the 1950s* (Westport, CT: Greenwood Press, 1998), 143-44.

8. Ibid.

9. Irving Berlin, "See You in C-U-B-A" (1920).

10. The Aeromarine Website, http://www.timetableimages.com/ttimages/aerom.htm, September 2004.

11. Harry Franck, *Roaming Through the West Indies* (New York: Blue Ribbon Books, 1920), 25-105.

12. Statistics compiled from *Foreign Commerce and Navigation*, 1890; René De La Pedraja, *The Rise and Decline of Merchant Shipping in the Twentieth Century* (New York: Twayne Publishers, 1992), 38-41; Franklin W. Knight, "Jamaican Migrants and the Cuban Sugar Industry, 1900-1934," in Manueal Moreno Fraginals, Frank Moya Pons, and Stanley L. Engerman, eds., *Between Slavery and Free Labor: The Spanish-Speaking Caribbean in the Nineteenth Century* (Baltimore: The Johns Hopkins University Press, 1985), 94-114.

13. Mark H. Goldberg, *Going Bananas!: One Hundred Years of American Fruit Ships in the Caribbean* (Kings Point, NY: The American Merchant Museum Foundation, 1993), 320; Basil Woon, *When It's Cocktail Time in Cuba* (New York: Horace Liveright, 1928), 27; Henry Albert Phillips, *White Elephants in the Caribbean* (New York: Robert M. McBride, 1936), 138.

14. The American community in Havana was described by Nathaniel P. Davis, Foreign Service Inspection Report, Embassy at Havana, April 23, 1935, Record Group 59, National Archives Building, Washington, DC; Robert E. May, *The Southern Dream of a Caribbean Empire, 1854-1861* (Athens: University of Georgia Press, 1989), 29.

15. Interview with Wayne Smith, Washington DC, July 8, 1997; Eric Paul Roorda, "Uprooting Clubland: The Demise of the American Colony in Havana," (working paper, 1998).

16. "Runnin' Down to Cuba," sea chantey collected by Stan Hugill from a West Indian sailor, researched and recorded on CD by Forebitter, *Link of Chain: Forebitter Sings Songs of America and the Sea*, vol. 1 (Mystic: Mystic Seaport, 1999).

17. Marifrances Trivelli, "Twenty Years Under Steam: Views of the Merchant Marine Career of Rupert Decker," *The Log of Mystic Seaport* 47:2 (Autumn 1995): 46-49.

18. Collection of Vice Admiral Dixwell Ketcham, 1928-30, Naval Historical Center, Washington, DC; Eric Paul Roorda, "Goodwill Gunboats: A Peacetime Role for the U.S. Navy," *The Log of Mystic Seaport* 54:4 (Spring 2003): 85-92.

19. First Secretary H. Freeman Matthews to Secretary of State Cordell Hull, March 18, 1935; Officer in Charge, U.S. Naval Station, Key West, W. Klaus to Chief of Naval Operations, October 13, 1935; Second Secretary Edward Lawton to Hull, June 8, 1938; "Cuban Exiles and Sailors Riot Here," *Miami Daily Tribune*, May 24, 1935; State Department Memo of Conversation, March 9, 1939, all contained in U.S. State Department files, correspondence with the U.S. Embassy in Havana, Record Group 59, National Archives Building, Washington, DC.

20. Pérez, *Lords of the Mountain*, 19-20; Bruce Blevin, "And Cuba for the Winter," *New Republic*, February 1928, 61-65, cited in Skwiot, "Itineraries of Empire"; Stan Hugill, *Sailortown* (London: Routledge & Kegan, 1967); Robert Stone, "Havana Then and Now," *Harper's* Magazine, March 1992, 36-45.

21. A. Hyatt Verrill, *Cuba Today* (New York: Dodd, Mead and Company, 1931), 62-63.

22. Advertisements from *Havanity* magazine, 1941, Biblioteca Nacional José Martí, Havana, Cuba; *Anglo-American Directory of Cuba 1956-57* (Marianao, Cuba: Imprenta Aldina, 1956).

23. *Weekend in Havana*, Twentieth Century-Fox, 1941.

24. Postcard of "La Playa, Havana, Cuba: One of the world's smartest bathing resorts—both in winter and summer," from Adele to Miss Marguerite M. Walker, New Haven, Connecticut, n.d., author's collection. Thanks to Marifrances Trivelli for this reference.

25. Spruille Braden, *Diplomats and Demagogues: The Memoirs of Spruille Braden* (New Rochelle, NY: Arlington House, 1971), 283-86.

26. De La Pedraja, *Oil and Coffee*, 144-45; Ernest Hemingway, *Islands in the Stream* (New York: Simon and Schuster, 1970), 242.

27. Holland America Line, *Nieuw Amsterdam* shipboard newsletter, *The Caribbean Mercury*, January 6-18, 1950, and assorted brochures and postcards from Havana, January 1950, Doyle-Roorda Collection.

28. De La Pedraja, *Oil and Coffee*, 145-49; Louis A. Pérez, Jr., *Cuba Between Empires, 1878-1902* (Pittsburgh, PA: University of Pittsburgh Press, 1983), 199-210.

29. Thomas G. Paterson, *Contesting Castro: The United States and the Triumph of the Cuban Revolution* (New York: Oxford University Press, 1994), 33, 69-70.

30. Roorda, "Uprooting Clubland."

31. *Anglo-American Directory of Cuba 1960* (Marianao, Cuba: Imprenta Aldina, 1960).

32. Paterson, *Contesting Castro*, 259; "Castro Retains Firm Grip 40 Years After Revolution," *Sarasota Herald-Tribune*, January 2, 1999.

33. Peter Wyden, *Bay of Pigs: The Untold Story* (New York: Simon and Schuster, 1979).

34. Paterson, *Contesting Castro*, 259.

35. Graham Allison and Philip Zelikow, *Essence of Decision: Explaining the Cuban Missile Crisis*, 2nd ed. (New York: Longman, 1999), 384-85.

36. Thomas G. Smith, "Negotiating with Fidel Castro: The Bay of Pigs Prisoners and a Lost Opportunity," *Diplomatic History* (Winter 1995): 59-86.

Chapter 5

1. William Shakespeare, *The Tempest* (1611; New York: Bantam Books, 1988), xvii; Peter Linebaugh and Marcus Rediker, "The Wreck of the *Sea-Venture*," in *The Many-Headed Hydra: Sailors, Slaves, Commoners and the Hidden History of the Revolutionary Atlantic, 1740-95* (Boston: Beacon Press, 2000), 8-35.

2. Jamestown ship dimension estimates come from Ivor Noël Hume, *The Virginia Adventure: -Roanoke to James Towne: An Archaeological and Historical Odyssey* (New York: Alfred A. Knopf, 1994): 113, 121, 123-25; other ship dimension estimates are from Lincoln P. Paine, *Ships of the World: An Historical Encyclopedia* (Boston and New York: Houghton Mifflin Company, 1997).

3. Alison Games, *Migration and the Origins of the English Atlantic World* (Cambridge, MA: Harvard University Press, 1999), 56, 61, 220, 250 n38.

4. Patrick Manning, *Slavery and African Life: Occidental, Oriental, and African Slave Trades* (New York: Cambridge University Press, 1990).

5. On the diplomatic and legal aspects of the African Squadron, see Hugh G. Soulsby, *The Right of Search and the Slave Trade in Anglo-American Relations, 1814-1862* (Baltimore: Johns Hopkins University Press, 1933), Warren S. Howard, *American Slavers and the Federal Law, 1837-1862* (Berkeley: University of California Press, 1963); for firsthand perspectives, see C. Herbert Gilliland, *Voyage to A Thousand Cares: Master's Mate Lawrence and the African Squadron, 1844-1846* (Annapolis, MD: Naval Institute Press, 2003) and Andrew Hull Foote, *Africa and the American Flag* (1854; reprint, Folkestone and London: Dawsons of Pall Mall, 1970); for a condensed discussion, see Calvin Lane, "The African Squadron: The U.S. Navy and the Slave Trade, 1820-1862," *The Log of Mystic Seaport* 50:4 (Spring 1999): 86-98.

6. Marcus Rediker, *Between the Devil and the Deep Blue Sea: Merchant Seamen, Pirates, and the Anglo-American Maritime World, 1700-1750* (New York: Cambridge University Press, 1987), 45-50.

7. Herman Melville, *Redburn: His First Voyage, Being the Sailor-Boy Confessions and Reminiscences of the Son-of-a-Gentleman, in the Merchant Service* (1849; New York: Penguin Books, 1987), 107-08, 112.

8. Ibid., 320, 322.

9. "By the Hush" researched and recorded on CD by Forebitter, *Voyages: Forebitter Sings Songs of the America and the Sea*, vol. 2 (Mystic: Mystic Seaport, 2000).

10. Stephen Crane, *New York Press*, January 7, 1897.

11. Stephen Crane, "The Open Boat" (1898), *The Norton Anthology of Short Fiction* (New York: W.W. Norton, 1978), 352-71.

12. Elisabeth Farrell, "*Golden Venture* Refugees Freed From Jail," *Christianity Today*, April 28, 1997.

13. Allen Freeman, "A Sense of Belonging," *Smithsonian* (March/April 1994): 28-34.

14. Frank Jacobson, "Empty Refugee Raft Is Found With ID Papers," *Key West Citizen*, September 17, 1969; Arnold Markowitz and Sandra Dibble, "Soviet Vessel Rescues Cubans," *Miami Herald*, July 29, 1989.

15. Dan Keating, "Rescues Don't Tell Number of Lost Rafters: Crossing Proves Fatal For Many," *Miami Herald*, June 13, 1991.

16. Dorschner, "Cuban Roulette," *Miami Herald*, July 4, 1993; Katha Sheehan, "Rafters Report Amazing Feats," *Florida Keys Island Navigator*, February 1994.

17. Dorothy and Thomas Hoobler, *The Cuban American Family Album* New York: Oxford University Press, 1996), 7; Felix Roberto Masud-Piloto, *From Welcomed Exiles to Illegal Immigrants: Cuban Migration to the United States, 1959-95* (Lanham, MD: Rowman and Littlefield, 1996); Norman Zucker and Naomi Flink Zucker, *Desperate Crossings: Seeking Refuge in America* (Armonk, NY: M.E. Sharpe, 1996).

18. Mirta Ojito, "My Escape From Cuba: A Mariel Boat-Lift Memory," *New York Times Magazine*, April 23, 2000, 68-78; photograph by Gail Swanson.

19. Joe Morris Doss, *Let the Bastards Go: From Cuba to Freedom on God's Mercy* (Baton Rouge: Louisiana State University Press, 2003).

20. Staff report, "In Mariel, Massive Boatlift a National Embarrassment," *Miami Herald*, April 21, 2000.

21. Thomas G. Paterson, *Contesting Castro: The United States and the Triumph of the Cuban Revolution* (New York: Oxford University Press, 1994), 226.

22. Mark S. Hamm, *The Abandoned Ones: The Imprisonment and Uprising of the Mariel Boat People* (Boston: Northeastern University Press, 1995).

23. Laurie Horn, "Mariel Artists Claim Their Place," *Miami Herald*, April 22, 1990.

24. Keating, "Rescues Don't Tell Number of Lost Rafters," *Miami Herald*, June 13, 1991; Richard Wallace, "Four Refugees Reach Keys in Rafts, But One Man Still Missing," *Miami Herald*, March 23, 1991; Chris Doyle, "More Refugees Brought Ashore," *Key West Citizen*, October 6, 1992; Mirta Ojita, "Crewmen Say Cubans Forced Boat to Keys," *Miami Herald*, September 25, 1989; Scott Hiaasen and Nancy Klingener, "Vacationing Family Watches Men Make Dash For Freedom," *Miami Herald*, July 10, 1993.

25. Dan Keating and Anglie Muhs, "Two Rafters Charged in Captain's Killing," *Miami Herald*, January 21, 1992.

26. Katha Sheehan, "Cubans Sail For Florida," *Key West Citizen*, July 5, 1989.

27. Liz Balmaseda, "The Great Escape: A Growing Stream of Daring, Desperate Cubans Are Rafting for Florida," *Miami Herald*, September 5, 1989; photograph by Gail Swanson; Jeff McNelly, "The Great Navigator," syndicated cartoon appearing in *Key West Citizen*, 28 August 28, 1994.

28. UN Ambassador Ricardo Alarcón quoted in Stanley Meisler, "Cuba, U.S. Still Far Apart on Refugee Crisis Solution," *Los Angeles Times*, September 2, 1994.

29. Frances Robles and Martin Merzer, "2,269: Record Number Picked Up In Human Tidal Wave," *Miami Herald*, August 23, 1994; William Booth, "U.S. Cutter Picks Up Cuban Rafters—'Like Fireflies'," *Washington Post*, August 27, 1994.

30. Jim Flannery, "Boaters Rescuing Cubans Risk Smuggling Charges," *Soundings*, November 1994.

31. Ibid.

32. Jim Hardie, "Rafters Add New Element to Keys Fishing," *Miami Herald*, August 25, 1994; Andy Newman, "Fishing Writers Find Refugees," *Florida Keys Keynoter*, May 16, 1990.

33. Anthony Boadle, "Film on Cuban Rafters Packs in Crowd in Havana," *Reuters*, December 2, 2002.

34. Pam Johnson, "Cubans Still Fleeing: 60 found in South County" and "123 Cubans Being held offshore," *Venice Gondolier*, February 15-17, 18-21, 1995; Jan Angilella and Stephen G. Reed, "More Cubans Found At Sea" and "Refugees Bound for Guantanamo," *Sarasota Herald-Tribune*, February 17, 18, 1995.

35. "Immigration Issue Strikes Venice Shores," *Venice Gondolier*, February 18-21, 1995.

36. Cathy Booth, "Desperate Straits," *Time*, March 7, 1994, 20; Katha Sheehan, "Volunteer Pilots Fly to Help Rescue Refugees in Straits," *Florida Keys Island Navigator*, February 1994.

37. Public Broadcasting System, *Eyes on the Prize II*, part 6 (1989).

38. Tim Golden, "Love in the Time of Castro: The Intimate Family History of Elián González," *New York Times Magazine*, April 23, 2000, 62-67.

39. Myrna Towner, "100,000 Defend Sovereignty of Cuba at Mariel," *The Militant*, June 5, 2000.

40. Warren Richey, "Cuban Rafters May Exploit Asylum Loophole," *Christian Science Monitor*, May 11, 2000.

41. Jennifer Babson, "Sickly Rafters Brought Ashore," *Miami Herald*, March 14, 2003.

42. Susan Candiotti and Tony Valdez, "Ferry Hijacking Ends, Cuban Government Says," *CNN News*, April 4, 2003.

43. "Cubans Try Floating Vintage Car to Florida," *Miami Herald*, February 4, 2004; "Cuban Car-Boat Family Sent to Guantánamo," *Sarasota Herald-Tribune*, February 12, 2004. With the assistance of the U.S. government, Luis Grass and his family were finally permitted to settle as refugees in Costa Rica in December 2004, *Miami Herald*, December 2, 2004.

Chapter 6

1. A. Hyatt Verrill, *Cuba Today* (New York: Dodd, Mead and Company, 1931); Basil Woon, *When It's Cocktail Time in Cuba* (New York: Horace Liveright, 1928); F.F. Hill Collection at The Mariners' Museum, Newport News, VA.

2. Medea Benjamin, Joseph Collins and Michael Scott, *No Free Lunch: Food and Revolution in Cuba Today*, 3rd ed. (San Francisco: Institute for Food and Development Policy, 1989), 102-03.

3. Staff report, "In Mariel, Massive Boatlift a National Embarrassment," *Miami Herald*, April 21, 2000.

4. Luciano Cuadras Fernández, interview by Fred Calabretta, interpreted by Miralys Milian, November 5, 2000, Oral History Archive, G.W. Blunt White Library, Mystic Seaport (hereafter cited as GWBWL).

5. Miralys and Julio González interview by Fred Calabretta, November 5, 2000, GWBWL.

6. *Miami Herald*, August 27, 1994, September 4, 1994, "Neighbors" section, 4.

7. Portions of the preceding came from interviews of Juan José Alfaro, Luís Cuadras, and Yadira Cuadras conducted by David Littlefield and interpreted by Lilliam Pancarbo, November 5, 2000, GWBWL.

8. Luís Cuadras Jr.'s autobiography, *Analuisa*'s registration and inspection documentation, telephone messages, notes, and internal memos are all contained in the *Analuisa* Accession File, 1994.130, Registrar's Office, Curatorial Department, Collections and Research Center, Mystic Seaport.

9. Robert Westervelt, "For Refugees, Emotional Reunion," *New London Day*, September 8, 2000; Al Lara, "Revisiting an Escape: Cuban Exiles Reunited with Boat that Brought Them to the U.S.," *Hartford Courant*, September 10, 2000.

Index

(Italic numerals indicate illustrations)

The American Maritime Library

Cuba, America and the Sea is the sixteenth volume in the American Maritime Library series, published by Mystic Seaport. Established in 1970, the American Maritime Library is intended to help Mystic Seaport tell the stories of America and the sea. The series includes accurate, nontechnical texts, with full illustration and documentation, that contribute to a broad public understanding of the nation's ongoing relationship with the sea.

With the exception of volumes III, IV, and VII, all works in the series are available. The titles are